*T*able of Contents

Part I:
Regional Dimensions

Part II:
International and
Transnational Dimensions

Illustrations

*F*oreword

*T*he demise of the Cold War has transformed US national security strategy from a perspective of global competition with the Soviet Union to one dominated by regional concerns. The implications of this landmark shift, assessed in national, international, and transnational terms, are the central subjects of this volume. Most of the essays are based on papers first delivered at the National Defense University Topical Symposium, "From Globalism to Regionalism—New Perspectives on American Foreign and Defense Policies." Several additional essays were written specifically for this book to add greater breadth than was possible at the symposium.

Collectively, these papers are a seminal source of discussion for what is surely the most profound shift in US strategy in half a century. Here one may study potential flash points of conflict likely to affect long-range US planning, as well as salient political, economic, and military developments likely to dominate particular regions of the world—from the Middle East and East Asia to Africa and Latin America. Here one also finds analyses of the growing importance of transnational factors—such as demographics, the environment, and resources—and examinations of the changing role of international organizations such as the United Nations. *From Globalism to Regionalism* is in effect a workbook for understanding national security in the 20th century's final decade.

PAUL G. CERJAN
Lieutenant General, US Army
President, National Defense University

Summary

How will future historians view the 1990s? Will they write about a decade of rampant international peace and democracy, the development of a new kind of warfare rooted in regional economic competition, or the growing tide of resource scarcity and population growth that spawned greater misery and unrest? How will they view America's altered role in the world? Will the US role in the last decade of the 20th century be portrayed as enhanced, diminished, or simply transformed? The events of the past few years have ushered in a revolution in thinking about the direction in which the world, and America's place in it, is headed. The foreseeable future no longer seems foreseeable. It may be impossible to provide definitive answers to these broad questions, but many clues, if not answers, can be found within this volume.

Despite the vastly differing backgrounds and approaches of the authors, four cardinal themes run through the following pages. The first is that, far from signalling the "end of history," the end of the Cold War has ushered in a new era in which the regions of the world can resume historic ethnic, religious and territorial disputes largely frozen by the superpower rivalry. In this sense, the world has moved from globalism to regionalism. For instance, in the Persian Gulf, the threat to the regional oil supply has now supplanted the global threat of Soviet expansionism; similarly, in Africa, the concern is no longer with Soviet-led proxy wars, but rather with the fragile African state system itself. A second, corollary motif found in this collection of essays is that, in addition to these traditional problems, there are some international and transnational problems that pose entirely new threats to the stability and quality of life globally, regionally and nationally. For example, unrestrained population growth means that today's great powers and industrial democracies will comprise a far smaller and older population than many developing countries. Furthermore, the wasteful use of natural resources and degradation of the environment equally may have a detrimental impact on international security.

A third theme of this volume is paradoxical: although the aforementioned problems are driven largely by a lack of regional harmony, the post-Cold War era provides a rare opportunity for greater regional cooperation that could enhance stability. While a clear international consensus for greater international collective security is not likely to materialize in the 1990s, all the regions of the world can make limited progress toward creating regional architectures or procedures which exchange ideas, reduce fears, and assist those most in need. A fourth and final theme is that the United States role in this emerging world can hardly help but to be transformed in the decade ahead. As the authors peer into the 21st century, they see good reason to believe that America's fundamental security and values—although not necessarily its unilateral action and clout—will remain intact.

This book begins with General Colin Powell's keynote address from the 1991 National Defense University symposium, *From Globalism to Regionalism*. Amidst the hurly-burly circumstances of recent years, Powell posits a couple of verities likely to persist throughout the decade ahead. According to Powell, while the United States must expend more effort to address its domestic challenges, it will retain a critical position of global leadership. Moreover, world history has not come to an abrupt halt; the trends of the moment will shift again in the future, and we should not dismiss Russia's residual military potential. In short, the Chairman of the Joint Chiefs of Staff advances a hedging strategy designed to deter large-scale aggression, respond to regional contingencies, and increasingly rely on our ability to reconstitute military forces in the event a global threat reemerges. The military wherewithal required to undergird this strategy is dubbed the "Base Force." While the requirements for that force will need constant reassessment, Powell warns against fine tuning it weekly, in response to the latest news reports; that, he admonishes, would only undermine the morale of America's volunteer forces.

Regional Dimensions

The first 7 essays of this book offer regional case studies, each of which demonstrates how the cessation of the Cold War contest has altered both the perception and reality of the Persian Gulf and Middle East, Asia, Latin America, and Africa. As David Long observes, "Regional specialists, both in government and academia, have long been frustrated that the Cold War, which viewed all international relations from a global, bipolar perspective, not only distorted the way the United States looks at regional politics but, more importantly, impaired US policies toward the region." Examining the Persian Gulf, Long notes that the United States historically viewed the Gulf as a mere subregion of the Middle East, which in turn revolved around the goal of containing Soviet expansionism. By the 1970s, American decisionmakers began to appreciate the strategic value of Gulf oil and placed it on a par with the military containment of the USSR; today, of course, oil and not Soviet expansionism is the salient concern. Concomitantly, more and more Americans—catalyzed by Britain's 1968 decision to withdraw "east of Suez" and terminate the military umbrella over the lower Gulf states—view the Gulf as a separate region. According to Long, this trend of the past two decades is likely to continue for the rest of the century. As the United States becomes more dependent on imported Gulf oil, the Gulf increasingly will be viewed as a discrete and vital region by Washington.

Marvin Feuerwerger, analyzing both the Middle East and the Persian Gulf regions, contends that America's traditional interests in this part of the world transcend the Cold War, namely, the protection of American citizens, the freedom of commerce and access to oil, the security of Israel, Turkey, and friendly Arab states, and general regional stability. While one of the traditional threats—the Soviet Union—has been eclipsed, the threats of interstate conflict, internal instability, and terrorism will continue to put US interests in jeopardy. Feuerwerger recommends going beyond containment and adopting an American security strategy for the Middle East and the Persian Gulf with four pillars. First, the United States should focus on constructing a more stable military balance. In contrast to those who wish the United Sates to erect a capability in place to defend the borders of Kuwait or Saudi Arabia against Iraq or Iran, however, Feuerwerger proposes that the United States instead should rely chiefly on a rapidly deployable contingency force. Second, the United States needs an arms sale and arms control policy to dampen the proliferation of weapons of mass destruction and ballistic missiles, while encouraging friendly states to but defensive arms. Third, even while reducing the size of the US Armed Forces, the United States should continue to improve its long-range power projection capabilities, including the ability to mobilize rapidly. Finally, the United States should help promote the settlement of regional conflicts through negotiations. Despite the obstacles confronting peace talks in the Middle East, Feuerwerger concludes that "even slow progress on any dimension—Israeli-Palestinian, Israeli-Syrian, or regionwide functional—can reduce tensions and promote the prospects for a more stable region."

Ralph Cossa argues that the United Sates is faced with a shifting balance of power among the major actors in Northeast Asia: Russia, Japan, China, and the Korean peninsula. While there are other regional military powers, these four will be decisive in determining the degree of stability or instability in the entire Asia-Pacific region. They will also be crucial in determining the future US military presence in Asia. While avoiding specific predictions. Cossa explains why the glass in Northeast Asia may be half empty rather than half full: A future Russian regime may revert to the military instrument in international relations; only the "lack of a nuclear arsenal" keeps Japan from becoming a superpower; even the next generation of Chinese leaders will remain "stubbornly committed to enhancing China's role in the region and world"; and North and South Korea may continue their tense standoff longer than many suppose. According to Cossa, the long-term challenge to US decisionmakers is to find creative and less costly ways to continue America's critical role in the Asia-Pacific region. He suggests a meaningful American presence can be preserved through a combination of exercises, exchange visits, port calls, civil and humanitarian projects, and a greater level of security assistance.

When viewing Southeast Asia, Kenneth Conboy simultaneously sees greater tranquility and complexity than in Northeast Asia. On the one hand, the end of the Cold War has unleashed many of the traditional animosities among Southeast Asian states. Indeed, Conboy believes the three decades of ideological conflict in Southeast Asia following World War Two were the exception to the rule of disputes occurring along racial, ethnic, and territorial lines. On the other hand, Conboy sees scant possibility of most of these skirmishes escalating into serious regional conflicts. For instance, the various small insurgencies within Southeast Asian states seem likely to remain self-contained within state borders. Even interstate territorial conflicts pose relatively little threat to regional stability, perhaps with the sole and important exception of conflict in the South China Sea. While Conboy offers a relatively benign regional outlook, he argues in favor of retaining a sustained US military presence in the region because of the continuing importance of the sea line of communication, the growing amount of US trade with the Asia-Pacific region, and the likelihood that a dangerous vacuum of power would result from a total US withdrawal.

South Asia, writes Seema Sirohi, is a veritable tinderbox of ethnic and religious conflict. Far from diminishing in importance in the wake of the Cold War, several factors may conspire to put South Asia high up on the agenda of US officials in the decade ahead. Widespread misery and discontent in a region in which one-seventh of the world's people reside, rising Muslim and Hindu fundamentalism, and the potential for expanded proliferation of weapons of mass destruction, ballistic missiles, and dual-use technology—all these factors make if difficult to ignore South Asia, according to Sirohi. Nor is Sirohi confident that the state regimes in Pakistan and India can control militant factions within their borders. This mounting tribalism poses one of the critical questions for post-Cold War American policy makers: By what criteria should the United States judge whether to support movements for national self-determination? This is a pressing global question and a major regional issue at a time when India, for instance, is fighting three separate insurgencies.

Patrice Franko-Jones suggests that perhaps the biggest challenge for American policy makers regarding Latin America is simply mustering the political will to help address its broad range of complex internal problems. In the post-Cold War era, the security challenge to the region is no longer a Monroe Doctrine-type external threat but rather the gradual "erosion of legitimating principles." There are, according to Franko-Jones, a number of "quiet crises" festering in Latin America, and unfortunately, the region lacks a homogenous view on how to cope with long-term challenges such as brittle democratic institutions, an increasing flow of illegal narcotics, potential weapons proliferation, and environmental degradation. The good news is that if enough political will and foresight can be found on both sides of the Equator, even relatively modest initiatives would have the potential of preventing conflict and chaos. Among the modest confidence-building measures between the Americas suggested by the author is the notion of a defense complement to the Enterprise for the Americas Initiative—focusing on the use of the market and private sector initiatives to meet our common security needs in the areas of drug trafficking, proliferation, and environmental security.

Jeffrey Herbst contends that the end of the Cold War may presage a new era of interstate unrest in Africa. Pressures for political and economic liberalization are likely to undermine the hitherto stable African state system, a system that since 1957 has not had one significant boundary change that was not agreed to by all parties concerned. Patrons will be harder to come by for those threatened by serious secessionist threats, local and international demands for democratization may rekindle long-subdued debates over national boundaries, and economic viability may require different national configurations. Consequently, writes Herbst, "some African countries may simply drift apart until a local leader or warlord realizes that no national political authority exists." Herbst predicts that the demise of the African state system may bring about widespread chaos, mass migration, and death "that makes the previous three decades seem tame by comparison." Herbst concludes that those policy makers bent on exporting Western political and economic liberalization to Africa should not be surprised when their policies lead to the unintended consequences of the wholesale breakdown of the African state system.

International and Transnational Dimensions

Part II of this volume explores international and transnational dimensions of security, including questions related to America's role in the post-Cold War world. Walt Whitman Rostow sets the theme of this volume by suggesting that regionalism offers a way of reaching the fundamental objectives of the United Nations Charter which appear beyond the reach of the United Nations. Rostow advances the notion that greater regional cooperation—perhaps led or guided by the United States—provides the most realistic way to maintain a regional balance of power and thwart the rise of regional hegemons. While Rostow recognizes a clear danger from regional powers, he argues that the end of the Cold War may not be "as clear a benchmark as it may appear." After all, he writes, the most tense episodes of the Cold War were chiefly regional disputes. Hence, Rostow contends that many US regional policies during the Cold War actually transcended that contest and may well be relevant to future crises in the decade ahead.

Nicholas Eberstadt suggests that today's prospective population trends highlight an impending moral problem in demographic form. Most demographers agree that global population is being redistributed away from today's industrial democracies and towards the world's lesser developed countries. The implications of this pronounced North-South shift are potentially far reaching. In even the recent past, great powers have possessed relatively large populations. Just over four decades ago, Eberstadt writes, 2 of the top 5 and 7 of the top 20 countries by population would have been considered industrial democracies. Thirty-five years later, in 1985, the industrial democracies accounted for only 1 of the top 5, and 6 of the top 20 countries. Thirty-five years from now, in the year 2025, Eberstadt forecasts a world in which not one of today's industrial democracies ranks among the top 5 and only 2—United States and Japan—remain among the top 20. In this future world, today's industrial democracies would account for less than one-fourteenth of the total population of the big countries. In other words, Eberstadt depicts a world in which the US population is less than Nigeria's, Iran's population is roughly equal to Japan's, and Ethiopia's population is double that of France. Concludes Eberstadt, "Imagine a world, indeed, very much like the United Nations today, but with today's rhetoric informing policy on a global scale, directing actions affecting the lives of millions of people on a daily basis. Even without an aggressive or hostile Soviet bloc, or the invention of new weapons, this would be a very dangerous place."

Peter Gleick writes that even as the threat of nuclear conflict is subsiding, a new period of international frictions is rapidly unfolding. "The seeds of this growing discontent," Gleick writes, "will be found, not in traditional territorial disputes, or religious and ethnic hatreds, or ideological competitions, but in growing economic disputes between rich and poor, transnational environmental pollution, and diminishing quality and quantity of resources. For the first time in history, the interactions between the geopolitical and the geophysical realms are reaching global proportions." Whereas in the past resources have been viewed as goals, targets or tools, they will have to be treated differently in the future. The deterioration of Earth's environment threatens fundamental alterations of biological and geophysical processes at the regional and global scale, whether by the overexploitation or degradation of nationally held resources through deforestation and desertification, or the abuse of resources held in common through the wasting of fresh-water resources, acid rain, and the depletion of the stratospheric ozone layer. Gleick prescribes several courses of action, from increased efficiency of resource use and recycling, to more concerted international cooperation. He also warns that global environmental problems cannot be isolated from underlying economic, political, and social causes. "The world cannot be considered 'secure' when billions live in poverty while others waste valuable resources, where the struggle for basic human services is a dominant factor in life, and where global environmental services are being degraded and destroyed."

William Durch focuses on the role of the United Nations, an organization that has emerged from the Cold War stronger than ever. UN peacekeeping missions are a common fixture of contemporary international relations, and Durch explains why the UN role in conflict containment and conflict resolution is likely to grow in the decade ahead. Traditional peacekeeping, Durch reminds us, adds to the self-help system of world politics "a formal element of disinterested outside assistance intended to help conflicting local parties disengage." As such, peacekeeping is a confidence-building measure; the objectivity and neutrality of the blue-helmeted forces are far more critical than their military capability. In a post-Cold World in which intrastate disputes threaten mass suffering and mass migration, the UN may have to consider peace enforcement without cross-border aggression. This would represent a fundamental shift in how the UN Security Council interprets "threats to international peace and security," but Durch believes we have already witnessed a watershed in how the United Nations operates. The United Nations has moved from "the Middle East model of peacekeeping" to "become an active champion of democratic principles and basic human rights." Concludes Durch: "As [the United Nations'] work in the field of cooperative security bears fruit, there may be that much less need in the future to implement the original, collective kind for which the United Nations was intended."

Patrick Cronin briefly retraces America's reluctant international leadership role and then outlines four major developments transforming the international political landscape: the terminal illness of Communism; the emergence of a tripolar balance of economic power; volatile trends in the developing world; and growing interdependence. For Cronin, these trends suggest the need to move from a Cold War *Pax Americana* to a post-Cold War *Pax consortis*. Rejecting competing paradigms for America's role in the world—from a fortress America, to a

unipolar moment, to global or regional collective security—
Cronin argues in favor of a more explicit concert with other key
industrial democracies. Cronin then makes a case for active
engagement on the basis that great powers can opt out of
international affairs only at the peril of international order.
The dangers of a leaderless world, the lack of suitable alternative centers of leadership, and America's military, political,
and even economic strength all make the United States
uniquely qualified for continued leadership on a broad range of
issues. At the same time, an active US role hinges on America's
own domestic renewal. Hence, the United States will have to
become more adept at sharing both burdens and decisionmaking. Cronin concludes that the new global environment requires a leaner, less domineering, but still active US role in the
world. "America can't go home again," he writes. "We cannot
easily regain our leverage and credibility if we now shatter the
patina of American power by disengaging militarily and politically. Yet we can no longer do so much on our own. Thus, the
best course is to pursue US interests internationally through a
concert of power with our key allies, by focusing on what we
have done well, by playing to our strengths in a period of
extended uncertainty, and by trying to shape the world more to
our liking."

In the concluding chapter of this volume, William
Woodruff writes that we are now "poised between the geopolitics of the Western Age and the geopolitics of a new world order
in which regional ethnic, religious and national aims are reasserting themselves." Woodruff predicts that the predictability
and relative stability of the Cold War will be lamented. Moscow and Washington are no longer the epicenters of international security. Peace in the post-Cold War era, he writes, now
hinges mostly on the behavior of Asians, Arabs, Persians and
other non-Westerners. In fact, this trend toward multipolarity
and regional centers of power has been developing for at least
the past three decades. But the implications of this trend will be
felt more acutely in the next decade than ever before, according
to Woodruff. "The temporary eclipse of Asia by the West
during the past half millennium is over. We can no longer take
it for granted that the American way is a universal gospel. Our

task is to adjust to a world in which the non-Western peoples are going to influence regional and world affairs more than they did in the Western Age; not only in terms of power but in terms of values." In setting forth a foreign policy agenda for the United States, Woodruff recommends, first, consolidating America's own hemisphere. He then goes on to recommend further US retrenchment but not total withdrawal from Europe. Third, he calls on the United States to recognize the "resurgence of Asia . . . [as] the outstanding fact of contemporary history." Finally, he predicts that, more than any other region, the Middle East will occupy our attention most in the decade ahead. As the United States moves toward the new century, Woodruff advises that "we should keep before us the basic objective of our foreign policy: to maintain the security of the United States and to uphold its fundamental values. In this task we are not faced by a new crisis, but by a new opportunity."

FROM GLOBALISM TO REGIONALISM:

New Perspectives on US Foreign and Defense Policies

*F*rom Globalism to Regionalism: Keynote Address

Colin L. Powell

*M*y entire life is devoted, these days, to regional matters. That's why this symposium is so important, and why the focus of this symposium is so appropriate. These are the kinds of problems that, increasingly, the people of the United States will be facing, that the leadership of the United States will be facing, and certainly that the Armed Forces of the United States and of our friends will be facing.

The simple fact of the matter—and I don't present this as a bulletin—is that the Cold War is over. More than the Cold War has gone by the wayside. We are witnessing the end of a period of history that began in the middle of World War I and manifested itself in the intervening 75 years in both fascism and communism. Fascism was defeated across the Atlantic and across the Pacific in 1945. Today, communism has ended in the Soviet Union and Eastern Europe, and it is fading fast among its few remaining adherents. Can there be any doubt in anyone's mind any longer that soon communism's final bastions—Cuba, North Korea, Vietnam—will discard their wornout and absolutely useless concepts?

The old international order of the Cold War that is disappearing before our eyes was a familiar thing to us. It was very comforting to us. It had form. It had substance. It had

General Colin L. Powell, US Army, was appointed the 12th Chairman of the Joint Chiefs of Staff, Department of Defense, by President George Bush on October 1, 1989. He was reappointed for a second term in October 1991. In this capacity, he serves as the principal military advisor to the President, the Secretary of Defense, and the National Security Council. Prior to this assignment, General Powell served as Commander in Chief, Forces Command, headquartered in Atlanta, GA. He also served as Assistant to the President for National Security Affairs from December 1987 to January 1989.

ideology. It could be seen. It could be touched. It could be studied. It could be heard. It had its demons. Its devils. Its Stalins. It had armies we could point to. It served as a very convenient and appropriate single point of focus for the Free World's response. As long as we responded to this monolith, surely we could handle any included regional problem that could come along.

That focus is now blurred. The form and substance are disappearing before our eyes, vanishing in a whirlwind of change, change, and still more change. If I gave a quiz right now and asked this distinguished group of scholars to tell me the name of the Autonomous Republic in the Soviet Union which in November 1991 declared its independence from Russia, requiring a great democrat, Mr. Boris Yeltsin, to declare marshal law only to be overruled by his own parliament, how many of you could tell me that the name of that Autonomous Republic was . . . *Chechen-Ingush?* In my 34 years of military service I had never heard of Chechen-Ingush.

This change is with us. This isn't bad news. This is great news. This is wonderful news. But however wonderful this news is, it is at the same time disconcerting. It is disconcerting because we are not sure what is coming in the place of the Cold War, as our grand nemesis, the Soviet Union—if one can still call it that—literally disassembles before our anxious eyes. We have no way of knowing what new form this beautiful and well-endowed rich land of 11 time zones will eventually take. Will it completely dissolve into an unstable nest of warring Republics? Or will it perhaps evolve into some kind of yet unclear, coherent federation that we can deal with as a single entity? We spend a lot of time discussing this question, but there isn't a whole lot we can do about it. We can only watch. We can only hope. We can offer our assistance to these people, where it is prudent, and where it is in our interest to offer that assistance.

Around the world, we see a proliferation of other nation-states seeking new ideologies, seeking new political systems, seeking new economic systems and new alignments, to deal with the challenges of the 21st century. We can be proud and we can feel vindicated that most of these nations are seeking their course and basing their systems on the democratic model, the model that we have pushed forward and demonstrated, and which has brought freedom and prosperity not only to the world but to the human spirit.

Four Constants in a Sea of Change

All this turmoil, all this dramatic change, still leaves us dazzled, as we try to keep up with it to determine the ultimate outcome. Yet at the same time, within all of this turmoil, within all of this change, it seems to me that there are certain realities, certain constants, that we can use like stars to help chart our course.

The first reality is that the United States will retain its position of world leadership. Our old friends in Europe look to us to continue the all-important trans-Atlantic link. The newly freed nations of Central and Eastern Europe now look west instead of east, and they look to us for their inspiration and—increasingly—they look to us to provide for their security.

In late 1991, NATO's leaders met in Rome to begin dealing with these fundamental questions. They approved the most dramatic revision of NATO strategy in four decades. They affirmed once again that NATO will remain crucial to the security and stability of a Europe that we hope now, finally, will be whole and free.

Our friends across the Pacific, similarly, look to us to stay engaged and to continue to be a stabilizing force in one of the world's most dynamic regions. In our own hemisphere, we have served as the model for the democratic reform sweeping Central and South America. That democratic reform—we have to caution ourselves—still rests on very, very fragile foundations.

In every region of the world, there are people who are counting on the United States for involved, engaged leadership. Only we could have put together the coalition that stood shoulder to shoulder in Saudi Arabia and reversed the brutal invasion of Kuwait. Only we could have served as the catalyst for the historic Middle East Peace Conference in Madrid. We cannot—we dare not—abandon our leadership role or retreat into a shell of isolationism.

After a titanic struggle of half a century, first against fascism and then against communism, America has found her home in the world. We are not locked into our territorial limits by the two great oceans to our east and to our west. Our home is the international community. Our home is with nations of the Free World. By being a part of that world, and by not withdrawing, America makes that world safer, more productive, more prosperous, and more humane.

The second reality is that, while the Soviet Union is transforming itself into whatever it is going to become, we must not lose sight of the fact that more than 27,000 nuclear weapons and a massive Red Army are still in existence, under increasingly tenuous control. This strategic nuclear capability can still destroy us in 30 minutes. Not a day as Chairman passes for me, when I don't remind myself of the reality of Soviet nuclear power. It must be deterred.

The Red Army, even in its weakened state, is still the most powerful army in Eurasia. It cannot be waved away or out of existence in the euphoria of the moment. In fact, in the next few months we may well see the Red Army begin to divide itself into several large, new, competing republican armies that will not see the United States as their enemy but might well see each other as potential competitors and even adversaries. This will bring a degree of instability to a part of the world that hasn't seen it in years.

The third reality that we can use to chart our course through these troubled times is that we must devote more of our energies and our resources to our needs right here at home in America. Our economy, our cities, our educational system, our minorities, and the poor who are yet to share in the national wealth of this great country must be tended to. You see that in your newspapers every day. You can see that that will be the major political issue in the months and years ahead.

Fourth, we must not close our eyes to the reality that we live in a world that is still very troubled, where danger, uncertainty, instability and crises will continue to lurk in many, many regions. We are not at the "end of history," where everything is going to be smooth and neat and where, for example, the Brookings Institution can predict what the world is going to look like in 1999.

The world we live in is a world where crises and war are very real possibilities. According to my staff, in the 25 months I have been Chairman I have been involved in 14 different regional crises of one kind or another. A crisis might involve just a few airplanes to be flown over an airfield in the Philippines on a December evening in 1989. It might involve humanitarian rescue. It might involve 541,000 men and women going to war in Southwest Asia. The one thing I and the Chiefs are absolutely sure of is that there is a 15th crisis out there waiting, and probably a 16th, and a 17th, and an 18th. We are not at the "end of history."

President George Bush, Secretary of Defense Richard Cheney, the Joint Chiefs of Staff and I, and the unified and specified commanders are fully aware of these constants—of these realities—and that we can use them to guide our course. We have used them to shape a new national security strategy that we believe will deal with this future environment and is also consistent with the resources we are likely to receive from the Congress and from the American people.

US National Security Strategy

The national security strategy we have developed recognizes that, first and foremost, the likelihood of a global war with the former Soviet Union is so small, so remote, and so unlikely that we can significantly cut back on the forces we have maintained for almost 40 years to deal with that possibility. The new strategy, however, at the same time makes sure that we maintain enough forces allocated for Europe, overseas, and at home to deter anyone from thinking that we are unable to defend ourselves, our friends, or our interests. It also preserves our ability to reconstitute forces, if this happy future we are looking at turns out not to be as happy as we had anticipated.

I am reminded of Winston Churchill's quip, some time after the turn of the century, when he said, "War is too foolish, too fantastic to be thought of in the Twentieth Century . . . Civilization has climbed above such perils. The interdependence of nations . . . , the sense of public law . . . have rendered such nightmares impossible." Then he paused and asked rhetorically, "Are you quite sure? It would be a pity to be wrong." And then, of course, he saw two world wars unfold. So I remind everyone, and I remind my colleagues up on Capitol Hill, "Pity to be wrong." We have to hedge our plans and our bets, to insure that we always have the capability to reverse course if—"pity"—our euphoric forecasts are wrong.

Our strategy insures that we are always able to deal with a regional conflict of the type we saw so vividly in the Persian Gulf during the past year. Our strategy insures that, in a world of proliferating nuclear weapons, our nuclear forces will be second to none. In the past few months, we have been working hard to reshape our Armed Forces to meet the demands of this new Strategy. As we went through this process, we first looked across the Atlantic to Europe. For years, we have maintained over 300,000 troops in Europe to deal with the Red Army. The Red Army is going home as fast as the Germans can build houses for them, and we can certainly cut back our forces there. Over the next several years, we will cut our forces in Europe by 50 percent, down to 150,000. Why 150,000? Why not 100,000? Wake up, Powell! The world has changed! Why not 75,000? Why not 50,000? What's magic about 150,000?

Nothing is magic about it, but for the moment we can visualize out only a few years, down to 150,000, because with 150,000 we can keep in Europe a robust Corps-sized unit, with two divisions, a headquarters, supporting air power, infrastructure, logistics, administration, communications and stockpiles so that—"pity if we are wrong"—we haven't taken it all out. We don't want to leave just constabulary forces in Europe, hanging around. We want the US force in Europe to be a real unit, able to perform a real mission in time of crisis, and to make a real contribution to NATO forces. That is why we believe 150,000—50 percent of the current force—is what we should be looking toward.

When we reach that point, we can take another look at what the world looks like. We have started the process of closing over 200 European bases. We are also cutting back here in the United States on the forces that are earmarked for Europe, to include reducing some of the large Reserve Component organizations that we put in the force structure simply for a war in Europe. Over the last 10 years, we added some 250,000 Guardsmen and Reservists. What for? To deal with the Red Army. To come reinforce Europe in the event of a European war. It is right and sensible to reduce this number.

I cannot tell you what a problem this is causing for the Department of Defense. We are in a death fight of a kind that I have never been in before in my career in Washington. I have had intense negotiations with congressional members up on Capitol Hill and with the Controller of the Department of Defense, to get just a part of this reduction started. But Congress is determined to try keep as much Reserve Component force structure as possible, because of its very attractive political nature. I have tried to convince a number of members that, when you take out an entire Army Corps and several Tactical Fighter Wings from the Active Force, it is only reasonable to take out the supporting Reserve units that are in the structure solely to support that Active Component element. I did not make my point. I failed miserably. But we will go at it again tomorrow.

Across the Atlantic there are other areas besides Europe. That is one of the reasons I talk about "Across the Atlantic." Our focus can't simply be on Europe. We have to maintain a presence in Southwest Asia. In our immediate response to Iraq's invasion of Kuwait, we proved how vital our interests are in that part of the world. "Across the Atlantic" has to take a much larger focus.

Next, after looking across the Atlantic in our strategy, we looked across the Pacific, to our friends and our allies in that vast and dynamic region. We can be very proud of the role that our Armed Forces have played in making the Pacific region-a place of stability and a place of progress. We firmly believe we can continue that stability and progress with fewer forces. We will be making modest, prudent reductions in Korea and

Japan, and, of course, we will be closing out our presence in the Philippines. We must, likewise, in all of this change, not withdraw or give the impression to our friends in the Pacific that we are withdrawing from this critical region of the world.

When we looked at the requirement to deal with instability and uncertainty in other parts of the world, we knew that we had to maintain in the United States a pool of forces ready at a moment's notice to respond to the contingency that nobody told us was coming that night, the crisis that erupts at two o'clock in the morning, the regional problem that was festering and then suddenly it appears one morning and has to be dealt with. A pool of contingency forces is needed for that.

Finally, as the last package in our strategy, we had to make sure that our strategic nuclear forces—offensive, defensive, command and control—are as good as we can possibly make them. It is the one area where we must not be second to anyone.

The Base Force

When you add up all the force requirements associated with this strategy—the forward presence requirements, the reinforcement requirements, the reconstitution requirements, the strategic and contingency requirements—you have what we are calling the Base Force. We define the Base Force as the minimum force the Nation needs to accomplish the new strategy and also to be consistent with the funding we are likely to get from the Congress. This is the first time the Joint Chiefs of Staff have tried to take a cold, hard look at both strategic and fiscal reality and match them together so that we can present a convincing case to the American people and to the Congress.

As a result of this process and under the leadership of Secretary Cheney, in 1990 we announced a 25 percent reduction from our Cold War force. We will cut one-third of the Army's active divisions, from 18 to 12. The Navy will lose more than 100 ships and close to 20 percent of its people. The Air Force will drop from 36 Tactical Fighter Wings down to 26.

The Marine Corps will be cut by close to one quarter. We've canceled or are terminating 100 programs. In the last 18 months we have reduced our civilian force by 85,000 through attrition alone, and we are looking for more opportunities to cut. We are closing out or withdrawing from over 300 different installations.

The cuts and the closures are a mixed blessing. When we cut back 500,000 troops in the Active Force—and that is what we are planning—we are also eliminating 500,000 jobs from the American economy—jobs that go to young people. Close to a third of those jobs go to minority young people. Those jobs will not be there any longer. Industries and communities will be affected by our cuts and by the various closures we are planning. I wish it could be otherwise, but cutting the budget means cutting the budget.

I keep telling this to my congressional friends and they keep saying, "You can't cut the Reservists. That affects my community, so don't cut the Reservists." They have told Secretary Cheney, "You can't force anybody out of the Active Force that does not wish to leave—no involuntary separations. But we are not going to give you the tools needed to encourage people to leave. We don't want any bases closed, so—rather than us decide—give it to an independent commission. However, with all those constraints, Mr. Secretary, we want our peace dividend. Go ahead and cut the budget." You can't do it.

Cutting the budget means cutting the budget, and it will have an impact on our capability and it will have an impact on our economy. I am not trying to justify the defense budget as a transfer payment to our economy, but there should be no doubt that the reductions that we are now undergoing will have an impact on that economy. I think many of you in the room will agree that it is starting to be felt.

The Base Force is no longer resting on a specific threat. The Red Army is gone. Fulda Gap is gone. The Soviet "blue water" Navy is a thing of the past. At the moment, notwithstanding what this conference has discussed, there is no regional power in the world that could stand up to the Armed Forces of the United States today or even after we have gone through this reduction that we are planning. We want to keep it that way. We want our friends to be reassured. We want all nations to understand that we have the capability and we have the will to defend our interests.

So the threat is no longer the Red Army or a monolithic hostile political regime. The threat is now instability. The threat is now uncertainty. The threat is an unclear future. The threat is 27,000 nuclear weapons that may no longer be under the control of a monolithic Red Army within the next few months. Complacency is the challenge and the threat if we think the demons are gone and that none of them is coming back again.

We were a superpower in this position several times before in our history, and we saw no dangers. It was wonderful in 1918. We were at the top of the world, a superpower. Nobody could challenge us. Then World War II came along a couple of decades later. In 1945, we had a force of 12 million men that had defeated fascism in two oceans and on three continents. Five years later we were unable to deal with the army of a fourth-rate power. It was in 1953 and again in 1973, when we said we would never again get involved in any new regional entanglements. Wrong.

We don't want to repeat those mistakes again. This time we don't want to leave any fertile ground for a new demon to find root in. The Base Force is being designed to be capability oriented, to provide a capability—a tool box, I call it—to deal with the uncertainties of the future, to handle the next crisis in whatever region it arises—but the next crisis that most certainly will come. The changes we designed last year—the 25 percent reduction—were not based on last year's situation. They were based on our assessment of a more promising, less demanding future. We are now moving into that more promising, less demanding future. The future is accelerating, but it is not now time to throw out all our thinking of last year, and abandon the plan that we put out then to take us to 1995 and 1996. It was a sound plan last year. It is still a sound plan, and you will find your President, your Secretary of Defense, and your Joint Chiefs of Staff swinging from the bleachers to keep Congress from ripping it apart.

The question before us, once again, is the eternal question of, "How much is enough?" How much is enough for a capability-designed Base Force? Defense spending is going to 3.6 percent of the gross national product, down from 5.6 percent. It is going to be only 18 percent of the Federal budget by 1995, down from historic numbers of 24 percent to 30 percent and—in time of war—much, much higher. Politicians and analysts all over town have visions of sugar plums dancing in their heads, as they anticipate how much more they can get out of the defense budget. Defense budget cuts are now seen as political matters solving every problem in the nation, from acne to the Federal deficit.

But, I can tell you, squeezing 18 percent of the Federal budget is not going to solve all the Nation's problems. Squeezing 18 percent of the Federal budget won't get you there, if you are not prepared to deal with the other 82 percent of the Federal budget. The Joint Chiefs of Staff and I and Secretary Cheney believe that the course we are on is the correct one. The savings will come over time, and it would be unwise to try to get them all in 1992 and in 1993. I can assure you that we are going to fight for the Base Force.

There is another aspect to all of this that is of a more qualitative nature. It doesn't lend itself to analysis that easily. My understanding of this issue derives from my responsibility, not just as the principal military advisor to the President and to the Secretary, but as the senior GI in uniform in the Armed Forces of the United States. My concern is that there is a risk of breaking apart the proud force that we now have.

I don't have—you don't have—any draftees clamoring to go home. There is no demobilization waiting to happen. I have got proud volunteers who volunteered to serve their Nation and who want to stay in the Armed Forces. Now they all can't stay, and we can't take in as many as we would like to, or who would like to come in the future, but we have to do this reshaping, this downsizing, in a way that takes into account this very human dimension—proud Americans wanting to stay. -

We can't redesign our strategy and our Base Force and our plans every Monday morning, based on what happened in Red Square that previous Saturday, or on what they said on

Meet the Press the previous Sunday. If we do that, if we constantly fiddle around, if we are not given some time to shape this properly, we will break that proud force of volunteers. It also has to be understood that we cannot go below a certain level of military coherence. With worldwide responsibilities, you cannot have an Army of six divisions and a Navy of a few carriers and a couple of Marines and a couple of Airmen. We need a rational base. We need a training base. We need a sustainment base. We need a development base. We need great educational institutions like the National Defense University and our other great war colleges. We need proud troops who believe in what they are doing, who believe they are serving the Nation's interest, and who believe they are getting the very best equipment, training, and support the Nation can provide them. That's the difference, in 1991, from any previous period of hope.

Our troops are enormously proud. They are enormously capable. They are proud because the American people are proud of them. As we reshape, we have got to ensure that we don't break that love affair that now exists in this post-Desert Storm environment between the American people and their forces.

It will take us time to do this in a very prudent and careful way. And in the final analysis, it is the Congress that provides for and maintains a Navy. It is the Congress that raises and supports an Army. I believe that Secretary Cheney and I and the Joint Chiefs of Staff can help the Congress choose the right course for the challenging years ahead. I know that the National Defense University will, in the months ahead, help to give us the guidance, the vision, the constructive criticism, and the support that we need, in order to ensure that our smaller Armed Forces of the future are even better than the magnificent one we have today.

PART I:

REGIONAL DIMENSIONS

The Persian Gulf Region in Nonglobal Perspective

David E. Long

Regional specialists, both in government and academia, have long been frustrated that the Cold War, which viewed all international relations from a global, bipolar perspective, distorted the way the United States looked at regional politics and, more importantly, impaired US policies toward the region. George Kennan and the policy of containment was no friend of regional studies. With the Cold War over, therefore, hope springs in the hearts of the regionalists that the parts of the world in which they specialize can at last be studied and understood in their own terms.

Those who focus on the Persian Gulf region are no exception. For years, Gulf specialists were forced to deal with such extraneous (for them) issues as how events facilitated the historic Russian quest for a warm-water port, and whether the Soviet-built Iraqi naval facility at Umm Qasr served such a function. (With the benefit of hindsight, it obviously never did.) Most regionalists now hope one can finally concentrate on the problems and issues of the Gulf without artificially injecting global considerations that do not significantly impact on Gulf political dynamics. Although there is a sense of relief that bipolar geopolitics need no longer distort analysis of and policy toward the Gulf as it did only a few years ago, a word of caution

---

David E. Long joined the US Foreign Service in 1962 and has spent most of his career dealing with the Middle East and the Gulf, including tours in Sudan, Morocco, Saudi Arabia, and Jordan. Dr. Long holds several degrees, including a doctorate from the George Washington University, and he has taught at a number of universities, most recently the US Coast Guard Academy. Among his books are *The Anatomy of Terrorism, The United States and Saudi Arabia: Ambivalent Allies,* and *The Persian Gulf.*

17

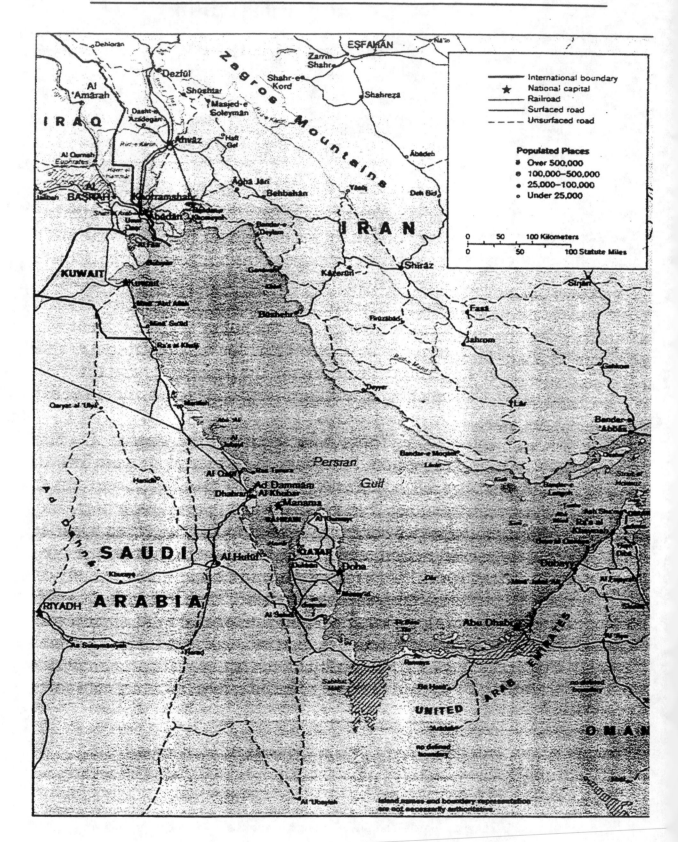

Figure 1. *The Persian Gulf Region*

is needed about how to view the Gulf in the post-Cold War world.

Defining the Gulf Region

How one deals with the world or any part of it, either intellectually or in policy terms, is more than anything else a matter of perspective. There is nothing inherent in the social, political, or economic makeup of the Gulf that compels one to look at the region in a certain way, or even look at it as a region at all. Indeed, for many, it is not a region, but a subregion of the Middle East. Ironically, the term Middle East itself was originally coined around the turn of the century to refer area lying between the "Near East" and the "Far East," that is, to the same region we now call the Gulf.[1]

The most prominent integrating geographic factor in the Gulf is that the states in the region—Iran, Iraq, Saudi Arabia, Kuwait, Bahrain, Qatar, the United Arab Emirates (UAE), and Oman—all have a shoreline on the Gulf, even if only a few miles, such as Iraq and Oman. Economically, all the Gulf states have oil resources, albeit in vastly different amounts. Saudi Arabia has the world's largest proved reserves, and in Bahrain, the reserves are almost exhausted. There is also a degree of cultural integration in the Gulf in that the societies in all the Gulf countries are overwhelmingly Islamic.

There are, however, as many disparate characteristics among the Gulf states as integrating factors. Geographically, none of the Gulf states is exclusively concerned with Gulf politics. Saudi Arabia, Kuwait, Bahrain, Qatar, the UAE, and Oman are also Arabian Peninsula states, which Iran and Iraq are not. As such, they share a political affinity with Yemen which is an Arabian state but not a Gulf state. Oman also has non-Gulf ties. Geographically closer to Bombay than to Beirut, Oman has close ethnic and commercial ties with the subcontinent. Until recently it owned a small conclave that is now part of Pakistan and, in an earlier time, also owned Zanzibar, off the African coast. The southeastern most province of Oman,

Dhufar, has far more ethnic and historic affinity with neighboring Yemen than with the Gulf states.

Saudi Arabia bounds the Red Sea as well as the Gulf, and is only a few miles by sea from Israel across the Gulf of Aqabah. It is thus geographically as well as politically concerned about politics in the Horn of Africa as well as being an important player in the Arab-Israeli dispute. Indeed, although the Kingdom has never considered itself a "confrontation state" with Israel, the latter still occupies two Saudi islands in the mouth of the Gulf of Aqabah, Tiran and Sanifir, that it seized in the 1967 Arab-Israeli war.

Iraq is a Fertile Crescent state as well as a Gulf state. Despite the enmity between it and the other Gulf states evidenced by the Iran-Iraq war of the 1980s and the Iraqi invasion of Kuwait in 1990, Baghdad has long considered its most implacable foe to be Syria, primarily the result of the personal enmity between Iraqi President Saddam Hussein and Syrian President Hafiz al-Asad.

Iran, in addition to being a Gulf state, has major interests in the politics of neighboring Pakistan and Afghanistan and was greatly involved in the Afghan insurgency. Iran also has centuries-old ties to Russia—mostly conflictual—and with the collapse of the Soviet Union, Tehran is already seeking to extend its political influence into the Muslim states of former Soviet central Asia. With Turkey and Iraq, it shares a Kurdish irredentist problem.

There are also great economic and social disparities within the Gulf region. Saudi Arabia and the small Gulf Arab states have few economic resources other than oil (and gas) and the revenues derived therefrom. They also have relatively small populations in proportion to their economies. Thus, unlike Iraq and Iran, which have large populations and the attendant need for high state revenues and are historically oil-price hawks, they are generally price moderates within the Organization of Petroleum Exporting Countries (OPEC). OPEC itself is not exclusively a Gulf organization, although the Gulf producers comprise the most important component. It was founded by Venezuela and has members from Africa and the Far East as well.

Social disparities include both ethnic and religious confessional differences. Although there are a few Arab speakers along the Iranian Gulf coast, the great majority of Iranians are not Arab, and a clash in Arab and Persian nationalisms has existed for centuries. Even the name of the Gulf is contested; the Arabs call it the Arabian Gulf and the Iranians call it the Persian Gulf. Moreover, segments of Iran's population have ethnic ties in central Asia the subcontinent. Tribes in western Afghanistan speak a dialect of Persian, and Baluchis, found in southeastern Iran, are also located in neighboring southern Afghanistan and southwestern Pakistan. The clash between Arab and Persian nationalisms is exacerbated by confessional split. All the Arab regimes in the Gulf are dominated by Sunni Muslims (even though there are numerical Shi'a majorities in Bahrain and Iraq), whereas Iraq is solidly Shi'a. Thus, confessional rivalries as well as Arab-Persian nationalist rivalries are a major feature of internal Gulf politics.

With all these disparities and extra-regional ties among many of the Gulf states, the question still remains, what set of characteristics define the Gulf as an autonomous region? The answer is that there is no single set of characteristics. For the cultural anthropologist, for example, ethnic ties are more important than national borders. For the economist, natural and financial resources and commercial patterns are determining factors. For political scientists, inter-regional political dynamics are defining characteristics, and for the outside student and practitioner of international politics, one's own political interests, and by extension strategic interests, constitute the determining factor. It is generally the latter, however, that dominates perceptions of what constitutes the Gulf, at least in the public mind.

Thus, we come full circle. For 45 years, the overriding US interest perceived to be at stake when one looked at this part of the world was the Soviet political and military threat. It assumed the highest priority of national interests, and more parochial interests were seen as subunits of an overall global focus. That in itself was not necessarily bad. Rivalry with the Soviet Union was indeed our most pressing foreign policy interest during the Cold War years, whether it was manifested in the Gulf or anywhere else in the world.

The main problem with our bipolar focus was that our order of political-military priorities in the Gulf was not necessarily shared by the political actors of the Gulf itself, nor were regional politics driven by our priorities; they had their own dynamics. For example, the cordial relations the Shah maintained with the United States were not driven by any affinity with democracy or friendship with the West but by self-interest. He calculated that the Soviets on his border comprised a greater threat to Iran than the Americans, thousands of miles away, and that the Americans would defend him against the Soviet threat.

Similarly, Iraq's Friendship Treaty with the Soviet Union was a product of Iraqi priorities that saw more to be gained from cordial relations with America's enemy than in distancing itself from a Soviet imperial threat. At no time did communism versus democracy ever come into the equation of Iraqi foreign policy interests. Without fully understanding what motivated the local actors, we were at a disadvantage in pursuing our political interests in the Gulf.

The United States and the Gulf

Before looking at what US interests will be in the Gulf in the post-Cold War era and how best we might deal with the region in furthering those interests, it might be instructive to review briefly the development of US policies in the region. In the years immediately following World War II, the United States did not look on the Gulf as a separate unit of policy interest, but rather as a subregion of the Middle East. Moreover, policy interests in the subregion were overwhelmingly preoccupied with military security, particularly in containment of the Soviet Union, which bordered the so-called Northern Tier states—Iran and Iraq as well as Turkey and Pakistan.

By the 1970s, the strategic importance of Gulf oil began to rival military containment of the Soviet Union in the priority of interests in the region. The two interests together provided the impetus for looking at the Gulf as a separate unit of policy interest for the first time. The catalyst that first caused US policy makers to perceive the Gulf as a region was the British government's announcement in 1968 of its intention to end the British protective status over the lower Gulf states by 1971. Prior to the announcement, the United States looked on the Gulf as basically a British sphere of influence within a broader Middle East policy arena.

Because the Soviet military threat and maintaining secure oil supplies complemented each other initially, the initial US policy toward the Gulf was predominantly defense oriented. This was the so-called Two Pillar policy of the 1970s, through which the United States hoped to enlist Iran and Saudi Arabia (the two pillars) to maintain regional security in the Gulf with US support but without a direct US military presence. The policy was driven by concern that the Soviet Union, either directly or through surrogates such as Iraq, would exploit the "power vacuum" created by the departure of the British, and attempt to displace Western influence among the remainder of the Gulf states, all of which were conservative, pro-Western oil producing states.

In fact, oil security and containing the Soviet Union were not as compatible as they first seemed. US and Western dependence on Gulf oil was dramatically underscored by the energy crisis of the 1970s and created highly ambivalent attitudes toward the region. Reacting to what was seen as gratuitous US support of Israel in the 1973 Arab-Israeli war, the same conservative Arab Gulf oil-producing states that the United States believed needed protecting from the Soviet Union and its surrogates initiated the Arab oil embargo which initiated the energy crisis, and were thus seen as much antagonists as allies, particularly by American supporters of Israel. As a result, US policies toward those states, particularly Saudi Arabia, were highly inconsistent. Nevertheless, the dual focus on military security and oil, while it encouraged ambivalent policy responses, did reinforce the US perception of the Gulf as a separate region in policy terms.

The transformation of the Gulf from a subregion of the Middle East to a major political-military arena in US foreign policy was completed in the early 1990s. The Iraqi invasion of Kuwait in August 1990 placed the Gulf in international focus and resulted in a multinational military effort led by the United States to forcibly eject the invading force the following January. For the first time since the United States has viewed the Gulf as a separate policy area, regional Gulf security was not linked to the Soviet threat, but rather to the threat to vital oil supplies. Indeed, the Soviet Union, however reluctantly, gave political support to the US-led coalition against its former friend, Iraq. Later in the year, the Soviet Union collapsed and ceased to be a threat to the Gulf at all.

In the space of fewer than 20 years, oil evolved from a benign interest to a major strategic interest, first rivaling and then superseding the Soviet threat. Looking to the future, Gulf oil is likely to remain a vital interest to the United States and the West generally for the foreseeable future. The United States is becoming more, not less dependent on imported oil, and the Gulf remains the residual oil supplier for the world. The end of the Soviet threat, however, does not mean the end of a strategic military interest in the Gulf. It simply means that maintaining the security of Gulf oil supplies has become a major strategic interest in itself. The combined interest in oil and regional security is sufficient to insure that the Gulf will remain a major focus of U.S. policy interest for years to come.

Conclusions

The knowledge that the Gulf is likely to remain a region of high policy interest does not insure that US policy toward the countries of the region will effectively further those interests. In times of crisis, good crisis managers are needed. This was borne out during *Desert Storm* and *Desert Shield* when not only military but diplomatic personnel in the area did an overall superb job of managing the crisis. During noncrisis periods, however, a keen understanding of Gulf political dynamics and the ability to communicate that understanding to nonarea specialists in Washington are essential; the only way effectively to persuade Gulf leaders to take policy measures supporting our interests is to couch them in terms that support their interests, and to do that we must have a sound understanding of what their interests are. In that area, our record is less bright. Misunderstanding and miscommunication have greatly hindered the US ability to follow up on a number of important policy objective such as working our military prepositioning agreements with a number of the Gulf states. The dearth of regional expertise is a major contributing factor to this state of affairs. If we are to promote more political cooperation and avoid differences arising from miscommunication, there must be a concerted effort to create and maintain the expertise necessary for better understanding of our friends.

Notes

1. See Roderic H. Davison, "Where is the Middle East?" *Foreign Affairs* (July 1960), 665-675.

The Post-Gulf War Middle East and US National Security Strategy

Marvin C. Feuerwerger

*A*merican interests in the Middle East are a subset of US interests in the post-Cold War world.[1] In the most general sense, the United States must seek to preserve its own independence, freedom, and economic well-being. But American interests can best be served if the United States, in cooperation with like-minded nations, can also work to promote greater stability and the peaceful resolution of disputes. This would be one important element of what President Bush has labeled the "new world order."

In many ways, Iraq's aggression against Kuwait provided a stressful test case for America's approach to regional conflict in the 1990s. Iraq's initial success demonstrated the importance of sustaining a stable global security environment—including the maintenance of sturdy regional military balances in key areas—so that local aggressors will be unable to determine the fate of their neighbors. The collective approach taken by most of the international community toward Iraq's assault against Kuwait constitutes an ideal model for future coalition efforts, should they prove possible in future crises. Iraq's unconventional weapons programs highlighted the importance of preventing the proliferation of destabilizing weapons of mass destruction.

Marvin C. Feuerwerger is Senior Strategic Fellow at the Washington Institute for Near East Policy and Professorial Lecturer in International Relations at the Johns Hopkins University's School of Advanced International Studies. He previously served as the Acting Director of the Pentagon's Policy Planning Staff and as Director for Regional Policy in the Office of the Principal Deputy Under Secretary of Defense for Strategy and Resources.

During the Cold War, the United States vigorously opposed Soviet presence and influence in the Middle East because the Soviets were antagonistic to American interests. This circumstance has clearly changed. Today the former Soviet Union is unable to assert its influence throughout the world, and in the Middle East, in the manner to which we had become accustomed over the past two decades. There is little doubt that the traditional interest Russia had in the Middle East will again reassert itself over time, but it is impossible to know when and in what manner.

The ending of the Cold War and the retrenchment of Soviet power has already significantly eased superpower competition throughout the world. As it has moved toward democracy, Russia has abandoned some of the practices that were the hallmark of Soviet policy in the Middle East. It has significantly reduced its military and aid relationships with erstwhile allies like Syria. It has curtailed support for terrorist activities. And it has urged both Arabs and Israelis to abandon "old thinking" and open the door to peace.

These Russian policy changes—including the resumption of diplomatic relations with Israel and the promotion of free emigration for Russian Jews—have enabled the United States and Russia to work together to foster regional peace. This joint activity was most clearly demonstrated by the co-hosting of the Madrid peace conference in October 1991.

US Mideast Interests: Continuity Amidst Change

Despite the changes wrought by the end of the Cold War and the Persian Gulf War, America's traditional interests in the region will, for the most part, remain the basis for US involvement in the Middle East. Perhaps the most traditional and constant interest will be the safety and protection of US citizens and property, which have always been a foremost goal of American governments. Americans have faced bombings, assassinations, and other forms of terrorism in the Middle East, and Iraq took American hostages in 1990.

Apart from the protection of American citizens, America's interest in the Middle East include: (1) freedom of commerce, especially access to oil at reasonable prices; (2) commitment to the survival and security of Israel; (3) commitment to the security of friendly Arab states and Turkey; (4) support for regional stability and conflict resolution; and (5) freedom of the seas.

First, the United States will continue to have a vital interest in maintaining access to Mideast oil at reasonable prices. In 1990, oil products comprised over 40 percent of US energy consumption and the US imported over 50 percent of its oil requirements. According to Department of Energy predictions, the United States could import up to two-thirds of its oil by the year 2010.

Almost two-thirds of the world's proven reserves are concentrated in the Gulf region, and the cost to recover this oil is among the lowest in the world. A predominant share of the world's excess production capacity also lies in the Gulf area. Such factors led former CIA Director William Webster to predict in 1990 that the percentage of US oil coming from the Persian Gulf would rise from about 10 percent in 1990 to about 25 percent in the mid-1990s.

Significant oil disruptions, when they have occurred, have had an important, deleterious effect on the US economy. At the outset of the Gulf War, the loss of Iraqi and Kuwaiti oil from world markets initially doubled oil prices and aggravated recessionary trends in the United States. The US gross national Product (GNP) declined by 5 percent as a result of the recession resulting from Arab state petroleum production cuts in the wake of the October 1973 War. The oil shock of 1979-80 caused by the Iranian revolution and OPEC's success in increasing prices contributed to a 3 percent loss of GNP for the United States. Clearly, assured access to Persian Gulf oil at reasonable prices remains important to the stability and health of the world economy. In order to preserve the free flow of oil, it is important to prevent any single power—particularly a hostile power—from dominating the supply of oil. This was the basis of the Carter Doctrine, which was issued over a decade ago to deter Soviet aggression in the Gulf. With the end of the Cold

War, the main threats to the free flow of oil from the Persian Gulf are likely to come from local states such as Iraq or Iran.

Second, the United States will continue to have a strong interest in supporting Israel's survival and security, in the context of American global interests and America's interests in the Middle East. The United States and Israel share democratic values and a unique historical relationship, close people-to-people bonds, and religious and cultural ties. Beyond backing for Israel's well-being, the United States will continue to have an interest in close strategic relations with Israel—although perhaps not at the level that some had imagined. As an American ally, Israel can be important in future Eastern Mediterranean contingencies. However hard these may be to define in the new world setting, it appears certain that an American presence and interest in this region will remain.

It is important to recall that the United States has, on occasion, relied on cooperation with Israel for military cooperation that was in no way linked to the Soviet Union. The best known case occurred in 1970, when Syrian forces threatened to invade Jordan. At that time, Secretary of State Henry Kissinger turned to Israel, which postured its forces in a manner that helped deter Syrian aggression. America's military cooperation with Israel evolved in important ways in the 1980s—to involve combined planning, prepositioning, and exercise activity under the guidance of the US-Israel Joint Political-Military Group. In the 1990s, Israel will continue to offer excellent training opportunities for US military forces—increasingly hard to find in post-Cold War Europe. Should the US need to use force in Israel's neighborhood, it can be confident of a politically friendly environment and competent military support.

Of course, at the request of the United States, Israel did not directly participate in *Operation Desert Shield/Storm*. This should not have been particularly surprising, since U.S.-Israeli planning never envisaged the use of Israeli forces in the Persian Gulf. At the same time, Israel did contribute to the international effort in a number of ways, by furthering America's diplomatic strategy and providing equipment and intelligence to U.S. forces. Indeed, Israeli forbearance in the face of provocation was appreciated in Washington as one of the key elements in maintaining the anti-Iraq coalition. One of the important lessons to be learned from *Desert Storm* is that the United States can maintain a strategic relationship—even during crises—with both Israel and friendly Arab states.

Of course, America's ability to cooperate militarily with Israel would be much enhanced if there were significant progress toward a resolution of the Arab-Israeli problem. If Israel had been at peace with its Arab neighbors, the United States and its coalition partners would have been likely to turn to Israel for more direct logistics support during the course of *Operation Desert Shield/Storm*. While this is hardly a strong motivating factor for American diplomacy, it is a factor that should not be entirely overlooked.

Third, the United States will maintain a strong interest in supporting the security and independence of friendly Arab states, either because of their centrality to the stability of the region or because of their importance for access to oil. Supporting Egypt will continue to be an American interest because of Egypt's commitment to peace with Israel, its central role in the Arab world, and its demonstrated position (as during *Desert Storm*) as a counterweight to radical regional powers. The United States will also support preservation of the independence of Saudi Arabia and other Gulf oil-producing states that cooperated with the US in response to Iraq's aggression. The United States has already expressed its intention in this regard by negotiating new agreements with Kuwait and Bahrain to help foster regional security and by seeking additional understandings with other Gulf states.

The United States also has an important interest in helping to protect Turkey from external threats. As a key North Atlantic Treaty Organization (NATO) ally with the largest ground forces in Europe, Turkey is a critical bridge between Europe and the Middle East. Its *Desert Storm* role in the anti-Iraq coalition demonstrated Turkey's renewed importance in the Middle East.

In the new international setting, a fourth interest of the United States is to help insure regional stability and ameliorate international conflicts in order to protect American friends and avoid unnecessary American military involvement. The Gulf crisis illustrated the extent to which American interests could be threatened when a regional imbalance develops in the Middle East.

As American policy makers survey the world scene, there are only a few areas in which it is easy to envision the large-scale involvement of American forces in the 1990s. These include the Korean peninsula, the Persian Gulf, and the Eastern Mediterranean. Obviously, American diplomacy and strategy will focus considerable attention on preventing the outbreak of major conflict and on the resolution of underlying disputes in these areas. To promote the resolution of regional conflicts, it will be essential to ensure that a balance of power exists to deter radical powers from challenging American friends. This may require a combination of American presence, access arrangements, security agreements, arms sales, and foreign assistance.

Improved regional stability will also require a strong focus on arms control concerns in the post-Cold War and post-Gulf War period. The United States should continue to strive for a reduction in the levels of armaments in the region and the elimination or control of weapons of mass destruction and their delivery systems.

The end of the Cold War created a cruel paradox. As disarmament agreements were being negotiated and implemented in Europe, the Middle East arms race was growing apace with the introduction of chemical and biological weapons, nuclear weapons technologies, and ballistic missiles into the arsenals of the principal regional powers. In the hands of an aggressive power like Iraq, these weapons pose a menace to neighboring states and a danger to those who oppose them. It might have been far more difficult for the United States and its Arab and European partners to oppose Iraq militarily if Baghdad had a serious nuclear capability. It is clearly in the interest of the United States to prevent such an eventuality and to promote control over arms and technology movement to potential aggressors in the Middle East.

The United States traditionally has perceived an interest in helping to resolve regional disputes such as the Arab-

Israeli conflict. Although the Gulf War demonstrated that the Arab-Israeli conflict is hardly the only threat to U.S. interests in the Middle East, it clearly is a potentially destabilizing element both in the Eastern Mediterranean and throughout the region. This is one of the key reasons motivating American policy makers to bring the parties to the dispute to the negotiating table.

Fifth, as the world's greatest maritime power, the United States requires freedom of the seas. US trade is overwhelmingly waterborne; the US and all developed countries rely on seaborne trade. Many billions of dollars worth of imports and exports must transit the Persian Gulf and Suez Canal each year. The geostrategic centrality of the Middle East, at the crossroads of three continents, means that maintaining access to that region will continue to be an important American interest.

Freedom of navigation and overflight also ensures that the US military can maintain an effective regional presence in peacetime, or respond rapidly in a crisis—as during *Operation Desert Storm/Shield*. US maritime superiority in that crisis also ensured that—as long as Iraq's neighbors restricted the flow of key materials overground—the United States and its allies could effectively cut off Iraq.

Threats in the Post-Gulf War Era

In the wake of the Gulf War, the United States has a strong interest in the creation and maintenance of a more stable balance of power that can protect American friends and preserve the free flow of oil from the region. Traditionally, American friends in the Middle East have faced four different classes of threats: the Soviet Union; interstate conflict; internal instability; and terrorism. With the end of the Cold War, the Soviet threat—which had galvanized American defense planning for the region—has basically disappeared.

The interstate threat posed by Iraq in 1990 was a nightmare that could have affected all basic American interests. With its conquest of Kuwait and the prospective threat to the independence of Saudi Arabia, Iraq could have intimidated many OPEC members and dictated the oil production policies of most Persian Gulf states. From such a position, it could have restricted the free flow of oil and manipulated world prices in a manner harmful to the fundamental interests of the United States and all oil-consuming countries. In addition, Iraq's increased revenues would have permitted it to amass additional military power to threaten others in the region, including Israel. United Nations revelations of the extent of Iraq's unconventional weapons programs indicate just how great a threat Iraq would have become had Saddam Hussein not led his country into war prematurely.

With Iraq's defeat, all friendly Mideast states enjoy an improved security environment. Member countries of the Gulf Cooperation Council have seen the two prior greatest threats to their security, Iran and Iraq, suffer significant recent military setbacks, reducing the interstate threat to the lowest level in many years. US actions have strengthened deterrence, which should contribute to regional stability. Israel has also benefitted strategically from Iraq's defeat and the deterrent impact of America's successful intervention on potential future aggressors.

At the same time, threats to America's friends remain. At the interstate level, Saddam Hussein continues to rule Iraq. Today he is weak and apparently powerless to attack his neighbors, but Middle Eastern states have little doubt that he will seek to avenge Iraq's defeat should the opportunity arise. Although Iran has moderated its political approach toward Gulf states in the recent past, it could still seek to rebuild its military capability, attempt to oust the United States from the region, and threaten traditional pro-American regimes. The evidence of Iraqi and Iranian unconventional weapons programs also heighten concern about the scope and destruction of future interstate conflicts in the Middle East. In the longer run, all the states of the lower Gulf will face security problems caused by their wealth (which makes them attractive targets), their limited military capability, and the tensions within their own societies. Israel will also face threats from its Arab neighbors, although these can be eased by greater progress toward a resolution of the Arab-Israeli conflict.

Beyond the interstate, threats to internal stability in many Middle Eastern states are likely to intensify. Rising groups in different societies such as the army, intellectuals, and the middle class are likely to increase their demands for power. Among the masses, social change may weaken traditional bonds of authority; many may turn to the sense of identity and purpose offered by Islamic fundamentalism. Fundamentalist groups themselves may grow more assertive.

In the broader Middle East, unresolved conflicts and the persistent threat of terrorism will also create security challenges. Despite the reduction in international terrorism in the Middle East over the past 2 years, the most likely threat US citizens will face in the 1990s is the threat of terrorism from the disaffected. Any survey of threats in the Middle East would not be complete without recalling just how poor a track record the United States has had in predicting threats to American interests and allies during the past 20 years. Few anticipated the timing of the downfall of the Shah of Iran, the Soviet invasion of Afghanistan, the outbreak of the Iran-Iraq War, or the Iraqi conquest of Kuwait. With this history, the best course is to anticipate that threats will emerge—but to avoid overconfidence about whether it will be possible to determine how and where they will arise.

Elements of a Post-War Regional Security Strategy

In the wake of the Gulf war, the United States has a strong interest in the creation and maintenance of a more stable regional setting that can protect American friends and preserve the free flow of oil from the region. President Bush addressed this question directly in his March 6, 1991, address to Congress, when he stated:

> We must work together to create shared security arrangements in the region. Our friends and allies in the Middle East

recognize that they will bear the bulk of the responsibility for regional security. But we want them to know that just as we stood with them to repel aggression so now America stands ready to work with them to secure the peace.

This does not mean stationing US ground forces on the Arabian Peninsula, but it does mean American participation in joint exercises involving both air and ground forces. And it means maintaining a capable US naval presence in the region, just as we have for over 40 years. Let it be clear: Our vital national interests depend on a stable and secure Gulf.

An American security strategy for the Middle East must address a number of essential elements, including:

● Appropriate security arrangements to create a more stable military balance, including a suitable American presence

● Arms sales and arms control policy

● Improving American "long-reach" military capabilities

● Promoting the settlement of regional conflicts through negotiations.

Appropriate Security Arrangements

With Iraq's defeat, considerable effort has focused on the regional security arrangements necessary to preserve stability in the Persian Gulf area and throughout the Middle East. How to preserve such stability is a vexing problem. The military balance between Iran and Iraq in the 1970s and 1980s was an important element in limiting the aggressive capabilities of each of these powers. Having each been defeated in military hostilities in the past several years, they pose only a limited threat to their neighbors for the first part of this decade.

Nonetheless, there is reason to believe that Iraq or Iran may again try to threaten regional stability in the future. Though President Bush encouraged American friends to assume the "bulk of the responsibility" for regional security, it is difficult to envision circumstances under which these states could be expected to defend themselves against major threats without assistance. Accordingly, they will look to the United States to provide a safety net.

For at least the near term, America's approach to regional security must ensure that Iraq cannot reemerge as a threat to its neighbors. The United States will have to continue to make sure that the special measures detailed in UN Security Council Resolution 687 and subsequent resolutions, including destruction of Iraqi unconventional weapons, are carried out in full. The United States also should continue to work to enhance US bilateral ties with Gulf Cooperation Council states and encourage the strengthening of the GCC itself. In the wake of the Gulf War, the US signed security cooperation agreements with Kuwait and Bahrain; similar agreements with other states may be on the horizon. In addition to multilateral exercises and high-level visits and exchanges, the United States should engage in planning with GCC states for future contingencies. In general terms, the United States must be ready to respond positively to reasonable requests to assist in the defense of GCC states.

Although President Bush ruled out a permanent US ground force presence on the Arabian peninsula, the US does require an enhanced presence in the region to help defend American friends. Beyond an enhanced naval presence, the US is seeking the prepositioning of heavy equipment and munitions in the region. We should increase combined exercises with the states of the region and seek better support ashore for the peacetime presence of US forces.

In the long run, the United States should not plan to build a capability *in place* to defend the borders of Kuwait or Saudi Arabia against a resurgent Iraq or Iran. Unless a significant conventional threat reemerged the maintenance of such a force level is unnecessary and politically and economically foolish—particularly at a time when the United States is drawing its own forces down. Instead, a suitable US presence should be designed to facilitate a speedier US return to the Persian Gulf and enhance deterrence at minimal cost with little danger of turning American soldiers into catalysts of regime instability. The contingency force planning concepts set forth by Secretary Cheney and JCS Chairman Powell appear suitable for this task.

Arms Sales and Arms Control

President Bush's May 1991 Middle East arms control initiative sought, among other measures, to limit the sale of conventional arms to the Middle East. A key feature was the effort to establish an arms sales code of responsibility, which was accepted by the Permanent Five members of the United Nations Security Council—who account for the great majority of arms sales to the Middle East.

Given that the Middle East region is the largest importer of arms in the world, it is clear that damping arms sales could make a major contribution to reducing local threats and enhancing regional security. At the same time, it is also clear that as long as the root causes of instability and conflict continue to exist, local states will continue to seek arms. And if they have the financial resources, chances are that they will be able to find a supplier.

While one cannot be overly optimistic about controlling the flow of conventional arms to the Middle East, there may be a greater capability to control unconventional weapons and missile technology. Fewer suppliers are available for such systems, and international norms against their supply are stronger. However, the scope of Iraq's secret unconventional weapons programs and reports of serious unconventional weapons programs underway in a number of Middle East countries do not occasion great optimism for leak-proof constraints in this area as well.

The United States has a clear interest in the full implementation of President Bush's arms control initiative. At the same time, as long as threats to America's friends continue, the United States will want to sell them arms to meet their legitimate defense needs. The United States has been committed for many years to preserve Israel's qualitative edge against prospective foes. The United States is also interested in helping friendly Arab states modernize their militaries to face prospective threats.

The tension between American arms control policy and arms sales policy may create a dilemma, because the United States is unlikely to agree with arms suppliers like China, North Korea, or even France about a definition for legitimate defense needs or about appropriate arms recipients. One need only remember the criticism the United States faced in the wake of the Gulf War after announcing limited arms sales to Gulf states, Egypt, and Israel. Moreover, as military spending through much of the world decreases, the competition for remaining markets is likely to intensify. In the region itself, the United States can also expect disagreement among its friends over the question of whether sales to a prospective opponent meet legitimate defense needs or could provide the means for aggression. Managing this situation could be difficult, although the fact that none of America's traditional arms recipients in the region is cash-rich today could ease the problem. In this potentially difficult situation, the United States should approach arms sales with some caution—trying to minimize the prospect for spurring regional arms races or destabilizing friendly regimes.

In the Gulf, rather than supporting dubious efforts to double or triple the size of existing armies, the US should encourage defense expenditures for two purposes: (1) initial defense and (2) facilitating the ability of the US to come rapidly to their assistance. Areas of focus for initial defense might include technologies to slow ground forces (tank traps, mines), mine sweeping and clearing equipment, antitank weapons, integrated air defense, and improved intelligence and communications.

Improving American "Long-Reach" Military Capabilities

The Gulf crisis provided a unique display of international cooperation against aggression. Yet, when Iraq threatened to invade Saudi Arabia and a quick response was required, only the United States had the political will and military capability to respond in a timely manner. The US and coalition success against Iraq may enhance deterrence of similar future aggression in the region because of increased respect for US capabilities. Nonetheless, there will be a continuing expectation of a rapid American response in the event of future significant crises. Although there is much to be said for coalition efforts, the United States still must plan to be largely self-reliant militarily in the early stages of a crisis.

This lesson has a number of important ramifications for US forces. Even as it reduces defense spending, the US will have to focus increased attention on the maintenance of a rapid deployment capability. We have already mentioned the US requirement for some peacetime presence, and prepositioning and access to local facilities. The United States will also require cooperation with capable local militaries and highly deployable US forces with long reach.

Most discussions of a suitably sized force have focused on being able to deploy about two heavy ground force divisions to the region within a month. Such a capability should provide a potent deterrent and a capable initial defense. This force capability would be equally applicable to future contingencies in the Persian Gulf or for the defense of Israel. Indeed, given Israel's superior self-defense capabilities against its threats as against the capabilities of US friends in the Persian Gulf against their threats, we may consider the defense of Israel a lesser included case.

Additional acquisition of airlift and sealift would be helpful to the United States in meeting future Middle East contingencies. In addition, future American forces may have to be tailored more toward contingencies requiring quick and distant deployment. High priority will have to be given to forces with long reach, and to special units and high technology systems that can provide leverage against middle-level powers like Iraq.

Helping to Resolve Regional Conflicts

The Middle East is a region rent by border disputes, religious strife, and regional rivalries. Outside powers cannot determine solutions to these problems, but the United States should continue to vigorously support the efforts of local states to settle their disputes. Foremost among these disputes is the Arab-Israeli conflict. During the Gulf crisis, Saddam Hussein tried to play on Palestinian grievances to undermine American interests. In spite of Saddam's efforts—including the launching of Scud missiles against Tel Aviv—the United States resisted the linkage that Saddam Hussein tried to draw. At the same time, American leaders rededicated themselves to actively promoting a settlement of the Arab-Israeli conflict. A solution to this problem can help stabilize the region by enhancing the security of Israel and its neighbors, slowing the regional arms race, and permitting the nations of the Middle East to devote their energies to more constructive purposes. In addition, it would remove the possibility that the United States might have to deploy forces to this region.

The current negotiation process fostered by President Bush and Secretary Baker is an important step forward. It is designed to address the concerns of all parties to the dispute, and includes a mechanism—through multilateral negotiations—to explore the possibility for regionwide arms control. Given the wide gaps that separate the parties on a range of issues, it is hard to be optimistic about rapid progress toward a solution. But even slow progress on any dimension—Israeli-Palestinian, Israeli-Syrian, or regionwide functional—can reduce tensions and promote the prospects for a more stable region. US efforts are in keeping with the values of the American people and with concrete American security interests in the new international setting.

Notes

1. Much of this discussion is based on the work of The Washington Institute for Near East Policy's Strategic Study Group. See, for example, *Restoring the Balance: US Strategy and the Gulf Crisis* (Washington: The Washington Institute, 1991) and *After the Storm: Challenges for America's Middle East Policy* (Washington: The Washington Institute, 1991).

The Shifting Balance of Power in Northeast Asia

Ralph A. Cossa

*E*ven the most dedicated cold warriors now agree that the great battle is over. While we can continue to debate whether the United States, Germany, Japan, or the world at large was the real winner, it is clear that the immediate threat caused by the Cold War's main protagonist, the Soviet Union, has clearly diminished on all fronts. This reduced threat has lead, rightfully, to a call for the US military to reassess its overall force structure and its overseas basing requirements, not only in Europe—where dramatic cuts have already taken place and more are planned or contemplated—but worldwide.

As part of this effort, a fresh look at the US force presence in the Pacific seems appropriate. The first attempt at this actually occurred a year before the Soviet Empire officially crumbled. In an April 1990 Defense Department Report to Congress, *A Strategic Framework for the Asian-Pacific Rim,* "measured reductions" in US Pacific-based forces were proposed in three phases. Phase One entailed a reduction of some 15,000 forces over a 3-year period. This is in fact underway. Phase Two called for "proportionally greater reductions" 3 to 5 years out. Phase Three promised, in 5 to 10 years, to "further reduce forces and stabilize at a somewhat lower level as circumstances permit."[1]

There can be little doubt that further Asian force reductions will occur. Given America's quest for the ever-elusive peace dividend, and the example provided by the rapid pace of

Colonel Ralph Cossa, US Air Force, is currently Chief of the Policy Division on the staff of the US Commander in Chief, Pacific (USCINCPAC). Formerly, he was a Senior Military Fellow at the Institute for National Strategic Studies, National Defense University.

troop reductions in Europe, how "measured" these reductions will be is less clear. This essay is designed neither to argue against, nor define the level of, future reductions. Instead it simply pleads that the continuing (and necessary) assessment of future Asia-Pacific force levels be based on an accurate representation of what American interests are—and on what a US force presence does and can accomplish. One perhaps obvious point needs to be made at the onset. Namely, European parallels do not necessarily apply to Asia; that the Asia-Pacific region is in most significant aspects completely dissimilar to Europe. For example, there exists no common military alliance on either side of the threat equation in Asia similar to the former Warsaw Pact versus NATO match-up. In fact, there has never even been a unified Asian perception as to who or what constitutes the principal threat.

Unlike Europe, the Pacific has always represented an "economy of force" theater for the US. In a theater encompassing half the Earth's surface, the United States has a total of 135,000 forward-deployed forces—less than the drawdown number of US forces currently proposed for the Europe of the future. These forces are largely concentrated in Japan and Korea (and until recently the Philippines), or afloat in the Pacific and Indian Oceans.[2] This modest overseas presence is augmented and underscored by a series of (largely bilateral) security alliances, periodic overseas deployments and military exercises, and a modest (and shrinking) security assistance program.

As with Europe, "containing communism" was the primary motivating factor behind the various Asian security alliances. However, the threat historically emanated not just from the former USSR but from the People's Republic of China, North Korea, and Vietnam, with each of these nations presenting a threat in its own right. The degree to which each threatened its neighbors—and US interests—has varied over time.[3]

There is also a (usually subtle) ethnocentric bias on the part of most Americans toward the region. Although in economic terms America is becoming more and more Pacific oriented, culturally and emotionally we remain a European nation. We have also been "twice-burnt" in Asia—the lack of a clear-cut victory in Korea and a defeat in Vietnam—as opposed to our string of victories in Europe and elsewhere. A defense commitment in Asia appears harder to "sell" to the American people and to Congress, especially at a time when the balance of payments is tilted so heavily in Asia's favor.

Europe and the Pacific do share one major characteristic, however. Both have fallen under an American security umbrella since World War II, and the presence of this umbrella has provided the sense of security essential to their social and economic development. Few nations in either region are eager to see this umbrella close, even as they acknowledge that some change in its size and orientation appears inevitable (and necessary).

A useful parallel can also be drawn between Asian fears of a resurgent, remilitarized Japan and Europe's lingering fears over a resurgent, reunified Germany. Like Germany, Japan already is an economic superpower. And, with the world's second- or third-largest annual military budget (measured in total expenditures rather than as a percentage of GNP), it is already seen by most Asians as a regional military power—one who previously cast a long shadow across much of Asia. Although the United States may not fully share the fears of Japan's (and Germany's) neighbors, we must understand these security concerns and ensure that our policies assuage rather than exacerbate their fears.

The United States is faced with a shifting balance of power among the major actors in Northeast Asia: Russia, Japan, China and the Korean peninsula. While there are other regional military powers, these four actors will be decisive in determining the degree of stability or instability in the entire Asia-Pacific region. They will also be crucial in determining the future US military presence in Asia.

Russia

When all the dust created by the rise and fall of the ill-fated Commonwealth of Independent States (CIS) finally settles, it seems safe to assume that the Russian Republic will still control one of the world's largest standing military forces and a strategic nuclear capability and arsenal second to none. Dramatic changes still underway within Russia may impact on the likelihood that the Kremlin will ever employ these forces, and may make Moscow more amenable to both unilateral and negotiated force reductions. But, given the size of its military and a national history of expansionism that predates the Bolshevik Revolution by several centuries, to say that the Russians no longer represent a potential threat is to deny both history and reality. The threat needs to be reassessed and put in proper context, given the changes sweeping the world—but, it should not be completely dismissed or wished away. An old Russian proverb says it best: "Dwell on the past and lose an eye; forget the past and lose both eyes." We need to look at Russia's future role in Asia (and globally) with both eyes open.

As mentioned earlier, there has been a significant reduction in the Soviet/Russian threat on all fronts. But, the reduction has not been as dramatic or as seemingly irreversible in Asia as it has been elsewhere. With the exception of those ground forces positioned specifically against China, Russian force levels in the Asia-Pacific region have not declined significantly in recent years.[4]

Traditionally, threat has been viewed as a function of capabilities and intentions. Since intentions can and do change overnight, and since a genuine reduction in capabilities is one method of demonstrating long-term peaceful intentions, prudent planners normally focus on capabilities when defining the threat. In Europe, the threat facing NATO has significantly declined. One major factor has been the transformation of a former staging area (Eastern Europe) into a neutralized buffer zone. The breakup of the USSR and the apparent inability of the CIS to establish a unified military force adds to this security blanket, as far as Europe is concerned.

The end of the Cold War and subsequent breakup of the former Soviet Union have not resulted in any significant border changes in the Asia-Pacific region, beyond the liberation of the People's Republic of Mongolia from Moscow's yoke. True Mongolian independence (it was a sovereign state in name only before 1989) and the emergence of several independent former Soviet Central Asian Republics may reduce China's fear of encirclement, but do little to lessen Moscow's potential to project power elsewhere in Asia. The only significant reduction in capabilities involves the much-heralded Soviet withdrawal from Cam Ranh Bay. Soviet TU-16/Badgers capable of sea lane interdiction have been based in Vietnam since the early 1980's.[5] At present, six remain. Their withdrawal will not only signal peaceful intentions but reduce capabilities as well.

Even if Russian military power projection capabilities in the Pacific region are reduced dramatically, concern will remain in some quarters.[6] This is particularly true in China and Japan; their rivalries with the Kremlin date back centuries. In the case of China, the rivalry proved to be too great for even the force of "monolithic world communism" to overcome. Mr. Gorbachev was successful in reducing tensions between his nation and both China and Japan. How effective Mr. Yeltsin will be in this endeavor remains to be seen. At best, it seems safe to predict that a healthy level of paranoia appears destined to remain. Future Russian peace initiatives notwithstanding, centuries of history will prevent Japan and China from discounting totally the threat from Moscow. In this regard, even a dramatic gesture such as the return of the Japanese Northern Territories will do little to reduce deep-seated Japanese fears. Returning what most Japanese believe already rightfully belongs to them may relieve a certain amount of tension, but will do little to alter long-standing threat perceptions.

Japan

The US-Japan security relationship serves a number of mutually supportive objectives. It provides a common security

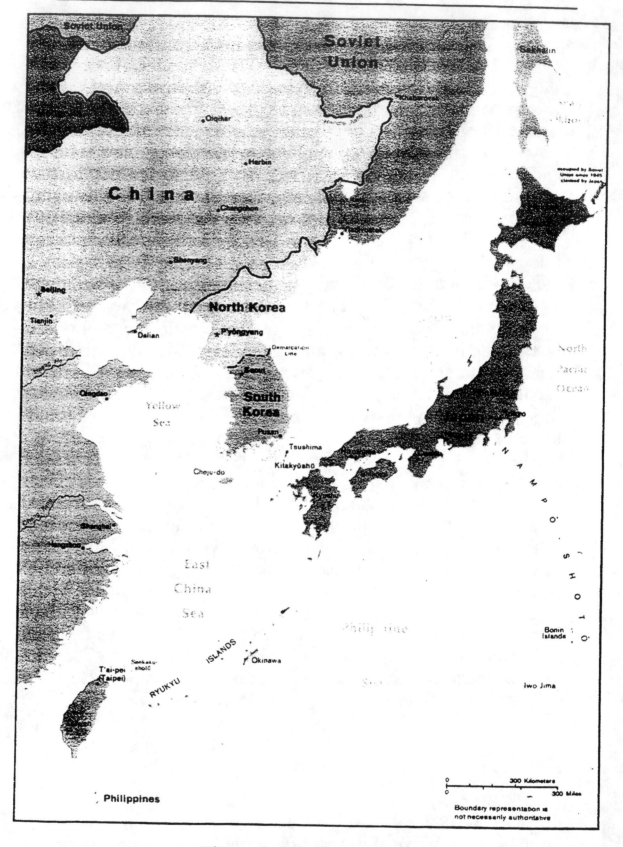

Figure 2. *Northeast Asia*

bond between two major powers, based on defense cooperation rather than competition. It provides US military access to Japanese facilities, to assist both in the defense of Japan and in the protection of US security interests throughout Asia. Most importantly, it provides an alternative to a massive Japanese military buildup that neither side (or anyone else in Asia) wants to see. As one strategic analyst observed, "it serves to keep the Japanese in a box that they want to remain in."[7]

The fact of the matter is, that the only thing that stands between Japan and true world superpower status is Japan's lack of a nuclear arsenal. Economically, Japan is already there. In terms of conventional military power, it has one of the best equipped, most capable armed forces in the region, if not the world. Its limited ability to project this power far from its shores (no aircraft carriers, long-range bombers or strategic missiles) could easily be overcome—it previously built carriers, has a burgeoning aircraft industry, and already has sufficient rocket technology to place satellites in orbit. It is the presence of the US-Japan security relationship that removes the need for Japan to develop an independent nuclear capability. To the extent that the US relationship and presence persuades Japan not to expand its military capabilities, regional security is enhanced. If Japan were to remilitarize, and particularly if it were to "go nuclear," the global balance of power equation would be significantly altered. Even the North Koreans—who otherwise would prefer to see the United States as far away from their shores as possible—would prefer a U.S.-Japan security relationship to a remilitarized, and particularly a nuclear, Japan.

Make no mistake, most Japanese share this preference. The sentiments against remilitarization in Japan run deep. There is no need to convince Japan in this regard; there is a need to avoid policies and actions that will convince them to modify or abandon these beliefs. Tokyo realizes that its economic health is totally dependent on overseas sea lanes. To argue, therefore, that a withdrawal of the US security umbrella would not result in Japanese remilitarization, is to argue that Japan would not take whatever steps are necessary to insure that its security interests remain protected. If Japan were denied the US nuclear umbrella, it would have only two reasonable options: develop its own nuclear capability, or align itself with another nuclear power—and it appears difficult to imagine Japan placing its security in Soviet or Chinese hands.

Given Japan's current military capabilities and past history, US calls for Japan to increase its defense spending raise concerns throughout Asia. Such demands reflect a lack of awareness regarding both current Japanese capabilities and the extent of regional concerns. They are not even genuine. What we are really seeking is for Japan to spend more on our defense—to share a greater portion of the cost of US forces based on their territory. There should be no hesitation about asking Japan to spend more to keep us there, on the basis they certainly can afford it. But, we must recognize that Japan already pays more toward the maintenance of US forces on its soil than any of our other allies and, more importantly, that these forces are present not just to protect Japan but to preserve and protect our own and other regional nations' interests as well.

There is another aspect of the US-Japan security relationship that needs to be addressed. As US economic leverage over Japan continues to diminish, the importance of our security relationship conversely grows. This does not mean we can or should wave the security umbrella over Japan as a sword, but it does indicate that the security link, as the strongest link bonding our nation's together, provides our greatest degree of leverage in dealing with Japan. As long as Japan's physical security is tied to the United States, we enjoy a special relationship that should, if properly managed, pay dividends in the course of economic and other nonsecurity related discussions— provided the various US agencies involved figure out how to cooperate on Japanese issues, rather than engage in internecine warfare.

China

China's role in the Asia-Pacific balance of power equation needs to be more clearly defined. It should come as no surprise that China looks out for China first. It distrusts both the Russians and the Japanese but desires normalized, if not cordial, relations with both nations. It seeks closer cooperation with the US, but on its own terms and not as a "card" to be played against Moscow or anywhere else. The US, for its part, has never needed China as an ally in the traditional sense of the word. During the Cold War, China's role in the event of a global conflict was to tie down a half million Soviet forces by virtue of its presence alone. Even a neutral China could serve this purpose.

Nonetheless, it is clearly in the US interest to maintain a dialogue with the world's largest nation, one that by virtue of size alone is destined to remain a regional power and whose nuclear capabilities and expanding Third-World ties make it a major global power as well. More importantly, most definitions of a "new world order" place increased emphasis on a multinational approach toward conflict resolution and tension reduction, with the United Nations as the most likely vehicle. This enhances China's international power and prestige, given its veto powers as a permanent member of the UN Security Council. (Ironically, many proponents of increased UN involvement are also proponents of hardline policies that would isolate and alienate China; these policies seem uncomplementary.) It is also essential to put current developments in proper perspective. Tiananmen notwithstanding, China has come a long way in the past decade in terms of economic and political reform, and Deng Xiaoping has recently provided strong signals that he remains committed to liberalization.[8] But, Deng continues to move cautiously, ever-mindful of not going so fast as to destroy his own power base.[9] More importantly, he has seeded the bureaucracy with like-minded reformers who are poised to lead China even further along the path of reform once the current generation of leaders passes from the scene. But, regardless of their policies, the next generation of Chinese leaders will likely be just as stubbornly committed to enhancing China's role in the region and world.

China's three largest neighbors (Russia, Vietnam, and India) all place the PRC high on their list of potential adversaries, and a deep sense of mutual distrust lies not-so-deeply buried beneath the currently cordial Sino-Japanese relationship. Recognize also that in many parts of Southeast Asia, China is seen as part of the problem rather than as part of the solution. In fact, one of the greatest fears among our Southeast Asian friends in the early 1970s was that the quid pro quo for China serving as a balance to Soviet power in Northeast Asia would be US acquiescence to a predominant Chinese role in their region. These fears of US-Chinese collusion have been largely overcome, but concerns about long-term Chinese intentions remain, especially in nations with large ethnic Chinese communities.

Sino-Russian relations are expected to improve, because both sides need a period of reduced tensions in which to undertake widespread economic reforms. It is important to note, however, that the initial improvement in Sino-Soviet relations engineered by Gorbachev came about almost exclusively on Chinese terms. To the extent that there was ever any self-doubt among China's leaders as to the wisdom of stubbornly holding one's ground until the other side finally comes around, their success in dealing with Gorbachev removed it. As a result, Chinese diplomatic inflexibility is likely to increase (and not just when dealing with Moscow).

Korea

Now that East and West Germany have reunited, is the reunification of the two Koreas close at hand? The answer, regrettably, is "not necessarily." While the dream of reunification is as sincere in Korea as it was in Germany, the level of mistrust and animosity between the two Koreas make progress more difficult. North Korea remains one of the most closed, repressive, heavily armed, and economically backward societies in the world; the prospects of significant reform from within appear slim as long as North Korean President Kim Il Sung is alive. Most analysts also predict a potentially volatile leadership transition following Kim's death, given his desire to have his son replace him.

The US presence in South Korea has been instrumental in preserving peace on the Peninsula. It has provided the security shield behind which the Republic of Korea's economy has blossomed to the point that Korea stands today as a model of economic development, in sharp contrast to the North. US force levels in Korea have never been sufficient to defeat an all-out North Korean attack but are aimed at deterring such an attack, by presenting a symbol to the North of US commitment. Politically, they serve in a "tripwire" capacity, one that "guarantees" the North that the United States will be involved. Militarily, they are there to help delay a North Korean advance until US reinforcements arrive. The amount of forces required to serve as a tripwire is open to debate, but the need to continue sending a strong signal of US commitment and support appears essential, especially during a time when North Korea's future direction is uncertain and potentially volatile.

Of note, the US commitment to Korea is also seen as a signal of US regional resolve. Of all of America's security agreements, the US-Korea arrangement is the least susceptible to the charge of having been rendered obsolete due to the absence of a credible threat. To appear to renege on this commitment would raise considerable doubts as to the viability of all other US defense commitments.

Conclusions

US forward deployed forces, in conjunction with our treaty relationships, represent a force for stability in the Asia-Pacific region. The US presence has traditionally served to balance not just the former Soviet threat but the overall mosaic, which includes a nuclear China, a Japan with unrivaled economic power and growing military potential, a volatile North Korea, and many other security concerns and issues. First and foremost, however, they protect and promote US security interests in Asia.

Discussions on appropriate US force levels need to proceed, but they should be based on a realization of how important a US presence is in maintaining the current balance. Also of importance is the realization that, as our relative economic clout declines—and it has and promises to continue to drop—our military presence becomes more important. This is not to predict that the United States is destined to become a one-dimensional power in Asia—we remain a major player economically and we continue to provide a political and economic model that, with minor modifications to fit Asia culture, continues to be attractive. We should recognize, however, that our security commitments, and thus our military presence, represent a powerful instrument of goodwill and potential influence even in peacetime, given regional threat perceptions that do not always coincide with our own.

Defense Secretary Cheney's planned Phase One cuts in US Asia-based forces have been accepted as reasonable and nonthreatening by most Asians but are unlikely to appease Congress or escape further challenge as defense cuts continue. The question of how low we can safely go remains to be answered. Forward-deployed forces cannot be addressed in a vacuum, however. They underscore the various regional defense commitments that promote our own economic and security interests and hold intraregional rivalry in check. Force cuts that undermine the regional security mosaic obviously will work to our long-term detriment.

Ultimately, it is the viability of the US defense commitment to Asia that will ensure continued stability and thus protect our political, economic, and military interests. The real challenge for the US, over time, is to break the mindset that equates commitment with presence. Instead, we must seek more creative, less-costly ways to continue playing the role that only we are equipped to play. More frequent exercises, exchange visits, port calls, civil engineer and other nation-building projects, more access to our military schools and training programs, and a greater level of security assistance all provide alternative means of demonstrating commitment and building good will. The challenge will be to find the proper mix between forces on the ground and alternative, more creative means of demonstrating that the United States intends to remain a force for peace and stability in Asia.

Notes

1. Office of the Assistant Secretary of Defense for International Security Affairs (East Asia and Pacific Region), Report to Congress, *A Strategic Framework for the Asian Pacific Rim: Looking Toward the 21st Century* (April 1990), 7-8.

2. Ibid., 5, for a breakdown of US forward-deployed forces.

3. Of note, three of the four still pay lip service to Marxist-Leninist principles, although the desire and ability of each to spread its ideology has arguably been reduced. Of the four, only North Korea clings stubbornly to Stalinist traditions. Vietnam is beginning to at least consider economic liberalization, while China is literally being over-run by capitalists, both homegrown and from the various overseas Chinese communities.

4. For example, the Russian Pacific Fleet remains the largest of the former Soviet fleets, with no other Republics contesting for partial ownership. For a breakdown of Far Eastern forces, see Department of Defense, *1991 Military Forces in Transition,* map insert, and earlier versions of the *Soviet Military Power* series of publications.

5. For information on Soviet activity and capabilities at Cam Ranh Bay, see Ralph A. Cossa, "Soviet Eyes on Asia," *Air Force Magazine,* August 1985, 57-58.

6. It is useful to note that US concern over the Soviet threat was never universally shared within the Asia/Pacific region. The further one gets away from Northeast Asia, the less of a threat the Soviets appeared to be. Among the Southeast Asia nations, for example, the Soviets traditionally have been the least of their worries.

7. Expressed by an Asian specialist during not-for-attribution discussions on Asian security issues.

8. "In Victory for Deng, Beijing Urges Century of Market-Style Reforms," *New York Times,* 13 March 1992, A8.

9. In my discussions with Chinese officials, they constantly stress that they are following the "Asian Model" of development that calls for economic liberalization first followed by gradual political reform.

They cite South Korea, Singapore, and even Taiwan as examples. They also point out with a certain degree of self-satisfaction that Mr. Gorbachev tried to do it the other way around and the result was chaos (and loss of power).

Conflict Potential in Southeast Asia and the South China Sea

Kenneth Conboy

Throughout its pre-colonial history, Southeast Asia was heavily influenced by outside powers. Located midway between India and China, this should come as no surprise. Yet even more than external influences, Southeast Asia historically has been the scene of intense internal competition, the result of the dynamic expansion and contraction of empires and kingdoms within the region.

This competition has been significant for several reasons. First, it produced deep, lasting animosities among various ethnic groups that continue to cloud foreign relations to the present time. Examples of this include the hatred between Vietnamese and Cambodians and, to a lesser extent, the sense of superiority felt by many Thais toward neighboring Laotians, Burmese and Cambodians.

Second, the historical ebb and flow of the major Southeast Asian kingdoms led, in many cases, to the mass migration of populations. A good example is the Thai victories over Laos in the 19th century, which resulted in much of the population on the east bank of the Mekong River being forcibly moved to the west bank, which now is part of Thailand. So great was the migration that today more ethnic Laotians can be found in Thailand than in Laos. Shifts in population such as this are significant because they often provide seeds of conflict when defining contemporary borders.

Kenneth Conboy conducts risk analysis for an Indonesian bank in Jakarta. Prior to this, he spent 6 years at The Heritage Foundation, first as a Policy Analyst for South and Southeast Asia, then as Deputy Director. He has published extensively, including several books on Southeast Asia.

The Colonial Experience

By the late 1800s, Southeast Asia had been effectively divided among the European colonial powers of Britain, France, Portugal, the Netherlands, and Spain. With the Europeans came Western religions, language, and culture, and political and economic systems. With the Europeans, too, came artificial borders that reflected the desire to conveniently safeguard lucrative colonial holdings rather than an attempt to divide the region into coherent ethnic groupings. Laos is a perfect example: the French fused together a conglomeration of diverse "states" in order to form a buffer between their rich colonies among the Vietnamese people to the east and the expansionist Siamese and British in Burma to the west. Burma, Indonesia, and the Philippines have similar diverse compositions.

When World War Two came to Southeast Asia, the indigenous peoples of the region for the first time saw an Asian power (Japan) defeat the Europeans (and Americans). This instantly shattered the myth of European invincibility, and gave a critical boost to the numerous fledgling nationalist movements throughout the region. Significantly, as the outcome of the war became inevitable, Japan began to actively assist these nationalists in an attempt to prevent the Europeans from retaking their former colonies.

World War Two had the added result of shifting several of the borders in Southeast Asia. For example, when the Japanese intervened on behalf of their quasi-allies, the Thais, the French were forced to turn over entire border provinces of Laos and Cambodia to Bangkok. The French also shifted the border in the Mekong Delta, putting most of the region, with its ethnic Cambodian majority, under the administrative control of Vietnamese-dominated Cochin China. As will be seen, some of these border adjustments have been extremely problematic in more recent decades.

Post-World War Two

In the three decades immediately after World War Two, conflict in Southeast Asia largely shifted away from the traditional struggles between countries and instead focused largely on the political tensions within individual nation-states. Initially, this was manifest in the independence movements against the resurgent colonial powers. By the late 1950s, however, the anticolonial struggle was replaced by Cold War battles waged between Soviet and Chinese proxies against the United States, Britain, and their allies. These battles were conducted primarily as civil wars (with foreign assistance) rather than conflicts between the Southeast Asian states.

During this period of Cold War struggles, many of the traditional animosities in Southeast Asia were temporarily suspended in the name of political cooperation. The ultra-nationalistic Khmer Rouge, for example, publicly cooperated with their historical enemies, the Vietnamese, against the US and its allies. The Pathet Lao, too, suspended their traditional suspicion of the Vietnamese and worked closely with Hanoi. Such cooperation was not limited to the Communists. The pro-Western Lon Nol regime in the Khmer Republic worked closely with Saigon. Lon Nol also cooperated with Thailand, despite the tension that had characterized Thai-Cambodian relations since the 13th century. While ideology was a primary source of conflict during the Cold War period, the more traditional sources of conflict—territory disputes and ethnic tensions—had by no means ended. Examples include:

● The Konfrontasi between Malaysia and Indonesia. The cause: Indonesian claims of sovereignty over portions of Malaysia and Singapore.

● Filipino support for a guerrilla movement in Malaysia. The cause: Manila claimed control over the Malaysian state of Sabah.

● Border clashes between Cambodia and Thailand in the early 1960s. The cause: Bangkok claimed control of the border temple at Preah Vihear.

● Armed conflict between China and South Vietnam in January 1974 over control of the Paracel Islands.

● The massacre of Vietnamese civilians in Phnom Penh in early 1970. The cause: Cambodian nationalist extremism in the wake of a military coup d'etat.

● Anti-Vietnamese insurgency by FULRO hilltribe minorities. The cause: ethnic discrimination on the part of lowland Vietnamese.

Post-Vietnam

Today, with 16 years of hindsight, it appears as if the three decades of *ideological* conflict in Southeast Asia following World War Two were not the exception to the rule. No sooner had the pro-Western regimes in Saigon, Phnom Penh, and Vientiane fallen to communism than the primary source of conflict in the region was tilting once again toward disputes involving *race, ethnic differences,* and *territory.*

The most dramatic example of this was the bloody conflict between the Khmer Rouge and the Vietnamese waged after 1975. The animosity between these two ethnic groups, which predates the arrival of the Europeans into Southeast Asia, was exacerbated by the French ceding the Mekong Delta to Vietnamese administrative control. The Khmer Rouge and the Vietnamese had cooperated briefly between 1970 and 1973, but by early 1974 there were widespread reports of fighting between Cambodian and Vietnamese Communist guerrillas. Soon after Saigon and Phnom Penh fell in the spring of 1975, the ultra-nationalist Khmer Rouge began a series of maritime and ground assaults against Vietnamese-held islands and border garrisons, apparently to bring at least some of these regions under what they deemed historical Cambodian control. What initially began as cross-border skirmishes quickly escalated into full-scale infantry assaults by both sides in 1977. By early 1978, entire Vietnamese divisions retaliated by occupying huge enclaves in eastern Cambodia. Then, in December of that year, Hanoi mobilized three of its four Strategic Army Corps to conduct what was at that time the largest military campaign since World War Two. Vietnam's occupation of Cambodia would last slightly more than a decade. Significantly, aside from a border war with China in early 1979, the conflict never expanded beyond Indochina; although the Thai military feared Vietnamese intentions beyond Indochina, Hanoi was stretched thin having to contend with counterinsurgency tasks in Cambodia and the threat from China.

Conflict Potential in Contemporary Southeast Asia

During 1988-89, in the face of heavy international diplomatic and economic pressure, Vietnam withdrew the bulk of its military forces from Vietnam. While numerous problems remain before peace comes to Cambodia, resolving that conflict has now become a problem for Cambodians, international humanitarian organizations, and the United Nations to solve. Cambodia aside, what, then, are the prospects for peace and stability in Southeast Asia? In general, two forms of potential conflict exist—and will continue to exist—in the region. The first of these are the numerous, small insurgencies burning across Southeast Asia. These have little chance of expanding across borders and, as a result, have only a limited effect on the region's stability. The second and much more serious source of conflict involves territorial disputes.

Insurgencies

Five major insurgencies loom or remain on the horizon in Southeast Asia:

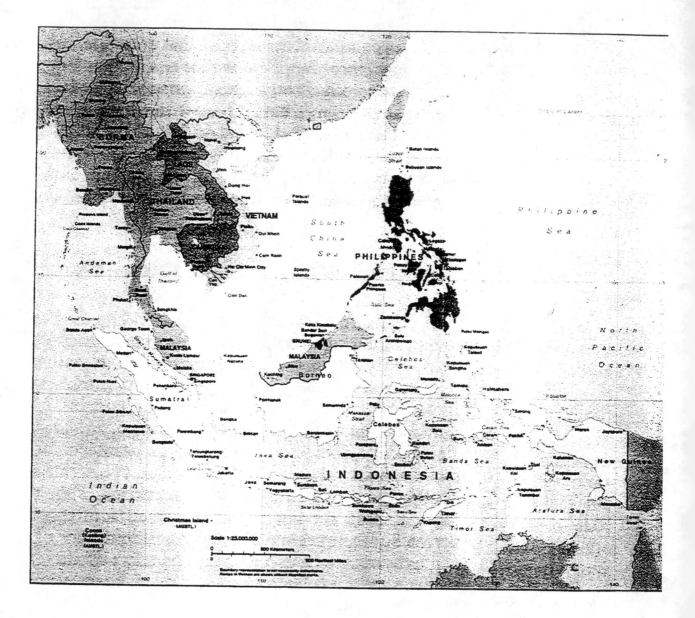

Figure 3. *Southeast Asia and the South China Sea*

1. Burma's highly fragmented ethnic composition is a perfect recipe for disunity. Rangoon is caught in a permanent Catch-22: the numerous guerrilla forces have little chance of expanding beyond their current limits of territorial control, yet the central government, because of its own ethnic limitations, has little hope of succeeding in its counterinsurgency campaign.

2. There are enough hidden weapons caches in Cambodia to fuel fighting for years to come. At best, these excess guns will be used by disunified bandit gangs; at worst, a civil war will resume between more organized guerrilla forces. The current UN plan does not call for elections in Cambodia until early 1993, so there is plenty of time for its peace plan to fall apart, leading to a resumption of open warfare.

3. The Philippines has the dubious distinction of having the fastest growing Communist insurgency in Asia. This is all the more remarkable given the fall of communism elsewhere in the world. Although the government has made limited progress in its counterinsurgency program, it is unlikely to completely extinguish the revolutionary movement completely.

4. Laos is host to several small anti-Communist guerrilla movements, all of which suffer from a lack of foreign support and are little more than an irritant to Vientiane.

5. Indonesia faces small pockets of guerrilla resistance in Aceh, East Timor, and Irian Jaya. Their ability to inflict casualties on the central government is minimal.

In all these cases, the negative effects of the insurgencies are felt almost entirely within the borders of each respective country. Moreover, there is little likelihood that fighting will expand such that neighboring countries will be drawn into the conflict.

Territorial Disputes

There are six potential territorial disputes in Southeast Asia which will need to be monitored for the foreseeable future:

1. Thailand and Laos: Since the victory of Pathet Lao forces in 1975, relations between Thailand and Laos have been strained. From Bangkok's point of view, Soviet-supported communism was now along its border. As for Vientiane, tens of thousands of anti-Communist refugees were camped just inside Thailand, some of whom were launching cross-border raids inside Laos while Bangkok turned a blind eye. By 1977, there were armed clashes between both nations after Laos began to aggressively patrol the Mekong River, which forms part of its common border with Thailand. Then, in 1988, full-scale fighting broke out over control of seven border villages. In this brief conflict, Laotian troops held the advantage of terrain and inflicted minor yet embarrassing defeats to the Thai forces. Although as recently as this January both sides traded charges of border violations, bilateral relations have improved somewhat since the military coup d'etat in Bangkok this February, making the chances for open warfare between Laos and Thailand slim for the near future.

2. Vietnam and Cambodia: In 1985, Hanoi and the puppet Cambodian government it installed in Phnom Penh reached several bilateral agreements that in effect gave Vietnam control over several disputed islands and a large chunk of Cambodian territory near the city of Svay Rieng. The Khmer Rouge and both non-Communist members of the current coalition have called for a cancellation of these agreements. To underscore their

concern, these three factions have fashioned a new national flag for use during the interim period of UN control. This flag, significantly, features an outline of Cambodia showing the borders recognized in 1954. Keeping in mind that border disputes were the cause for the Khmer Rouge forays after 1975, should Vietnam continue to claim control over the territories gained in 1985, this affront to Cambodian nationalism undoubtedly will provide the seed for future border conflicts.

3. Malaysia and the Philippines: Since the 1950s, Kuala Lumpur and Manila have clashed over control of the Malaysian state of Sabah. In 1968, then Filipino President Marcos secretly authorized training of Sabah rebels to battle the Malaysian government. Before it could be launched, the plot was exposed, to the embarrassment of Manila. Formal delineation of the border remains controversial. Border discussion broke down in July 1989 when a group of Filipino senators reasserted their country's claim to Sabah. Kuala Lumpur says that the border dispute will never be resolved until Manila drops this claim. Despite these lingering differences, the chances of this dispute escalating beyond a war of words is minimal.

4. Indonesia and Malaysia: Border disputes between these two nations date back to the Konfrontasi of the early 1960s. Since the rise of President Suharto in 1965-66, Jakarta has had cordial relations with Kuala Lumpur. Still, since 1969 there has been conflicting claims over ownership of two islands located east of Borneo and Kalimantan. In 1988, both nations agreed to maintain the status quo on the islands until a final agreement had been reached, but in mid-1991 Malaysia began to develop one of the two islands. Discussions were held in July, but no final decision was reached. Jakarta continues to protest Malaysia's moves, but insists that any differences over the islands will not endanger good bilateral ties.

5. Gulf of Thailand: Malaysia, Singapore, Cambodia, and Vietnam have declared Exclusive Economic Zones (EEZs) extending 200 nautical miles out to sea. Several of these claims overlap in the Gulf of Thailand, and even intrude on Thailand's territorial waters. Should any of these nations attempt to enforce these EEZs with military or paramilitary maritime patrols, tension in the Gulf of Thailand is likely to rise considerably.

6. The South China Sea: This vast area, which includes the Paracel and Spratly Archipelagos and the Natuna Island group, is the most serious flashpoint in Southeast Asia. The Paracels already have been a source of conflict in recent decades. Located about 200 miles equidistant from the coast of Vietnam east of Danang and south of China's Hainan Island, this island chain was claimed by the Chinese as early as the 15th Century. Vietnam, meanwhile, dates its claim to 1802; by late that century, France (which colonized Vietnam) and Chinese were arguing over its control. During World War Two, the Japanese took over the islands. After the war, Tokyo in 1951 ostensibly relinquished control to the Chinese. However, Vietnam, still under French control, repeated its claim over the island chain. Although the islands were thought to be of little economic value in the 1960s, the Saigon government quietly established a weather station and introduced a small militia garrison on three of the islands. With the oil crisis beginning in late 1973, the South Vietnamese government signed several oil contracts in the area south of the Paracels. The Chinese, as a result, showed renewed interest in the Paracels and dispatched a fishing fleet with navy escorts in January 1974. Saigon reinforced its garrison, and the Chinese responded with an 11-ship naval flotilla that sank one South Vietnamese ship and sent four limping home. In the aftermath of the clash, South Vietnam protested, but was ill equipped to reassert its control. North Vietnam, in the name of communist solidarity, supported the Chinese claim of control. Taiwan pro-

tested the move by Beijing, claiming that it was the rightful owner of the Paracels. The United States maintained a completely neutral position.

The Spratly Archipelago, stretching 600 miles south of China's coast nearly to Brunei, also is highly contested. Like the Paracels, South Vietnam occupied part of the chain through the early 1970s. China, meanwhile, claimed full control of the archipelago, despite the fact that it was 600 miles from its closest border. Taiwan also claimed historical control of the Spratlys, and maintained a small garrison on Itu Aba Island. In February 1974, after losing the Paracels to China, Saigon reinforced its garrison with three platoons of SEAL naval commandos. South Vietnam was especially keen to control the island chain because a study by the UN's Economic Commission for Asia and the Far East had hinted at promising oil deposits being located under the archipelago.

During the final week before the fall of South Vietnam in April 1975, the North Vietnamese 126th Naval Sapper Group conducted a surprise amphibious raid and occupied Saigon's garrison on the Spratlys. Little was heard about the chain until 1988, when the Chinese navy began to assert its control over the islands. In the process, they scored several small but decisive victories over Vietnamese naval forces. Since then, Vietnam and China have refrained from further fighting, although the war of words persists.

The conflict over the Spratlys is complicated by two important factors. First, it is not simply a bilateral issue. A total of seven nations claim control of part or all of the archipelago. These include mainland China, Taiwan, Malaysia, Brunei, the Philippines, and Vietnam. In addition, just southwest of the Spratlys, Indonesia and Vietnam have conflicting claims over part of the Natuna Islands.

Second, there is ongoing speculation that oil may lie under the Spratlys. Already, the Philippines have leased some portions of the Spratlys for drilling. In addition, Vietnam may offer 30 deep-water blocks for bidding in the near future.

Should oil or natural gas be found, those nations claiming control will undoubtedly try to enforce their claims.

To help head off what appears to be a future showdown in the South China Sea, Indonesia announced it would host a "workshop" on the Spratlys and Paracels. The meeting was held in July 1991 and was attended by diplomats, lawyers, and ex-military from mainland China, Vietnam, Taiwan, the Philippines, Malaysia, and Brunei. In addition, observers were sent from Indonesia, Singapore, Thailand, and Laos. At the workshop, there was basic agreement by five of the participants on joint development of the archipelagos. They agreed that, with Vietnam fading away, China and India are the next military threats to Southeast Asia. China, alone, refused to agree to joint development of the islands, saying it would take place only if Beijing's sovereignty was recognized.

At present, the Chinese maintain on the Paracels a helicopter landing facility and a small port. Missile boats and patrol craft are permanently stationed there. On the Spratlys, the Chinese occupy seven reefs and islands. There they maintain small garrisons and artillery; two minor ports are expected to be completed by next year. In late 1988, a major naval task force operated in the vicinity; since then, the islands are periodically patrolled by destroyers and frigates. In May 1991, Beijing announced that it would increase the number of combat drills in the Spratlys, upgrade their marines, and improve the fleet's ability to respond to "emergency needs." It is believed that once the two ports are completed, patrol craft will be permanently deployed to the Spratlys. Vietnam occupies 25 coral reefs and islands in the Spratlys. It occasionally flies light planes to a small runway built on one of the islands. Taiwan occupies Itu Aba Island, in the northern part of the Spratlys. There it has maintained a company-sized garrison since the early 1970s; Taipei ceased regular naval patrols of the vicinity in the mid-1970s. Malaysia occupies three islands in the extreme south of the Spratlys. It has long maintained a token troop presence on the islands. In September 1991, Kuala Lumpur announced its intention to build a 1500-m airfield on the island of Terumbu Layang, 165 nmi off the coast of Malaysia's Sabah state. Earlier this year, Malaysia opened a small hotel there and announced plans to promote it for tourism. The Philippines occupy eight islands in the northwest portion of the Spratlys. A small number of troops are garrisoned there.

Power Projection in the Region

Given that perhaps the most serious flashpoint in Southeast Asia is in the South China Sea, the capacity of the various nations in the region to project military power and to conduct extended naval operations has become increasingly important.

China: Although China is not a major world naval power, compared to its competition in Southeast Asia, Beijing has the largest and most sophisticated navy available for deployment in the South China Sea. Should China flex its military muscles in the South China Sea, the People's Liberation Army-Navy (PLA-N) can call upon 45 major surface combatants; slightly over 100 submarines; a proven ability to keep a naval task force at sea for at least 30 days; and a marine brigade that reportedly is being upgraded. Although the PLA-N suffers from poor command and control and many of its weapons systems are obsolete, it still could be expected to enjoy success against most Southeast Asian navies during any potential conflict in the Paracels or Spratlys. It should be noted, however, that Beijing is somewhat limited in interdicting civilian shipping in the South China Sea because it would make its own large mercantile fleet extremely vulnerable.

Thailand: The Royal Thai Navy has been undergoing an ambitious modernization program since the mid-1980s. Among its more recent acquisitions are three indigenous-built antisubmarine corvettes to be commissioned by the end of this year; two Chinese-made frigates launched in June 1990 and two launched this year; and two Chinese-made frigates with helicopter decks set for delivery by the spring of 1992. In addition, Bangkok discussed with the United States this summer the purchase of four Knox-class frigates and 30 A-7E aircraft to form a naval combat air wing. With these acquisitions, the Royal Thai Navy by 1996 will have an anticipated force strength of one German-built 7,800-ton Helicopter Support Ship, possibly equipped with Harrier V/STOL aircraft; six Chinese-built frigates, five US and Thai-built corvettes; three 1970s-vintage frigates; nine fast attack craft, and five large patrol boats. Thailand also maintains Marine Corps and Navy SEAL commandos.

Malaysia: Like Thailand, Malaysia has begun an ambitious modernization program for its fleet. Among purchases discussed this year were a contract for two British-made corvettes and an open competition for four diesel submarines. Malaysia, moreover, regularly exercises with Australia, New Zealand, England, and Singapore as part of the Five Power Defense Arrangement. In May 1991, for example, Kuala Lumpur hosted STARFISH 91, a maritime exercise with 39 aircraft and 34 warships from all five countries. An air defense exercise, ADEX 91, was held at the same time.

The Philippines: Of the various nations with claims in the South China Sea, the Armed Forces of the Philippines is one of the least capable of serious power projection into the South China Sea. Much of its maritime forces have been tasked with coastal defense and riverine counterinsurgency. This September, Manila announced plans to buy three missile boats from Spain, three other gunboats from Australia, and two logistics support vessels from China. Manila, significantly, claims that its 1951 mutual defense agreement the United States extends to its claims in the Spratlys; Washington disagrees.

Vietnam: In terms of sheer numbers, Vietnam in the 1980s had over 70 surface combatants, giving it the largest navy in Southeast Asia. These figures, however, are misleading when determining power projection. Much of the equipment captured from the South Vietnamese regime, for example, is obsolete. In addition, the Soviet Union has slashed its military assistance program, which could make it difficult for Hanoi to maintain all of its Soviet-made ships. Economic pressures in Vietnam are causing further military cutbacks. Already, it is believed that Hanoi may have disbanded two of its five naval infantry brigades.

Conclusion

Despite simmering insurgencies in Southeast Asia, greater conflict is not inevitable. Given the region's growing naval muscle, however, and the fact that no resolution to the overlapping territorial claims in the South China Sea appears in sight, perhaps a better than average chance exists of at least limited maritime clashes in the region. The United States has two treaty allies in the region—the Philippines and Thailand—and last year signed a limited defense agreement with a third nation—Singapore. Washington, however, has gone to great pains to remain neutral in the South China Sea dispute. Moreover, with the end of the Cold War and America's likely departure from Subic Bay, it will be increasingly difficult to keep Washington's attention focused on Southeast Asia. Still, there are several reasons the United States should sustain a presence in Southeast Asia. First, 90 percent of the oil destined for America's allies in Northeast Asia passes through the South China Sea and the Strait of Malacca. Second, US trade with the Asia-Pacific region already is larger than US trade with Europe; by the end of this century, trade across the Pacific is expected to be twice that of trade across the Atlantic. Lastly, any power vacuum left by a US withdrawal from Southeast Asia might be filled by China, not an appealing option to America or its Asian allies.

The Outlook for Stability in South Asia

Seema Sirohi

*T*his chapter explores the significance of the historic changes over the past 4 years in the context of India and Pakistan, recently dubbed, "the two most crazy nations in the world" by a Pakistani professor of political science. While the world has been on a constant fast forward, shattering old ideas and ideologies, politicians in South Asia seem reluctant to embrace the changes. We have seen the collapse of East European regimes, the unification of Germany, the slow implosion in the Soviet Union, the Gulf War, the agreements in Angola, Afghanistan, and Cambodia and the beginning of change in South Africa.

But the winds of change have barely touched one of the most difficult relationships between nations—the one between India and Pakistan. The two seemed locked in eternal mistrust and a constant game of one-upmanship. It is almost the dialogue of the deaf. They talk of confidence-building measures on the ground while their armies are eyeball to eyeball in Kashmir, exchanging fire with an intensity that would constitute war between any other two nations. This is the maddening reality of South Asia, a region racked by religious and regional disputes, a region that has seen four major wars and one that appears continually on the edge to Western eyes.

The end of the Cold War jolted South Asia politically, economically and strategically. In reality the region has had to warm up to the end of two Cold Wars—one between the United

Seema Sirohi is the Washington correspondent for *The Telegraph,* India. Ms. Sirohi covers major US domestic and foreign policy issues with special emphasis on South Asia and writes a fortnightly column on trends in the United States. Prior to her current position, she was the Washington correspondent for the international wire service, *Interpress.*

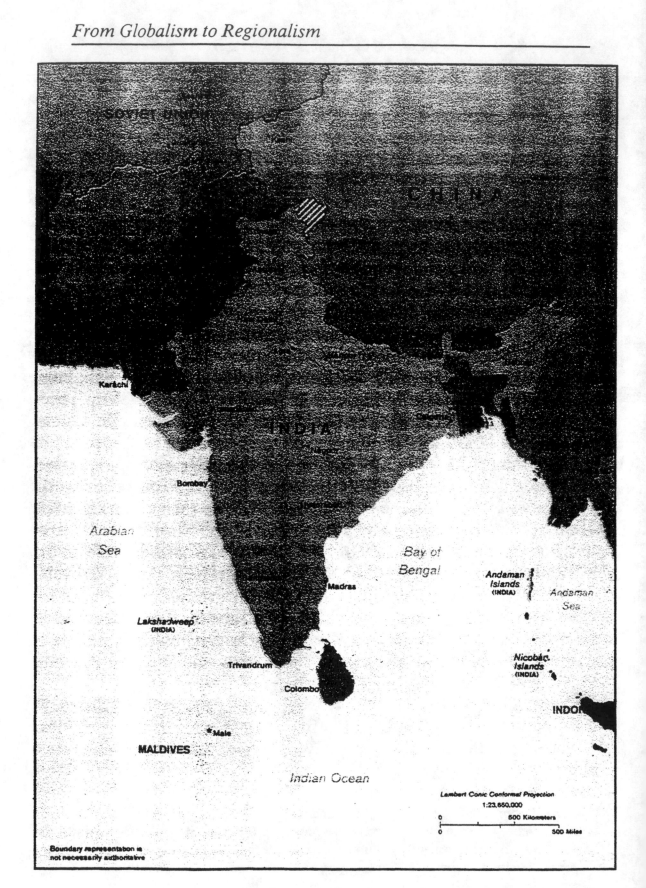

Figure 4. *South Asia*

States and the Soviet Union and the other between the Soviet union and China. The changes have come when both India and Pakistan are in a severe economic crunch. They are mourning the loss of their respective patrons while trying to adapt to a unipolar world. For decades, they had been comfortable under their respective nuclear umbrellas, satisfied in the knowledge that the could call upon external support if things got rough. But today, they must increasingly address each other directly. They process of transformation has produced new twists in their bilateral and multilateral relationships.

The state of confusion was most recently exemplified by India's bewildering response to the attempted coup in what was the Soviet Union in August 1991. Sections of the Foreign Ministry seemed to want to go back to the days of the bipolar world when life was simple and trading was easier. The loss of the psychological pillar of the Soviet Union was difficult to bear for Indian strategists. One response has been confusion, the other a refusal to acknowledge the changes, as exemplified by the two Communist parties in India that have defiantly decided to carry the mantle of Marxism into the next century and condemned the former Soviets for giving up halfway.

With Mr. Gorbachev reduced to being an international party guest, the Indian government is not sure who will pick up the burden of the Indo-Soviet Friendship Treaty that was renewed after a long tantalizing act by the Soviets just before the attempted coup. Will the republics be responsible or will Mr. Boris Yeltsin go to bat for India? Who will supply spare parts for India's defense forces? The grim reality has forced a fast indignation and production of Soviet spare parts. Defense Minister Sharad Pawar said in the fall of 1991 that India will export guns, ammunition, and electronic systems to collect hard currency. Nearly all plans to modernize the Navy and the Air Force are at a standstill. In terms of trade, India has suffered from the dismantling of the ruble-rupee arrangement with Moscow. The Soviets have faltered in their commitments to supply newsprint, steel, and coal. Amazingly enough, India to some extent has provided credit to the faltering Soviet economy while increasing its own budget deficit. But this cannot go on much longer.

Pakistan faces a similar set of problems. The end of the Afghan War has also meant the end of the massive US aid and military hardware for an ambitious army. Isalamabad is under constant pressure from Washington to roll back its nuclear program and take effective measures against the narcotics smuggling. Feeling insulted by being summarily dismissed by Washington, Pakistani leaders speak in two languages—one filled with nationalist belligerence about retaining the nuclear option, the other showing their moderate credentials among hard-line Islamic states. The question of identity continues to boggle the country that must constantly fight a crisis of confidence—striving to be a modern nation state while wearing an Islamic badge.

It is this search for identity among nations—which intensified after new assertions by ethnic groups—that makes South Asia susceptible to a military confrontation. I hesitate to use the word "war" because both governments are faced with tremendous domestic and international constraints to refrain from adventurism. Ironically, although Pakistan lays claim to Kashmir on purely religious grounds, in 1971 Bangladesh was born of Pakistan on these same grounds. India is equally insistent that the issue is closed after Kashmiri Muslims voted in Indian elections. India also cites its democratic system as proof that religious differences can be accommodated within a secular framework. While Pakistan might have implicitly accepted the status quo in the past because it was beyond its capability to change it by force, its hopes have been revived by the near total alienation of Kashmiri Muslims from New Delhi. Indian politicians have treated Kashmir like a political football, dismissing state governments at whim and willfully ignoring signs of trouble. The discontent has erupted onto the streets and an "AK-47 culture" is dominant.

India says that Pakistan is encouraging terrorism in Kashmir and Punjab, providing the militants with arms and money. Pakistan formally denies any hand in India's troubles but Pakistani politicians openly use the Kashmir issue to heat things up. While the birth of the Punjab and Kashmir movements took place in India, much of the rearing has been done by Pakistan. Militants living on Pakistan's side of Kashmir have openly acknowledged the presence of training camps for militants and channelling of money. Pakistani leaders, from Mohammed Ali Jinnah to Benazir Bhutto, have used Kashmir to rally domestic support for their political goals. Militants in Punjab and Kashmir also have been recently emboldened in their beliefs after watching a reassertion of ethnic identity by smaller and smaller groups around the world from Ethiopia to Yugoslavia, from the former Soviet Union to Canada. In this atmosphere, it becomes difficult to make real gestures of peace.

Why South Asian Stability Matters

Stability in South Asia should be a major concern for those interested in peace and a new world order. The current thinking in Washington appears to be that South Asia has declined in strategic importance because the Afghan War is over and the Soviets have "folded tent." That may be, but instability in a region that houses one-seventh of humanity is not in anyone's interest. The rise of fundamentalism—both Muslim and Hindu—should give anyone pause, especially when seen in the context of emerging Muslim states out of the former Soviet Union and the pan-Islamic ideals of some of the Arab regimes. The easy availability of weapons has changed the face of discontent in India. The country has long lived with discontent but the proliferation of conventional weapons has drastically altered the equation. The incentive for militants to make peace is gone because they can counter Indian security forces with better weapons easily obtained and often free of cost. Strategic experts in Washington should be equally concerned about the proliferation of guns and rocket launchers in South Asia as they are about nuclear weapons and dual-use technology.

But before passing judgement on who is right, one must consider the sheer tool of terrorism on India, a fact not fully appreciated by American analysts in their eagerness to condemn human rights abuses. While we should be critical about excesses committed by security forces, let us not fool ourselves that the militants are great defenders of democracy. To cite a few examples: Sikh militants have issued guidelines on how journalists in Punjab must report the news; they have dictated what young girls and women can wear; and Kashmiri extremists have kidnapped foreigners and killed vice chancellors of universities, government officials, and citizens. Sikh terrorists have set off bombs in trains, buses, and market places for maximum impact.

The numbers are chilling. In 1990, in Punjab alone, more than 2,300 civilians, 700 militants, and 500 security officers were killed. In the first ten months of 1991, more than 4,000 people died in Punjab and 500 in Kashmir. The haul of weapons in equally stunning. Over the same 22-month period, some 1,800 AK-47s were seized from Kashmiri extremists. Rocket launchers and rockets have also been seized. Some Afghan Mujaheddin, ready to share technology, have boasted that they are willing to give Stinger missiles to Indian extremists if need be. There have been kidnappings involving 143 people, including relatives of prominent Hindu and Muslim cabinet ministers. The area of attack has steadily expanded beyond Punjab and Kashmir into other Indian states. The tactics of militants are inhuman. In the fall of 1991, an attack by Sikh extremists not only involved setting off a bomb to kill innocent civilians but for good measure they also bombed the hospital where survivors may have been treated. Consider if this were to happen in rural Tennessee.

While many of the grievances of the militants are genuine, and successive Indian governments have been cavalier about resolving them, the violence against innocent civilians is unforgivable. India is fighting a bloody insurgency in three states. The army is stretched thin and battle weary after a disastrous intervention into Sri Lanka. More and more generals are heard complaining about having to clean up the mess created by politicians and bureaucrats. The militant Hindu party, the BJP, has been critical of the Indian government's dual-track policy of talking to Pakistan about confidence-building measures while Islamabad continues to support terrorism in Punjab and Kashmir. Reports of Pakistani troops providing fire cover for Kashmiri extremists as they cross the border into India have inspired strong editorials even in moderate newspapers.

But soon, changes in the international equation will force India and Pakistan to aim for negotiated solutions to their disputes and curb the arms race. War is not considered a possibility by most analysts, given the financial constraints on both sides and pressures from the international community eager to restrain regional conflicts. The deterrent capability that both countries have achieved rules out a decisive outcome. This is recognized by thoughtful policy maker son either side. Besides, any changes in the borders following a war will not guarantee an end to the migration of militants. The new border will remain just as porous. However, escalation on the Indo-Pakistani border is very much a reality. A Western diplomat told an Indian reporter in late 1991: "India very nearly went to war last year given a quarter of the provocation it is facing today."

Developing Confidence-Building Measures

Fortunately, New Delhi and Islamabad are engaged in semi-active dialogue on confidence-building measures to reduce the risk of war. Although desirable, such talks do not touch on the core issues of respective claims over Kashmir. Pakistan wants to raise the issue of Kashmir in a foreign policy context while India views the problem as essentially domestic. It thinks of Pakistan only in the context of supporting the insurgency. India will hang on and try to impose a semblance of normalcy on an alienated population while its army gets more and more tired from curbing civilian unrest. Meanwhile, for Pakistan, the continuing rebellion and severe Indian counterinsurgency measures would provide a useful rally cry. Kashmir is one of the issues that brings the Pakistani leadership closer to its people.

The Indian government is not keen to retaliate against Pakistan; therefore it has the option of outmaneuvering its rival on the political front by seriously engaging in dialogue with the militants. Indian politicians must attempt to reverse the alienation among the people and be prepared to grant more autonomy to the states. The events in Yugoslavia may force the government to see the need for a truly federal structure which can accommodating regional aspirations. This is where India can afford to make bold moves while Islamabad cannot.

But the United States must also decide what guidelines it wants to promote for new world order when it arrives. Will the United States support a change in the line of control in Kashmir? Or support India's claim that a secular setup can absorb religious differences or Pakistan's reading of history? The larger question that Kashmir and Punjab pose for the United States and indeed for the entire world is, How large or small must a group of people be before they can claim independence?

Conflict and Cooperation in US-Latin American Security Relations

Patrice Franko-Jones

*T*he end of the Cold War has turned US security policy toward Latin America upside down. Stripped of the mission of leading the hemispheric defense against the external threat of communism, the United States security posture toward the region is challenged by an erosion of legitimating principles. The absence of an extra-hemispheric enemy makes it difficult to generate a consensus in the United States that Latin America matters much at all. Among the wide array of competing demands on US foreign affairs resources, Latin America falls low on the priority list. Not surprisingly, the political will to address a broad range of internal, multidimensional challenges in Latin America is notably lacking in the United States.[1]

But low priority on the US global agenda is not the only impediment to a strong and coherent US security policy toward Latin America. The nature of the security concerns themselves make consensus problematic. The threats are diffuse and emanate from a variety of sources. Additionally, there is a fundamental asymmetry between how the United States defines challenges to its national security and how the same issue affects the security of the Latin nation. Because of this difficulty in defining a common agenda, there is a greater likelihood of conflict in security relations between the United States and Latin America.

The lack of guiding principles combined with divergent security interests among the nations of the hemisphere make

Patrice Franko-Jones is an assistant professor in the Department of Economics at Colby College. In 1990-1992, Dr. Franko-Jones served as a Regional Policy Fellow in the Office of the Assistant Secretary of Defense for Inter-American Affairs. She has also held teaching positions at Trinity College and the University of Notre Dame.

for a potentially volatile and crisis-driven relationship with Latin America. This chapter discusses the sources of this conflict and suggests policy alternatives to redirect the momentum toward cooperative approaches. It explores the implications of both US cooperation with Latin American countries as well as the ramifications of enhanced cooperation among Latin nations in the nontraditional security areas of counternarcotics, nonproliferation and defense of the environment. Relatively modest initiatives have the potential not only for avoiding conflict, but also for generating positive returns. The real trick, of course, will be mobilizing political energies on both sides of the equator to make the investment.

Changing Priorities in US Security Policy

US security policy toward Latin America has long been oriented toward an external enemy. Newly born Latin nation states were welcomed into the hemispheric system under the protection of the Monroe Doctrine of 1823, which restricted interference of extra-continental powers.[2] The postwar implementation of the regional collective security agreement, the Rio Pact, institutionalized by the creation of the Organization of American States, was, under US pressure, fundamentally anti-Communist in its approach.[3] While many recognized that not all problems in Latin America were directly caused by Soviet expansion and not all solutions resided in the containment of communism, the looming shadow of Soviet influence kept our Southern neighbors on the US policy agenda.

The vulnerability of weak regimes in Central and South America to the possibility of Soviet infiltration legitimized the provision of economic and military assistance.[4] The aid was not provided primarily for the augmentation of forces to be used against a common external enemy, but rather to strengthen domestic political and economic institutions against internal subversion promoted from abroad. From Truman to Nixon the containment of Soviet expansionism was seen to be advanced by purchasing political favor. Kennedy's

Alliance for Progress also called for special responsibilities of Latin nations in exchange for aid targeted at strengthening democratic, capitalist institutions.[5] The fight against the national infiltration of communism was embraced by most militaries in Latin America. While Carter's insistence that recipients of US assistance conform to minimal standards on human rights strained the friendly relationship, the Reagan era reaffirmed the importance of Latin countries in the fight against the expansionist impulses of the Soviet Union. Strong and thoughtful arguments against fighting communism with contra forces notwithstanding, the appeal to the defense of democracy against a foreign enemy dominated policy.

Despite the threat of external aggression, the attention given to Latin America under the regime of containment was rarely pro-active or sustained over time. United States actions in the Dominican Republic (1916), Guatemala (1954), Cuba (1962), Chile (1973), and Nicaragua (1980s) are testimony to the failure of a positive, long-term policy agenda. The result was the recourse of violent action. In contrast to these bursts of focus, there were periods of "benign neglect" during which the United States seemed to forget its Latin neighbors. But even during the dormant periods the ability to call forth the specter of an external enemy in the United States' backyard was present. Minimal levels of assistance were maintained and reciprocal relations nurtured to close the circle against communist encroachment. The anti-Communist threat was instrumental in achieving policy goals.[6] Indeed, the knowledge that this could be effectively done to counter a threat was probably an impediment to longer term political investments in the region. Nevertheless, when perceived as necessary, defense against an external threat could be could be relied upon to motivate support.

Latin Americans rarely attached as much importance as the United States did to Communist expansionism. Latin nations continued to maintain diplomatic and commercial ties with Soviet Union and Cuba. Particularly during the Reagan era Latins did not subscribe to the strength of the security argument. However, many Latin militaries did use the threat of Communist subversion as the rationale for internal wars. There was a domestic constituency within Latin America that could be counted on to share, at least rhetorically, US aims of anticommunism. Even after the period of internal wars against communism, support could be mustered for anti-Communist strategies. Despite the fact that the left in Latin America remained a vital part of their political culture, Latin volunteers for the war against communism created a political constituency sympathetic to US positions and actions. But the enemy has been vanquished. The Soviet Union has been transformed from a vilified aggressor to a favored competitor for scarce financial resources. Cuba is weak and isolated. With the metamorphosis of the Soviet Union and the emaciation of Cuba, the geostrategic rallying point for Latin American policy is gone.

Losing an external enemy is not bad; the absence of a foundation for Latin American regional policy is, however, problematic. Given the drama of the global stage, Latin America does not rank high on the foreign policy checklist. It is difficult to generate an enthusiasm on Capitol Hill for Latin issues. With a constrained foreign assistance budget even the counternarcotics fight is stalemated against formidable political barriers. Both Congress and the Administration seemed unwilling to consider Peru seriously when it takes time and resources away from Israel and Egypt—much less pursue a broader regional policy. Alternative investments of political energies appear more fruitful.

Is this a rational assessment of priorities? To make the case for the importance of the Latin region one can certainly invoke geostrategic arguments for ensuring free and open passage, political imperatives to support the consolidation of democratic institutions, or the economic potential of a reinvigorated Latin market.[7] It is strategically sensible to maintain good relations with Latin American and Caribbean neighbors and to encourage the economic and political growth fundamental to a stable inter-American system. Nevertheless, while heads might bob up and down in accord with the good policy sense of a strong Latin policy, little initiative is taken. There are no dramatic issues to capture attention on the Latin front. Unlike the Reagan era where Central America was the divide against which communism would be defeated, the Bush policy reverts to a historical pattern of downplaying US interests in the region.[8] The sound reasons for strategic involvement pale in comparison to the Middle East or the Soviet Union. Unwilling to invest token amounts of political capital in the short run, the United States loses leverage over time.

This isn't news. The Reagan period aside, Latin America has always been of secondary priority to the United States. What is different, however, is that when Latin American policies diverge sharply from US security interests, the ability to marshall a political response will have atrophied significantly. The costs of neglect are likely to be high. Although less dramatic than foreign infiltration, contemporary threats from Latin America to the United States have a greater probability of directly affecting the lives of American citizens. Economic Community Commission President Jacques Delors' commented before the International Institute for Strategic Studies:

> All around us, naked ambition, lust for power, national uprisings and underdevelopment are combining to create potentially dangerous situations, containing the seeds of destabilization and conflict, aggravated by the proliferation of weapons of mass destruction.[9]

With extremes of wealth and poverty and fragile political institutions, instability in Latin America is likely to present security challenges to the United States. Because it will be more difficult to muster support during a crisis, it is worthwhile to consider modest long-term alternatives. Cooperation with Latin partners and encouraging cooperation among Latin nations could serve to enhance the stability and security of the region. A discussion of the importance of these threats to the security of the United States and means of crafting realistic policy responses to counter them is therefore in order.

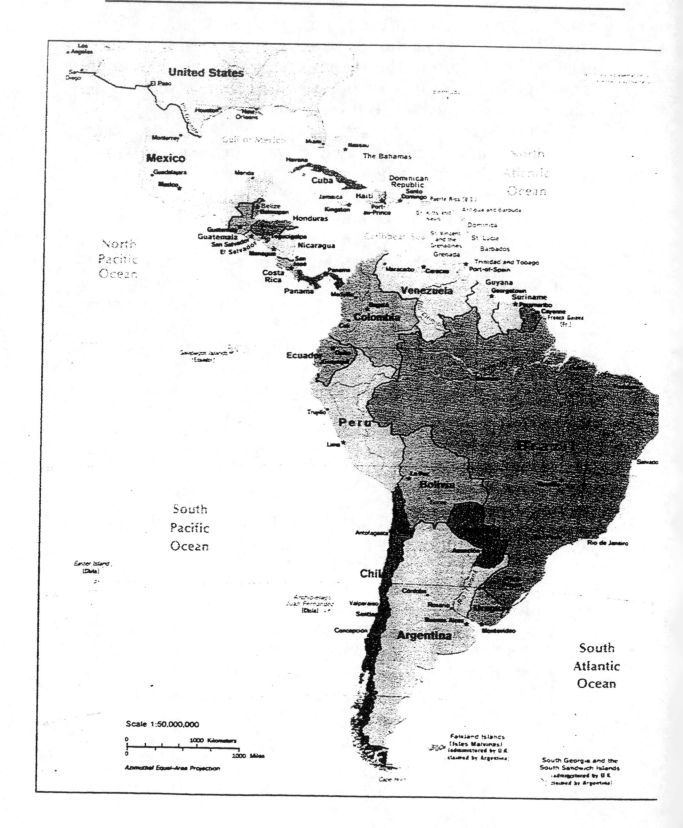

Figure 5. *Latin America*

Quiet Crises

The relegation of Latin concerns to a secondary tier unsupported by a political rapid reaction force is further complicated by the diffuse nature of the security challenges Latin America presents to the United States. There is little of immediate concern in the region. No country in the hemisphere is likely to attack the United States or impede free transit in international waters. The fall of a democratic government in the region will not radically constrain US foreign policy options. The US lost jobs because of the economic crisis in Latin America, but the loss was not dramatic. Economic and political hardship have prompted a steady stream of Latin emigrants; while their presence in the United States has at times been contentious, the cheap labor they provide has also been a benefit. Environmental concerns have been advanced on the policy agenda, but they have hardly provoked a crisis of state. Nonetheless, the "quiet crises" are exceedingly important. Support for the democratization and restructuring of regional forces, the counternarcotics struggle, problems of weapons proliferation, and sustainable, environmentally respectful economic growth have clear implications for US political and economic strength. But the problems do not scream for immediate attention. The failure to address these issues of critical concern is unlikely to inflict immediate political costs.

Furthermore, on each of the issues the Latin perspective is not clearly identified with our own. This dissonance amplifies the tendency toward policy inertia. Because of the lack of immediacy and the likelihood of disagreement with Latin Americans, the enhancement of regional security can only be achieved via deliberate, almost plodding measures to redress long-term structural issues. Increasing cooperation with Latin America is politically pragmatic. There are no immediate political costs, and the President is afforded a public policy platform decorated with warm and fuzzy feelings for the apple pie goodness of cooperation.

Counternarcotics

The most intractable issue on the Latin American security policy agenda and the one with the most visible support is the counter-narcotics program. The national security strategy of the United States defines the reduction of illegal drugs into the country as critical to its survival as "a free and independent nation, with its fundamental values intact and its institutions and people secure."[10] The Andean Strategy, presented in 1989, is the regional plan to achieve this national objective. A multifaceted program, the Andean Strategy is designed to "work with Andean governments to disrupt and destroy the growing, processing, and transportation of coca and coca products within the course countries, in order to reduce the supply of cocaine entering our country.[11] While the Department of Defense has the lead in detection and monitoring of narcotics entering the United States, the strategies are squarely lodged in a process of interagency coordination.

Of the security concerns on the US-Latin American agenda, the drug war is the issue most like anticommunism in its ability to create the specter of an external enemy. There is a broad US constituency that believes drugs are a major national problem. Although few contend that the problem can be eliminated from the supply side alone, the benefits of the international strategy are presented in the context of supporting demand reduction programs, thus minimizing deleterious effects until a decline in consumption takes hold.

But the characterization of drugs as an external enemy is neither neat nor politically satisfying. The multinational illegal narcotics industry is intricately woven into the economic, cultural and political activities of producer countries in Latin America. Production and distribution of illegal narcotics are indeed a threat to the Latin national fabric—but not one that can be characterized as a threat from an external enemy. Bolivia, for example, earned three times more in 1984 from the cocaine industry than it did from its major export, tin.[12] Forty percent of the economically active population in Bolivia and 15 percent in Peru depend on coca for survival;[13] drug trafficking activities register hard currency earnings of $1.8 billion a year, more than 50 percent of Peruvian legal exports.[14]

In the Peruvian case the narcotics infrastructure is tied to a culture of political violence via the Shining Path terrorist group, *Sendero Luminoso*. *Sendero's* involvement with the drug trade is a relatively recent phenomenon. *Sendero* reportedly establishes the rules of the game in the Upper Huallaga Valley, negotiating on the behalf of the peasants and taxing traffickers for the use of legal or clandestine airstrips.[15] Its ability to draw resources from the narcotraffickers makes Peru's domestic struggle against this terrorist organization more difficult. More constraining politically is the connection between Sendero and the coca-growing peasants. The surest strategy to stem the erosion of Peruvian political and economic institutions from illegal narcotics is a healthy increase in the legal sector of the economy. A strong legal economy not only creates economic alternatives, but also diminishes the relative weight of narcotrafficking in political and judicial systems. However, through violence and intimidation *Sendero* restricts peasant mobility between the legal and illegal sectors and sabotages the government's efforts to provide the developmental infrastructure critical to growth of the legal sector.[16] Political violence is estimated to be responsible for 20,000 deaths in 10 years, and terrorism has cost $23 million, the equivalent to the nation's foreign debt.[17] Narcotics is only a small part of Peru's critical problem with a brutal insurgency.

Until the 1991 agreement, US assistance could only be used in counternarcotics efforts; most recently there has been the recognition that drug trafficking and guerilla activities are "inextricably intertwined."[18] While it is important that the United States has recognized the connection between the dual threats facing Peruvian society, the dichotomy between US and Peruvian interests still remains. *Sendero* is clearly a greater threat to Peru than narcotrafficking. Requiring Peru to fight a full-scale war on two fronts because of US-defined security needs is begging for defeat. The military requirements for counterinsurgency operations are different from counternarcotics.[19] Indeed the Peruvian military has reportedly entered into alliances with the narcotraffickers in order to achieve its counterinsurgency aims. It is important that the United States fully appreciate the Peruvian priorities. Little is going to happen on the drug front until the counterinsurgency is under control; *Sendero* actions effectively block progress in the drug war.[20] Only by placing Peruvian interests first will US objectives be met.

Furthermore, from the Latin perspective the drug war is a US problem. As Peruvian Prime Minister Carlos Torres noted before the Peruvian Congress, "We have maintained that the phenomena of drug trafficking is multidimensional. Its origin is drug consumption and there must be a shared responsibility."[21] The drug war is indeed driven by the US demand problem. This creates conditions for the growth of suppliers, narcotraffickers that threaten the fabric of domestic life in Andean countries. The United States therefore had a shared responsibility. We are the cause of their domestic problem. As a nation we also have a commitment to the defense of democratic institutions, particularly fragile governments as in Latin America. The United States has responsibilities to the Andean ridge nations. But this responsibility can only be executed by the invitation and with the cooperation of the democratically elected host government.

Such invitations carry high political costs for Latin countries. Cooperation with the United States in the drug war is extremely risky for Latin governments. The arrival of US military advisors in Bolivia in April of 1991 prompted heated debate on the militarization of the drug war and raised issues of Bolivian sovereignty.[22] For citizens who lived under military dictatorships, the involvement of the military in the internal affairs of their country is a frightful prospect. Despite the clear message on the part of the Bolivian government that efforts would not be targeted against peasant growers, the General Union Confederation of Peasant Workers of Bolivia declared that the Bolivian government would be accountable for "the possible outbreak of violence, bloodshed, and mourning" due to US presence.[23] The Bolivian Labor Confederation called for a nationwide work stoppage to express opposition to "US intervention in our national territory," and "to protest the sellout of our natural resources."[24] This was not an isolated outburst of anger. Rather, external pressure from the United States has provoked the solidification of a national coca-growers movement determined to protect their rights.[25] Others argue that the military will be corrupted by kickbacks from narcotraffickers.

By requiring demonstrable efforts on the counternarcotics front, the United States is perceived as forcing the militarization of the drug war. The physical presence of US military advisors and personnel involved in training exercises was characterized by the Bolivian Labor Federation as a violation of national sovereignty.[26] Likewise in Peru the signing of the antidrug agreement with the United States sparked protests; the Provincial Peasants Federation charged that the Fujimori government was trying to "put coca producers in the hands of Yankee imperialism" and reserved the right to defend themselves against military action.[27]

Where is the line drawn between a US militarization of a national effort and cooperation with the United States? As President Fujimori noted in an address before the Peruvian Congress to request permission for the presence of US advisors, the drug war is already militarized. Pointing to the large number of troops and police personnel deployed in the coca zone, he contended that the issue was not a possible militarization but rather effective training to use forces in place.[28] Clearly diplomatic arm twisting takes place under US Congressional requirements for certification,[29] but it should also be remembered that the military trainers arriving in Peru originally were part of an agreement negotiated by a democratically elected government and approved by a freely chosen Congress. This is distinctly different from an accord with a host country military or a government propped up by military means.

The United States has an interest in the effects of the narcotics industry on national institutions. Our commitment to democratic ideals should not end with the Cold War. The difference now, however, is that democracy is not a fight against communism or a military dictatorship but rather a process of working with our hemispheric neighbors at long-term democratic institution building. Narcotics trafficking threatens those institutions. If the host government is committed to fighting this institutional corrosion, the United States has a responsibility to assist.

The expansion of the drug industry beyond the Andean countries creates possibilities for minimizing the cost of cooperation with the United States. Drugs are not only a problem of Peru, Colombia, and Bolivia. The fight against narcotrafficking in Latin America has broadened beyond the Andean ridge. Argentina announced in April 1991 its antidrug program, which included the provision for joint action with the United States to conduct a photographic survey of Argentine territory to detect clandestine landing fields and coca plantations.[30] Despite reticence on the part of Argentine military officers, President Menem signed a decree creating the Federal Service Against Drug Trafficking, which tasks the military with counternarcotics intelligence collection.[31] President Carlos Perez of Venezuela created an interagency unified command to attack drug consumption and drug trafficking.[32]

On a multilateral front, the security forces of Argentina, Bolivia, and Paraguay established a plan to carry out simultaneous operations in their border zone.[33] The illegal narcotics industry in Latin America is truly multinational. Transnational drug cartels are capable of quickly moving operations from one area to the next. Latin nations are well advised to take initiative today to restrict the movement of narcotraffickers into their territories. The United States should support their national efforts by providing training and equipment.

The United States, however, cannot and should not be the counternarcotics Santa Claus. With global commitments elsewhere, the pot is limited. Fiscal Year 1992 totals for security assistance to the Andean countries are proposed at almost $500 million economic assistance.[34] In the broader scheme, this is a small portion, but clearly similar levels cannot be replicated throughout the region. Further, it would not be in our political interest to do so. US security policy toward Latin America should not become simultaneous with the drug policy. Security concerns are broader, and unidimensionality is a fragile base.

The fact that narcotics are becoming a concern not only for the Andean countries creates interesting possibilities for US policy. The counternarcotics effort must rely on multilateral political will. Cooperation by other Latin America nations could decrease both the costs to the United States as well as lessen US visibility. Counternarcotics cannot remain solely a US effort; the political dangers of resistance to a new brand of Yankee imperialism defined by drugs threaten to undermine success. A broader base of nations thus decreases resistance to US activity as well as providing a more effective curtain against the multinational drug cartel.

A promising area for United States to counteract the threats of narcotrafficking and narcoterrorism involves the support of the European nations. The growth rate of narcotics use in Europe is increasing; 20 percent of the world market for coca is within the European community.[35] It is more difficult to generate opposition to European intervention in Latin America than to Uncle Sam; therefore, the United States should focus on multilateral efforts. The role of the Organization of American States (OAS) could be amplified, as could stronger support for initiatives of regional subgroups. Thus, multilateralism provides gains in sharing both the political and economic costs of the counternarcotics effort. The modest investment of energies and resources is likely to have a significant payoff.

Proliferation Concerns

In addition to counternarcotics, the United States' national interests are directly challenged by the proliferation of armaments. As outlined in the *National Security Strategy of the United States,* "it is the nation's objective to prevent the transfer of militarily critical technologies and resources to hostile countries or groups, especially the spread of weapons of mass destruction and associated high-technology means of delivery." But from the Latin perspective, restricting the growth of domestic defense industries and their freedom to exploit the international defense market directly challenges their national security. Domestic sovereignty is threatened. More importantly, according to Latin militaries and some civilian political elites, the ability to appropriate and absorb high technologies critical to competitiveness in the modern international economy is limited.

The war in the Persian Gulf underscored once more the difficulties proliferation of armaments by Third World countries presents to the security of the United States and the clear conflict with the security interests of Latin America. Brazil, which competes with Israel as the largest Third World exporter of weaponry, had sold armored cars and missiles to the Iraqi government during its war with Iran. Military sales with Iraq were part of a larger trade package which counterbalanced chickens and weapons against Brazil's pressing need for oil imports. After the United States, Brazil was Iraq's largest trading partner. Although European allies had also supplied Saddam Hussein's army, Brazil's defense industry was perceived as a threat to US security.

US attention to Brazilian defense exports was exacerbated by several factors. First, at the outbreak of the war Brigadier General Hugo Piva, the retired head of the Brazilian Aerospace Agency, was working on a missile program with the Iraqis. Piva, a nationalist, quickly let it be known that although he would comply with UN sanctions against Iraq, as soon as permitted by law he would return to resume the engineering project. Because of his former role as a government official, distrust of Piva's activities raised questions as to the Collor administration's commitment to the Gulf War effort.

Uneasiness in relations with the United States came at a time where the Collor administration should have been saluted for its aggressive stand against the secret nuclear program pursued by the Brazilian Army. In a dramatic display Collor threw lime in the nuclear testing hole in Cachimbo and vowed that Brazil would not pursue a nuclear program for destructive means. The secret army nuclear program pursued by the military was aired in the press, a concrete demonstration of greater transparency in heretofore clandestine military programs. Unfortunately in the context of Piva's Iraq activities, the playback in Washington on the unveiling of the clandestine nuclear program echoed more of the distrust based on activities of past military administrations than applause for asserting democratic, civilian control over the military.

US distrust has very strong implications for Brazil's achievement of its national security interests. Brazilians define the acquisition of advanced technologies as critical to their national security. US disapprobation for Brazil was made evident in the contentious sale of an IBM vector processing computer to EMBRAER, Brazil's state owned aircraft firm. The US government cited the need for stronger end-use monitoring in light of the fact that they perceived that the computer could be used in support of a nuclear or missile development program. The sale of the supercomputer—and access to high technology in general—soon became tied to demands on the part of the United States that Brazil bring the anti-nuclear proliferation Treaty of Tlatelolco into force and that it adhere to MTCR (Missile Technology Control Regime) guidelines in the export of material that could be used for missile production.[36]

Declaration of adherence to the Treaty of Tlatelolco was a simpler demand for the Brazilians to meet. Simultaneously, the United States required that Argentina bring this agreement limiting nuclear weapons programs into force. Germany, a partner in Argentine and Brazilian nuclear programs, also exerted pressure via a decision by the German cabinet that nuclear cooperation would only continue with those countries with those countries subjecting their facilities to full IAEA safeguards.[37] The jointness of the decision to bring Tlatelolco into force allowed both Brazil and Argentina to transform the national embarrassment at being told to do so by the United States into a proud declaration of shared regional goals and a commitment to the will of the people in a democratically elected government. On July 18, 1991, Brazil and Argentina signed an agreement for the peaceful use of nuclear energy, formalizing the declaration by the two presidents announced at Foz do Iguacu. As noted in the Brazilian press, the reason the agreement was signed was that the declaration would allow both countries greater reign in pursuing access to high technology from the United States.[38]

However, meeting the concerns of the United States and Germany involved the application of international Atomic

Energy Agreement safeguards, a step beyond a binational accord. According to Brazilian Science and Technology Secretary Jose Goldemberg, sovereignty would be maintained as inspectors of the most sensitive program would be would be Argentine and Brazilian.[39] Even with the binational inspection program, however, there are those who feel "there is really a war going on between the countries that have nuclear technology, and those who are attempting, independently, to gain that knowledge.[40] The Brazilian President of the National Commission for Nuclear Energy (CNEN) was forced to defend publicly the contention that the safeguards agreement to be signed with IAEA signified a retreat from the Brazilian commitment to the indigenous development of a nuclear program.[41] The domestic political costs of adhering to US pressure have been significant.

Given the strong resistance to even multilateral stances, unilateral initiatives have been harder to implement.[42] In response to US pressures, a proposal has been drafted to control Brazil's export of strategic technology. The political fallout surrounding the Gulf crisis made it clear to the Brazilians that in order to receive the technology necessary for national security, controls must be imposed on the export of armaments. As Foreign Minister Rezek noted, "Brazil today is simply convinced that it is essential to act with extreme prudence and make certain analyses relating to the political future before getting involved in that kind of trade." This is not simple.

The Brazilian Government is preparing a new policy for the conventional arms material sector. According to the foreign minister, "the most sensitive area" relates to exports and involves not only the sale of military material but the performance of services abroad. He said the latter aspect had become manifest recently with the activities carried out in Iraq by HOP consultants, a company owned by Brigadier General Hugo Piva. He quickly defended Piva's actions but stated a willingness to change. "The company's situation was perfectly legal; it was work done by private enterprise," Rezek maintained. "In other words, the government had nothing whatever to do with it, but we can improve our performance in this area."[43] Despite the desire to be perceived as accountable to first-world nations, Rezek has not come out squarely for strict controls of conventional weapons exports. In response to a reporter's query as to whether Brazil would sell weapons to potentially bellicose nations, including Iran, Rezek said:

> We have not ruled it out, but neither is it on our agenda. Moreover, any prospective deal with Iran would take a little longer, would require some reflection. Although from the point of view of the Brazilian Government, Iran has turned over a new leaf since that period. The Iranians are sensible; they know what Brazil is and what it stands for, and this must have influenced the Iranian decision to immediately offer us all the petroleum we need.[44]

In response to the question whether the government will allow exports of weapons to Iran, Rezek answered,

> Yes, but within a new perspective. We hope to establish three main guidelines for exports of national weapons. First, that the weapons we export be defensive, not offensive. There seems to be a very small difference here, but the military know how to differentiate between them very well. Second, that we will be completely convinced that those weapons will not be enough for the purchasing country to begin a war. Third, that the export of weapons will not figure as the main trade item with any country. You will see that if weapons are included on our list of exports to Iran, they will appear in a very small scale.[45]

According to Rezek, the Brazilian government "recommends" that businessmen consult diplomatic channels whenever a trade deal involves other countries.[46] This is an important rhetorical shift in the government "hands off" policy of arms exports. It is not clear, however, that it will be enforceable. After the Collor visit to Washington in June 1991, energies have been focused on designing a system of control to replace the Brazilian weapons export regime, PNEMEM.[47] While the intent to comply with US requests appears genuine, the logistical difficulties in both designing the system and gaining approval from the more nationalistic members of Congress appear problematic. The costs of not doing so, however, are high. Redefinitions of the list of restricted items on the Multilateral Coordinating Committee on Export Controls (COCOM) now include supercomputers with composite theoretical performance greater than 195 million theoretical operations per second, machine tools with a precision greater than 6m, high-speed disk drives, high-performance printing systems, equipment for processing signals, certain microchips used in personal computers, high-velocity optical fibers, and digital commutation in public telephone and data systems.[48]

The Chilean defense industry also poses new challenges for the United States. Unlike the Brazilian sector, which is facing a period of contraction, the Chilean defense industry appears to be growing. The Army Ordnance firm FAMAE has launched a new lightening rocket in coordination with Royal Ordnance of England, and an armored vehicle is being jointly developed with the Swiss firm Mowag.[49]

An area to which Argentina acceded unilaterally to US demands was in the dismantling of their Condor missile project, which was jointly developed in concert with Egypt.[50] Argentine Foreign Minister Domingo Carvallo admitted that, under a previous administration, the Condor 2 project was bankrolled by Iraq with the intention of technology transfer.[51] Weighing the international political gains as well as the high investment costs the project demanded, President Menem deactivated the Condor program.[52] The head of the Air Force at the time criticized this move, suggesting that the cancellation of the program at the US request made Argentina look like a banana republic. Although the general was fired and confined to house arrest for his comments, this sentiment is not unrepresentative of military views on conforming to US demands.

In responding to pressures from the United States on strategic technology, Latin governments open themselves to criticism from domestic nationalists. Argentine Foreign Minister Guido di Tella, for example, defended the greater openness to US demands by pointing to his belief that past policies of antagonizing the United States have not achieved the ends of greater sovereignty but instead were costly in terms of Argentina's trade and industrial growth.[53] The domestic political costs Latin governments face in adhering to US policy demands are high. If within a relatively short period there is little to show for cooperation, then there will be increasing pressure to diverge from US interests. It is important that the United States recognize that it ability to leverage change in national security issues in Latin America is not unlimited. The United States needs to expand the offering of carrots as incentives to convince Latin governments to realign their security interests with those of the united States. Given the importance placed on the acquisition of technology as a critical component of national security, the United States must explore concrete means by which Latins can achieve this security objective while also serving our own interests. As Brazilian President Collor noted, Latin America wants "reciprocity, mutual respect." He outlined the efforts being made in democratization and economic stabilization, but noted that "we must have access to new forms of technology."[54]

If the United States would like to modify Latin American weapons production and sales activities, it must give incentives to do so. For example, the US should provide Brazil the rationale to identify its security interests with that of the United States. Three programmatic means for doing so come to mind. First, because it is difficult to control the behavior of the defense firms legislatively, market incentives ought to be used. That is, if Brazilian defense firms had a vested economic interest in the US market, the calculus of export to undesirable nations versus losing the U.S. market would be a risky one. As mentioned earlier in the case of exports to the Middle East, relatively limited activity makes a difference. The Brazilian defense industry offers products of potential interest to the US Armed Forces because of the particular market niche that they fill. Weight should be given the foreign policy considerations of such a purchase. Joint ventures with US firms should be encouraged.

Of course, such initiatives would have to be sensitive to Latin demands for sovereignty. Rumors of a military agreement with the United States generated opposition from those within both the Brazilian defense industry and defense ministry. Aeronautics Minister Socrates Monteiro, for example, noted that there was no interest in a military cooperation agreement with the United States.[55] Given the sensitivities, initiatives must proceed through the private sector. Essentially what is being proposed here is a defense complement to the Bush Administration's Enterprise for the Americas Initiative. The most productive approach to improving relations with the Latin Americans in the area of proliferation of weaponry and the development of high-technology industries is commercial joint ventures. In addition to being respectful of Latin sovereignty in focusing activity on being commercial partners, the market approach is realistic in that it does not promise huge sums of money that cannot be delivered.

As with counternarcotics, there are also gains to Latin nations in complementing relations with the US with stronger regional ties. The chief of the National Space Commission in Argentina, Jorge Saade, noted that Argentina, Mexico, and Brazil will jointly develop a light, satellite-launching rocket.[56] Any kind of launch vehicle development program has been vehemently opposed by the US Government on the grounds that the technologies involved have applications to missile technology. Since it is more difficult to argue that the transfers of technologies would be made across multinational sectors, in this case regionalism may be a strategy on the part of the Latins to subvert declared US interests.

However, while Latin multilateralism in the drug war is likely to be in the US interest, joint programs in weapons development are not. In the drug war US and Latin interests are more clearly allied. In defense production, US interests in nonproliferation are pitted against Latin interests of geostrategic power and technology acquisition. Multilateralism in this case enhances the bargaining power of nations against the United States. A commercial response to nonproliferation concerns on the part of the United States might work to dissipate the effects of cooperation in Latin defense production to the degree that "carrots" of US market access or joint ventures with U.S. firms could weaken the incentives for cooperation among Latin firms.

Defense of the Environment

Latin Americans appreciate the environmental dimensions of national security. In a forum held at the Inter-American Defense College in April of 1991, it was concluded that the threat to the environment was one of the greatest perils confronting the continent. Nevertheless, despite general agreement that environmental challenges are to be considered as part of the broader threat to hemispheric security, action on the environmental front is problematic. Colombian President Cesar Gaviria noted in reference to problems such as the environment that "the ghost of interventionism has not disappeared," and that the Latin nations must assume a united stand against outside powers intervening in Latin affairs.[57] Various North-South tensions were readily apparent during the United Nations' Environmental Conference ECO, held in Brazil in mid-1992. Latin militaries have positive contributions to make to the protection of their national resources. An obvious area for expansion of activity is in radar control. A more comprehensive radar system would facilitate the detection of environmentally destabilizing activities associated with narco-trafficking while also aiding in the detection of deforestation. Joint exercises with US forces could be tailored in support of environmental protection. So called "Green Brigades" could be deployed in greater numbers to assist in water purification projects, well drilling, or other activities in support of the environment.

The biggest obstacle to such action, however, is the perceived attack on the sovereignty of the host nation. A broad spectrum of Brazilians, for example, belief that US activities in the Amazon—including the role of voluntary organizations—have the objective of colonizing that country's vital resources.[58] In the environmental area there are positive gains for enhanced multilateral action; joint environmental activities by Latin countries lessen the erosion of sovereignty from the United States. Common policies on the part of Latin nations improve the local political viability of environmental programs while contributing to the goals of sustainable development. The outcome of the 1992 environmental meetings has important implications for the broader US security agenda. Many agree that the environment constitutes an important national security agenda item,[59] but the concrete mechanisms for confronting this challenge remain problematic.

Clearly the tools of the Cold War security regime are not appropriate for confronting the environmental threat. You can't just send in the marines to prevent deforestation, but does acknowledgement of this fact preclude the involvement of the armed forces at all? Are there appropriate roles for the military in the preservation of the environment? For example, are there applicable lessons from the role of the US Army Corp of Engineers for Latin America? What kind of support can the United States provide? These questions merit US policy attention prior to the meetings to be able to explore concrete alternatives with our Latin neighbors. In particular, US policy makers should explore means by which multilateralism can help in the achievement of objectives and not degenerate into contentious and unproductive North-South debate.

Toward Cooperative Solutions

Defense of the environmental and the counternarcotics struggle highlight the case of positive returns for cooperative behavior in resolving security threats facing the Americas. Drug-free societies and sustainable growth are laudable goals easily shared by nations. In both the environmental area and in counternarcotics, cooperation among Latin nations has net positive returns. Despite the shared objectives, however, cooperation with the United States is not costless. From the Latin perspective, cooperation is almost surely to be thwarted by the hegemonic position of the United States. Cooperation is best achieved by relatively equal partners, yet the United States so clearly dominates the hemispheric equation. This is problematic not only because it allows the United States to impose its preferences but because even when the United States is encouraging equality in decisionmaking, the Latin countries assume that there must be some hidden agenda. Paranoia then obscures possibility for positive policies.

There is a need for confidence-building measures between the North and the South. Given the relatively low priority of Latin America for the Untied States, efforts and programs must be realistic and pragmatic. The US security policy toward Latin America cannot be conceptualized as a grand scheme. Indeed, beyond the financing concerns and the low level of political attention, by its very nature a grand scheme is patriarchal. Modest attempts at cooperative action fits both the US security agenda and Latin America's requirement for sovereignty and independence outside the aegis of the United States.

The US objective of nonproliferation is unlikely to be achieved by purely political cooperation, because US interests of global arms restraint stand in conflict with Latin interests of technological development and geostrategic power, Latin nations need to be compensated to realign their goals with those of the United States. Given fiscal and political constraints, the best mechanism for compensation is enhanced market access. A defense complement to the Enterprise for the Americas Initiative could go a long way in the economic and political realm for setting the context for such realistic policy making, as the Enterprise promises very little in the way of financial or political resources. Therefore a defense complement to the Enterprise is in order, one that focuses on the use of the market and private sector initiatives to meet our security needs in the areas of narcotrafficking, proliferation, and environmental security. Much more than this is unlikely to be achieved given competing priorities.

In all three nontraditional security areas—narcotrafficking, nonproliferation and environmental defense—the fact that a quick consensus cannot be mustered in the United States against an external threat is a blessing in disguise. The new security concerns in the region cannot be addressed by rapid intervention or force. But a modest, pragmatic approach to security relations that maximizes cooperation with our Latin neighbors is likely to have a more positive long-run effect than cycles of neglect and intervention.

Notes

1. A preliminary draft of this chapter was presented at the New England Council of Latin American Studies Meeting, Smith College, 5 October 1991.

2. See Federico G. Gil, "The Kennedy Johnson Years," ed. John D. Martz, *United States Policy in Latin America, A Quarter Century of Crisis and Challenge, 1961-1986* (Lincoln, Nebraska and London: University of Nebraska Press, 1988).

3. See Wayne S. Smith, "The United States and South America: Beyond the Monroe Doctrine," *Current History* (February 1991).

4. Thomas S. Bodenheimer and Robert Gould, "U.S. Military Doctrines and Their Relation to Foreign Policy," Augusto Varas, *Hemispheric Security and U.S. Policy in Latin America,* (Boulder, CO: Westview Press, 1989).

5. Robert Pastor describes this "special relationship" in his essay "The Carter Administration," Martz, *United States Policy.*

6. As Jorge Casteneda noted, " . . . it was also an instrument for rallying a domestic constituency around a policy often seeking other objectives. . . . But it was an indispensable ingredient of U.S. policy toward the region." "Latin America and the End of the Cold War," *World Policy Journal* (Summer 1990).

7. See for example, the testimony of Dr. Joseph P. Tulchin, Director, Latin American Program, Woodrow Wilson Center for Scholars before the Subcommittee on Western Hemisphere Affairs, Committee on Foreign Affairs, US House of Representatives, Washington D.C. February 19, 1991, for a discussion of issues on the US security policy agenda toward Latin America.

8. For a comparison of the differences in the Reagan and Bush administrations see William M. LeoGrande, "From Reagan to Bush: The Transition in US Policy Toward Central America," *Journal of Latin American Studies* (October 1990), 595-621.

9. In Zbigniew Brzezinski, "Selective Global Commitment," *Foreign Affairs* (Fall 1991).

10. *National Security Strategy of the United States* (Washington, D.C.: The White House, March 1990).

11. US Department of State, Bureau of Narcotics Matters, *International Narcotics Control Strategy Report,* Executive Summary (March 1991), 14.

12. Peter M. Sanchez, "The 'Drug War': The US Military and National Security," paper prepared for the 32nd Annual International Studies Association Convention, Vancouver, British Columbia, Canada 20-23 March 1991.

13. Ibid. The Peruvian Studies and Research Association for Peace, conducting a study with the financial assistance of the United Nations Fund for Drug Abuse Control, found that 11 percent of Peruvian GDP for 1989 came from coca and involved 600,000 Peruvians directly or indirectly. In the Upper Huallaga Valley, three-quarters of the peasants cultivate coca for a return of $4,000 per hectare. Foreign Broadcast Information Service-Latin America (FBIS-LAT) 90, 19 October 1990, "Paper Reports Research on Drug Activities," *La Republica,* 3 October 1990.

14. "Meeting Criticizes US Antidrug Policy in Andes," FBIS-LAT-91-068 9 April 1991, Madrid EFE 0029 GMT 8 April 1991. Rensselaer Lee, noted expert on the drug trade and author of *The White Labyrinth,* put this figure at 15-20 percent of foreign exchange earnings in a presentation at The Peru Roundtable, sponsored by the Central Intelligence Agency, Rosslyn, 13 September 1991.

15. "SL Links to Drug Trafficking Detailed," FBIS-LAT-90-164, 23 August 1990, *El Comercio,* 28 June 1991, A14.

16. "Invest and die," *The Economist,* 7 September 1991, 56.

17. "Fujimori on Human Rights, Trade, Other Issues," FBIS-LAT-91-170 3 September 1991, *Excelsior,* 22 July 91, 1-A, 10-A.

18. "In Peru, doubts on US aid plan," Boston Globe, 13 August 1991, 2.

19. Rensselaer Lee, The Peru Roundtable.

20. Ibid.

21. "Prime Minister Addresses National Congress,"FBIS-LAT-91-076, 19 April 1991, Lima National Radio, 1657GMT, 15 April 1991.

22. "COB Protests Militarization of Antidrug Effort "FBIS-LAT-91-067, 8 April 1991, *La Paz Radio Fides*, 1100GMT, 6 April 1991.

23. As quoted in "Peasant Group Issues Warning to Government," FBIS-LAT-91-066, 5 April 1991, La Paz Radio, 1100GMT, 4 April 1991.

24. As quoted in "To Protest US Intervention," FBIS-LAT-91-069, 10 April 1991, La Paz Radio, 1100GMT, 8 April 1991.

25. Kevin Healy, "Political Ascent of Bolivia's Peasant Coca Leaf Producer," *Journal of Interamerican Studies and World Affairs* (Spring 1991).

26. "Army Units to Be Ready to Join Fight in July," FBIS-LAT-91-062, 1 April 1991, Madrid EFE, 1740GMT, 29 March 1991.

27. "Cusco growers to fight," FBIS-LAT-91-128, 3 July 1991, *Cambio*, 23 May 1991, 15.

28. "Fujimori Presents U.S. Drug Accord to Congress," FBIS-LAT-91-095, 16 May 1991, Lima RTP Television Network, 0204 GMT, 15 May 1991.

29. Congress, House Committee on Foreign Affairs, "Review of the President's Narcotics Control Legislative Request: Should Certification be Repealed," 2 May 1991.

30. "President Menem Announces Antidrug Measures," FBIS-LAT-91-075, 18 April 1991, *Buenos Aires Argentina Televisora*, 2330 GMT, 17 April 1991.

31. "Military to Collect Antinarcotics Intelligence," FBIS-LAT-91-070, 11 April 1991, *Noticias Argentinas*, 1350 GMT, 10 April 1991.

32. "President Carlos Perez declares War on Drugs," FBIS-LAT-91-122, 25 June 1991, Venezuelan Television *Caracas Venezolana,* 1507 GMT, 21 June 1991.

33. "Antidrug Effort With Bolivia, Paraguay Announced," FBIS-LAT-91-074 17 April first published in *La Prensa,* 13 April 1991, 3.

34. US Department of State, "Fact Sheet: International Aspects of 1991 National Drug Control Strategy," *United States Department of State Dispatch,* February 18, 1991.

35. "Spanish Delegation Offers Antidrug Cooperation," FBIS-LAT-91-070, *Madrid* EFE, 1310 GMT, 10 April 1991.

36. Of course the United States would have preferred that the countries sign the NPT, the nuclear Non-Proliferation Treaty, but the language of this treaty has been consistently rejected by Latins as unfavorable and unfair to developing countries.

37. "FRG Reaction," FBIS-LAT-91-162, 21 August 1991, *Gazeta Mercantil,* 30 July 1991, 14.

38. As reported in an unclassified State Department cable 131318Z, August 1991.

39. "Reaction to Accords with IAEA, Argentina: Inspection not Intrusive," FBIS-LAT-91-162 21 August 1991, *Gazeta Mercantil,* 30 July 1991, 1, 15.

40. Ibid.

41. "Secrets Will be Preserved," FBIS-LAT-91-162, *Gazeta Mercantil,* 31 July 1991, 11.

42. This section of this paper draws from my forthcoming book *The Brazilian Defense Industry* (Boulder, CO: Westview Press, 1992).

43. FBIS-LAT-90-229, 28 November 1990, *Gazeta Mercantil,* 10 October 1990, 3.

44. *Journal do Brasil* (9 February 1991): 7.

45. FBIS-LAT-91-046, 8 March 1991, *Folha de Sao Paulo,* 1 March 1991, second section, 8.

46. FBIS-LAT-91-040, 28 February 1991, *Folha de Sao Paulo,* 23 February 1991, second section, 3.

47. "Bill on Export Control of Strategic Technology," FBIS-LAT-91-167, 28 August 1991, *Gazeta Mercantil,* 2 August 1991, 1, 6.

48. As listed in "Bill on Export Control of Strategic Technology," FBIS-LAT-91-167, 28 August 1991, *Gazeta Mercantil,* 2 August 1991, 1, 6.

49. "Details on Country's Weapons Industry Reported," FBIS-LAT-91-108, 5 June 1991, Santiago Radio Nacional, 1100 GMT, 31 May 1991.

50. "The Condor is Grounded," *The Economist,* 8 June 1991, 48.

51. "Carvallo Claims Iraq Financed Condor Research," FBIS-LAT-91-015, 23 January 1991, *Noticias Argentinas,* 2258 GMT, 22 January 1991.

52. "Ministers Decide to Deactivate Missile Program, "FBIS-LAT-91-087, 6 May 1991, *Buenos Aires Herald,* 5 May 1991, 1.

53. FBIS-LAT-91-166, 27 August 1991, *Noticias Argentinas,* 2322 GMT, 24 August 1991.

54. "Collor Views Debt Payment, NPT, GATT," FBIS-LAT-91-148, *Excelsior,* 16 July 1991, A1-10.

55. "Military Minister Oppose Agreement with US," FBIS-LAT-91-082, 29 April, *Fohla de Sao Paulo,* 24 April 1991, 4.

56. "Space Commission to Build Rocket for Satellites," FBIS-LAT-91-167, 28 August 1991, *Noticias Argentinas,* 2105 GMT, 23 August 1991.

57. "International Affairs Viewed," FBIS-LAT-91-171, September 1991, Madrid EFE, 0153 GMT, 3 September 1991.

58. "Rezek Diz que a soberania continuia," *Jornal do Brasil* (16 August 1991).

59. See, for example, Jessica Tuchman Matthews, "Redefining Security," *Foreign Affairs* (Spring 1989).

The Potential for Conflict in Africa

Jeffrey Herbst

The end of the Cold War, combined with the wave of political and economic liberalization sweeping the continent, heralded the beginning of a new era for Africa. While there is the potential for dramatic gains across Africa now that many countries are discarding self-defeating authoritarian economic and political strategies, the new era may also pose new dilemmas for African leaders and western policy makers. This essay will examine how the evolution of the superpower relationship combined with the dramatic domestic reforms now being contemplated will affect the stable system of boundaries that Africa has had for the last 30 years. The question of the future of Africa's boundaries is particularly important because, while many believe that the continent has experienced almost constant instability since the early 1960s, the secure system of boundaries has meant that there have been only a few attempts at secession and very limited interstate war.

Simply questioning Africa's boundary system is something of a revolution. Since the dawn of independence in the early 1960s, one of the central goals of African countries has been the preservation of the inherited system of boundaries. Dedication to the state system created by the colonialists may seem paradoxical as there is widespread consensus on the continent that many of the boundaries ignore local social groupings and guarantee the economic marginality of a significant number of countries. However, African leaders feared the chaos that widespread boundary changes might cause and were aware that dramatic changes in the inherited state system could

Jeffrey Herbst, an Assistant Professor of Politics and International Affairs at Princeton University, earned an M.A., M.Phil., and Ph.D. from Yale University. He was a Fulbright Research Associate, Department of Political and Administrative Studies, University of Zimbabwe, 1986-1987.

be particularly dangerous to those who had succeeded the colonialists. Indeed, boundary maintenance has been the great, although unheralded, accomplishment of African foreign policy: Since 1957, there has not been one significant boundary change that was not agreed to by all of the concerned nations.

However, the pressures for political and economic liberalization emerging in the 1990s will put enormous pressure on the African state system. The end of the Cold War will make it far more difficult for African countries to find patrons should they face significant secessionist threats. Also, demands for democratization from Western countries and from African citizens may reignite fundamental questions concerning the desirability of the current nation-states for particular ethnic groups. The norm of sovereignty, which African countries successfully used as a cover to repress those who challenged the existing nation-states, is also now being threatened in a world increasing concerned with self-determination. Finally, the demands for internal economic reform that became common in the 1980s may begin to challenge the fundamental basis of African nations. In particular, Western donors may come to the realization that some countries, as presently configured, are not viable no matter what set of internal policies are adopted. As a result, some African countries may simply drift apart until a local leader or warlord realizes that no national political authority exists.

The Successful Boundary Maintenance Regime

The Organization of African Unity (OAU) recognized that the borders drawn by the colonialists "constitute a grave and permanent factor of dissension." The OAU, and most African governments, believe that cohesive social groups were separated by the boundaries and that groups having little to do with each other, or that were overtly hostile, were brought together in the same nation-state. However, the OAU also recognized that there was no simple way of redrawing the map of Africa. Africa's topography does not provide much in the way of natural frontiers, and many social groupings are actually so fluid that it would be impossible to construct a set of boundaries that would assure ethnic peace. As a result, no African leader could be guaranteed when the dust settled after mass boundary changes that he would still have a country to govern. Since the OAU is fundamentally a leaders' club, it therefore declared that the inherited boundaries were a "tangible reality" and rulers pledged, "to respect the frontiers existing on their achievement of national independence."[1]

Several developments at the international level helped the African leaders in their effort to continue the inherited state system. First, the international community in the postwar era has greatly elevated the norm of sovereignty. Especially since the advent of African independence, the world community has allowed any country, no matter how underdeveloped its political and economic institutions are, to enjoy the full privileges of sovereignty. In contrast, the norm of self-determination, which Africans relied upon in the struggle against colonialism, was largely ignored. For instance, it was felt that it would be a violation of an African country's sovereignty if the world community supported a dissident ethnic group disaffected with its government. The precedent set by the lack of international support for the Ibo during the Biafran war, despite their suffering and the fact that they could make a credible claim to being a viable national unit, solidified the practice of ignoring claims based on ethnic self-determination. In the postwar era, the norm of self-determination has applied only to people under colonial rule.

Second, the Cold War had the effect of providing African countries with patrons when their boundaries were challenged. The superpowers were concerned with cultivating clients in all parts of the world and were therefore willing to help African nations crush ethnic rebellions or threats from neighbors. Thus, Zaire won crucial aid from the United States in turning back the Shaba rebellions, Chad relied on France to retain its territorial integrity in the face of Libyan aggression, and Ethiopia was given critical military support by the Soviet Union in order to resist Somalia's irredentist claims. The superpowers were also attentive to African sensibilities

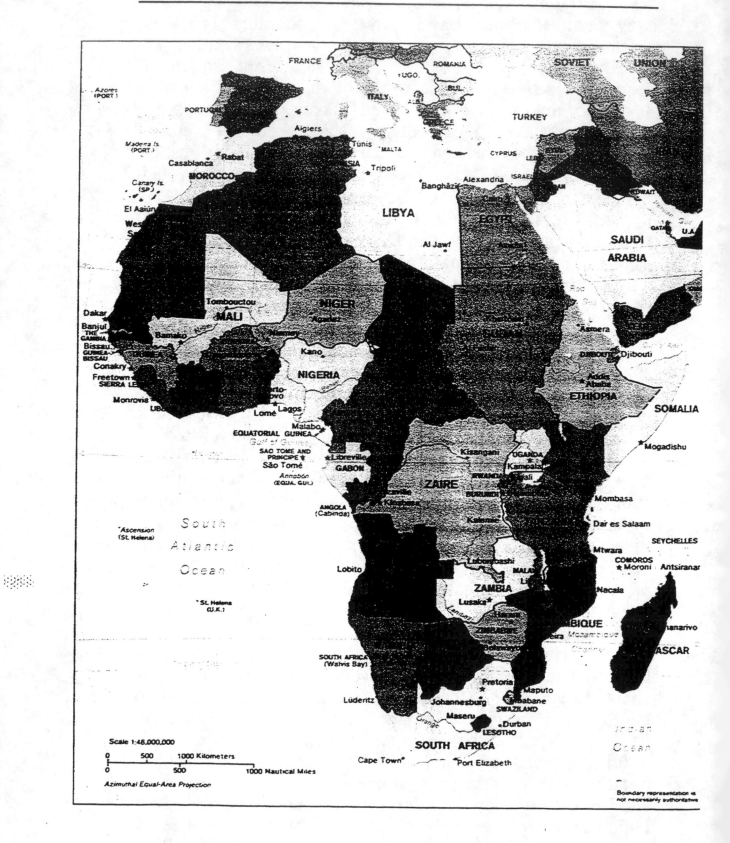

Figure 6. *Africa*

concerning boundary maintenance. Indeed, not once did either superpower, or any other power, support an African effort to overturn an existing boundary.

More generally, the superpowers created a global environment between 1945 and 1989 that made any attempt at boundary change appear illegitimate. The superpowers made clear their preference for stability—symbolized by a bizarrely divided Berlin—over the potential chaos caused by ethnic self-determination in a multitude of ways. Indeed, while the superpowers were in competition, their relationship was also partially managed. One of the implicit rules was that supporting efforts to change boundaries was not part of the competition. Thus, between the end of the Second World War and 1989, the only forcible boundary changes that were not related to the end of colonialism were the creation of Bangladesh and the absorption of South Vietnam.[2]

This was a remarkable development in a world where forcible boundary change was once a fairly common event. Indeed, the most stunning aspect of the Iraqi invasion of Kuwait in 1990 was not that it happened but that this sort of armed effort did not occur more often in a world made up mainly of weak states that cannot defend their boundaries.

Thus, the interests of African leaders and those of the great powers were almost identical on the issue of boundary stability. The Africans and the global community provided not only the arms but also a legal framework in the form of international sovereignty to justify African leaders taking almost any step to crush local rebellions. The system also greatly discouraged interstate war. Of course, few African countries even had the ability to invade their neighbors in the 1960's. However, even as African militaries have become more sophisticated, the fear of war between nations has not increased dramatically. Rather, most of the weapons African countries have purchased have been used to appease the military or turned against local citizens. The overthrow of Amin in Uganda is the only example of an African leader being displaced by invasion; even in this case it was obvious that the Tanzanians did not have any territorial ambitions. Even South Africa, which during the 1980s showed little hesitation in attacking neighbors and had a near monopoly on military power in the region, has never threatened the territorial integrity of any state in Southern Africa.

As a result, African boundaries have been unchanged since independence. This stability is especially remarkable given the domestic upheavals that have occurred in many nations. Indeed, boundary maintenance among so many weak countries for such a long period of time is an extraordinary occurrence in the history of international relations.

The End of the Cold War

After 30 years of boundary maintenance, powerful forces are now at work which threaten the existing African state system. First, the end of the Cold War means that African countries no longer have automatic patrons to turn to if they are threatened. The great powers no longer feel any incentive to aid troubled African countries. Indeed, Gorbachev's pressure on Luanda to come to an agreement with South Africa in 1988 heralded a new era in which Moscow and Washington (and now Paris) are willing to let old allies that have received significant aid twist in the wind. As a result, in just the last 2 years, governments in Ethiopia, Liberia, Chad, and Somalia, which had been able to attract significant security and financial resources from their patrons in the past, were abandoned and quickly overthrown. These upheavals were unprecedented because, while African governments were routinely overthrown by their own militaries in the past, only Museveni in Uganda had been able to lead a successful insurgency from the bush in an already independent African country between 1957 and 1990.

The reluctance of the superpowers to aid African countries in trouble occurs at a particularly treacherous time for many governments. First, many states have atrophied after experiencing 15 to 20 years of economic decline. The continuing fiscal crisis has meant that many governments do not have a significant presence in their countries outside of the major cities. Police, military, and even agricultural extension officers are not present in the countryside because they have not been paid or because the state lacks the transport and fuel to exhibit much of an institutional presence beyond the major urban areas. Thus, many governments are not capable of even detecting the development of a major insurgency in the rural areas, much less combat it.

Second, African society is becoming more militarized. It is now apparent that it is relatively easy for almost any group to collect several dozen machine guns in order to start an insurgency. Once the guerrilla movement begins, it can overrun local police stations and armories to collect more weapons. The example of the successful insurgencies listed above, as well as the MNR in Mozambique, indicates just how easy an armed threat to an African government can develop when the local army is underpaid and poorly equipped and has low morale.

While the governments that recently fell were replaced by internal rivals within the context of the existing state system, there is little reason to believe that the great powers would intervene more forcefully if boundary stability was at stake. Indeed, the specter of Assistant Secretary of State Herman Cohen welcoming the Tigrean movement into Addis, even though the rebel victory will probably eventually result in the independence of Eritrea, was an extraordinarily powerful symbol that the superpowers are ambiguous agents for boundary stability. The new world order may help prevent interstate war in Africa; the potential for successful secessionist movements, however, has improved dramatically now that the Cold War has ended.

The Reemergence of Self-Determination

In addition to the changes at the international level, there are a number of processes at work that may serve to promote threats to boundary stability in Africa, especially from ethnic groups bent on secession. First, the historic memory of African populations is changing. The recognition that they had achieved an unparalleled peaceful transfer of power made African leaders and their citizens especially cautious in their approach to potentially chaotic boundary changes in the aftermath of decolonization. However, two generations have been born since independence in most African countries. Indeed, half the population on the continent was born since 1975. The vast majority of citizens therefore have no historic memory of the peaceful transfer of power but are aware of how political arrangements in their nations have failed to guarantee them an adequate consumption level or a democratic political life. They may therefore be much less to new national structures that might promise them a better life.

Second, the demands for political liberalization—from both African citizens and the international community—may be especially dangerous to the existing state system. In the West, political liberalization is equated with democratization; however, in Africa, questioning domestic political arrangements may have the effect of reigniting debates as to the desirability of the nation itself. The first issue that emerges when politics are liberalized is what should the outlines of the political community itself be. There are, in fact, many groups that may emerge in a more liberal political environment to demand that they be allowed to leave the existing nation, join another, or create their own political institutions. Already, in Central Europe and the Soviet Union, political liberalization has had the effect of reopening old ethnic conflicts, and, as a result, some nations are under tremendous strain. There is no reason to believe that many African citizens have a stronger commitment to their nations than people in the Russia, Yugoslavia, or Czechoslovakia.

Pressures for liberalization also affect the African state system in other ways. Most importantly, the international community, which for so long offered unreserved support for the norm of sovereignty, is now less reluctant to interfere in the domestic affairs of African nations. Most noticeably, for almost a decade, the International Monetary Fund (IMF), World Bank, and bilateral donors have, through stabilization and structural adjustment programs, played very important roles in what were previously considered sovereign economic decisions. There is substantial evidence that as donors become frustrated with the slow pace of democratization, they will also begin to condition aid on political changes. In addition, there is mounting pressure to condition Western aid on a host of other reforms (e.g., decreasing military spending, promoting environmental protection) that at least some in the West find desirable. Thus, it is not too much of an exaggeration to say that Western donors are close to micromanaging many aspects of African countries' domestic policies. In this context, it is hard to say exactly what the norm of sovereignty means.

Correspondingly, with the decline in the norm of sovereignty, new attention has also been directed toward the right of self-determination. The world, including the superpowers, has now focussed on the need for certain ethnic groups to create their own national arrangements. For instance, German unification was widely perceived to be a question of self-determination, and there was widespread support for the right of the Baltic states to secede. Most important for African countries is the independence that Slovenia has achieved in all but name. Baltic independence could at least be rationalized by African leaders as unique because these countries were simply regaining the independence that they enjoyed before the Stalin-Hitler pact. However, Slovenia is the first example of a new country based on ethnic homogeneity emerging from an existing nation that had once been widely recognized as viable and legitimate. Between 1945 and 1990, global boundary stability reinforced the case for not interfering with African boundaries. Now, the world is sending a different message.

Consequently, in the future, the world may offer much more support for African groups asserting their right to self-determination. For instance, the Biafran rebels might get a much better hearing in the 1990s, when the global community is increasing concerned with democratization and self-determination and less fixated on sovereignty. Certainly, new concerns for political liberalization and democratization may make it much more difficult for African countries physically to repress those agitating for changes in the nation-state. Especially in conjunction with the strategic changes outlined above, it will be very difficult for African leaders to gain arms and other resources to suppress secessionist movements.

If African leaders and their citizens still do not understand that the world has changed, the imminent independence of Eritrea will serve as a clarion call for ethnic self-determination. Indeed, when independent Eritrea applies for membership to the Organization of African Unity, the era of African boundary stability may very well be over. It is, of course, true that the Eritreans have a better claim to independence than many, because successive Ethiopian governments violated the United Nations agreement that was supposed to give the Eritreans autonomy. However, this legal distinction may not be salient to many other ethnic groups or potential leaders of insurgencies who feel that the nation that they live in is not viable.

Economic Liberalization and the State System

In Africa, the main force behind economic liberalization has been the multilateral institutions that have promoted stabilization and structural adjustment programs across the continent for the last decade. Most analysts focus on the contrast between these policies and those previously adopted by African countries. However, in one respect the neoclassical policies of the IMF and the World Bank are the same as import substitution industrialization and all other policies pursued by African countries in the past: They assume that if African governments adopt the correct policies, economic growth and development are possible.

However, as donors expend more resources on aid and become increasingly engaged in day-to-day decisionmaking in African countries, it may soon become apparent to them that certain African countries are not viable no matter what set of economic policies are adopted. Some African countries are simply too small (e.g., Gambia, Burundi, Rwanda), while others are so bereft of natural resources (e.g., the Sahel countries) that they may never be able to develop. Therefore, Westerners may decide that some countries will never progress and place them permanently on the international dole with the only expectation that famine will be avoided. If there is enough frustration, Europe and the United States may finally abandon countries that they do not view as viable. Donor signals that some countries cannot develop may only further strengthen the sentiments of Africans who believe that their domestic political arrangements must change.

The potential for abandonment of nonviable nations is increased because of the end of the Cold War, but the fears that the entire African continent may be marginalized or abandoned are dramatically overblown. Those who believe this ignore the long-term interest of the West in Africa's resources, the humanitarian impulse, domestic constituencies (e.g., the Black Congressional Caucus), and the bureaucratic inertia in foreign ministries and multilateral institutions that compel them to continue to deal with Africa. Instead of abandoning a continent, Western nations and multilateral institutions will devote far more energy to picking winners in Africa. Selecting winners is the logical next step, given the increasing conditionality being imposed on African countries, and it appeals to many who want to be involved in Africa, although not necessarily with every struggling nation. In addition, now that the strategic impulse that caused the United States to have some kind of relationship in every African country is over, the United States is free to try and decide which countries will be successful and which will not and act accordingly. Of course, the analogue of picking winners is that some nations are deemed to be losers.

Indeed, gradual abandonment of certain African countries points to the other threat to African boundary stability. It may be that African countries come apart not only because of direct secessionist threats but also because of gradual disintegration of the center. In the context of continued economic decline, certain regions of some countries may simply drift away from the political center until local leaders realize that they are the head of a de facto independent country. As in China, many African countries may retain some nominal degree of territorial integrity but suffer from warlordism and continual clashes between subnational rulers who seek to occupy the political vacuum left by the disintegrating center.

Conclusion

African boundaries have remained more or less constant since the turn of the century. However, there are now powerful forces at work to weaken the state system that African leaders have established. In this context, the end of the Cold War and political and economic liberalization may be the critical factors which finally brings about fundamental challenges to the state system. Should the African state system be overthrown, the continent may see a period of upheaval and chaos, and the potential for massive loss of life in new state creation is high. Indeed, the chaos in Liberia and Somalia may be a harbinger of the future if the boundary system in Africa is seriously threatened. Also, one of the inevitable products of new state creation is the large-scale movement of people. The potential for massive conflict on the African continent is therefore clear.

Finally, African efforts to mediate violent domestic conflicts will probably be ineffective and may cause disputes to spill over into other countries. Certainly, the ECOMOG precedent does not suggest that African countries are particularly good at solving conflicts. Indeed, African militaries are not equipped to intervene in other countries, and African diplomats do not have the necessary administrative structures, intelligence mechanisms, or resources to resolve conflicts successfully in other countries. However, Liberia does clearly demonstrate the potential for domestic disputes to spread to other countries because of ethnic groups that straddle borders. Also, just as there is currently a "democracy contagion" crossing Africa, many groups may be emboldened to challenge their national political leaders if there is a successful secession nearby. If the issue is boundary change, the potential for an entire region to become involved may be high. This is not to say that political and economic liberalization are necessarily bad ideas. Indeed, boundary changes may be inevitable and liberalization may just accelerate the process. The problem is that it is probably impossible to know in advance if a boundary change will lead to a new, more viable national unit or simply cause an entire country to descend into chaos.

The implications for Western foreign policy should therefore be clear. In Africa, political liberalization in particular is not just a question of improving institutions or promoting democracy but, potentially, a fundamental threat to the entire state system. In the end, Western countries may decide they still believe that liberalization should be pursued and the right to self-determination promoted. However, they should then be prepared for the consequences if the African state system is threatened. American diplomats in particular will be faced with extraordinarily difficult situations where, for humanitarian considerations alone, there may be powerful appeals for the United States to intervene. For instance, in Liberia there was considerable pressure both within the United States and from our European allies to do something to prevent mass slaughter.

It is probably impossible at this time to develop general precepts by which American diplomats can react to the mass instability that may be caused by African boundary changes. Individual situations will probably vary too much to impose general decision rules. Certainly, the kind of flexibility that American diplomats exhibited in Ethiopia during the transition will be highly valuable. What can be done now is to recognize that many of the existing rules that have governed African politics are changing and that demands for political liberalization in particular may be highly destabilizing. Although the old practices were convenient for all the governments concerned, reliance on the old standby of African boundary stability will no longer be possible.

Notes

1. Organization of African Unity, "OAU Resolution on Border Disputes, 1964,"reprinted in Ian Brownlie, ed., *Basic Documents on African Affairs* (Oxford: Clarendon Press, 1971), 364.

2. Even Bangladesh could arguably be cited as a remnant of decolonization.

PART II:

INTERNATIONAL AND

TRANSNATIONAL DIMENSIONS

Regionalism in a Global System

Walt W. Rostow

*T*he underlying thrust of this book suggests that the United States is moving from a global confrontation with communism to a policy designed to protect our vital interests in the various regions of the world. Our task has ceased to be the containment of the global ambitions and enterprises of a superpower operating from the Kremlin and has become that of dealing with the ambitions and enterprises of the likes of Saddam Hussein, Kim Il Sung, or even a junta in Haiti. There is a certain obvious legitimacy in this perspective, as any reader of the headlines or viewer of CNN can attest.

Chaos or World Order?

How did the problem before us arise, and what is the nature of that problem? The end of the Cold War posed two questions: What next, and within what broad framework should we view the world and set our objectives? The key to answers to these questions lies in a curious fact: The forces that led the Soviet leadership to bring the Cold War to an end and to contemplate radical change in the Soviet system and its relation to the world are precisely the forces that the world community must confront and organize peacefully if we are to achieve and maintain a reasonably stable world order.

Walt Whitman Rostow is the Rex G. Baker, Jr., Professor Emeritus of Political Economy at the University of Texas. During the Kennedy Administration, Dr. Rostow served as Deputy Special Assistant to the President for National Security Affairs and Chairman of the State Department's Policy Planning Council. Dr. Rostow, the author of numerous books and articles, received B.A. and Ph.D. degrees from Yale University and attended Oxford University as a Rhodes Scholar.

First—and above all—was the progressive diffusion of power and technological capacity away from both Moscow and Washington. This process dates from 1948, when Yugoslav Premier Marshal Josip Broz Tito successfully broke with Soviet dictator Joseph Stalin and when the American Congress voted the Marshall Plan legislation, guaranteeing that in time a vital Western Europe would reemerge.

Perhaps accepting that fact, it was also in the late 1940s that Moscow's attention shifted away from Europe to the expansion of Soviet power and influence in the developing world. There it pursued a long campaign—for more than 40 years in fact—climaxed by the debacle in Afghanistan in the 1980s, a campaign basically defeated by the growing power of nationalism in the developing world. Meanwhile, it became apparent that an increasingly nationalist and assertive Eastern Europe would become progressively more difficult and expensive for Moscow to control. So Soviet President Mikhail Gorbachev cut the imperial knot, as British Prime Minister Clement Attlee had done 40 years earlier by granting India independence.

The Soviet decision had another dimension. The diffusion of technological capacity had the effect of spreading the capacity to manufacture nuclear weapons and other instruments of mass destruction into the developing regions, turning them into sources of anxiety for Moscow, rather than targets of opportunity. Soviet anxiety was further heightened by the character of the great technological revolution that came on stage in the mid-1970s: micro-electronics, genetic engineering, lasers, and a batch of new industrial materials. The pace and diversified character of that revolution proved impossible for a centralized command economy to manage, so the Soviet Union found itself falling behind Western Europe, Japan, the United States, and even such a precocious developing country as the Republic of Korea.

It is precisely this diffusion of power, combined with a new technological revolution, which produced Soviet "new thinking" in foreign policy, that also poses the central challenge for a new world order: Will the forces of diffusion that rendered the Cold War obsolete lead to chaos? Or can this arena of multiple centers of competence and initiative organize itself to preserve a stable peace? That is the central question now and in the foreseeable future.

The Potential Contribution of Regionalism

Regionalism can help tip the balance towards order. The role of regionalism in achieving and sustaining a benign outcome stems from the fact that regional organizations, at their best, can compensate for the inherent weaknesses of a centralized global organization such as the United Nations. It states in memorable prose three large objectives. Stripped of rhetoric, those objectives are:

- To prevent or undo military aggression

- To advance fundamental human rights and political freedom

- To promote social progress and better standards of life.

To what extent has the United Nations (UN) achieved these three objectives? The United Nations has twice undone major acts of aggression at great cost (1950-1953, 1990-1991), and it has sometimes played a useful role in organizing peacekeeping force in the wake of conflict. but it has not proved capable of preventing acts of aggression—neither in Korea nor the Persian Gulf nor elsewhere. The United Nations has, in some cases, supported fundamental human rights and political freedom; but its constituency is so large and diverse and its commitment to respect national sovereignty so deeply embedded that its contribution has been, on the whole, weak and dilute. Similarly, the United Nations has made some contribution to social and economic progress, but its contribution has been minor as compared to that of the specialized agencies, regional development banks, and more affluent individual governments.

With respect to the first of these objectives—security from external aggression—regional arrangements, supported by outside powers (and, if useful, by the United Nations itself) appear much more likely to create stable peace than the central body on its own. Although regional institutions also confront the limitations imposed by national sovereignty, they can be more effective in promoting economic and social progress and human rights.

In Europe, for example, the corrosive historical tension between France and Germany was greatly eased by institutionalized regional arrangements starting with the Coal and Steel Community; human rights were, to a degree, extended eastward by the Helsinki Accords even before the collapse of communism; and support for economic and social progress was extended to the poorer states of Southern Europe and, in part, to Africa by European regional agreement. Moreover, the European Community (EC) defined itself as a club of political democracies, and this had a quiet but powerful effect on societies throughout the region. For example the Spanish economic reformers who transformed their country starting in the late 1950s had their common market and the democracy it required.

In the Western Hemisphere, for example, despite recurrent US-Latin American tension, the region's fundamental, binding security agreement—the agreement that substantial external military power shall not emplace itself in the Western Hemisphere—has been sustained even in the test of the Cuban Missile Crisis. The ultimate commitment of the Hemisphere to human rights and democracy, incorporated in the Organization of American States (OAS) Charter, has had a rocky historical course, since John Quincy Adams noted Latin America's "feudal and clerical heritage" and questioned its capacity to manage democratic politics. The cause of democracy has gathered strength over the years, however, and asserted itself rather strongly in the 1980s. In early 1992 it was being tested collectively with the case of a junta in Haiti. Since the late 1950s, the principle of cooperation to advance economic and social progress in Latin America—symbolized by the Inter-American Development Bank—has been given considerable but varying substance and may be now entering another creative period with a focus on trade agreements and on the accelerated diffusion of the new technologies, especially to the region's smaller countries.

Against this background, it is natural that current diplomacy towards the Middle East appears to envisage a sequence of steps not unlike that which evolved in Western Europe:

● Settlement of the major corrosive political issues; i.e., Arab-Israeli problems as opposed to the Franco-German problem in Europe

● A reliable arms limitation and control agreement that would bring the production of weapons of mass destruction definitely under control and rule out the temptation for any Middle East nation to seek regional hegemony by military means, backed, as in Europe, by the United States and perhaps by other extra-regional powers

● A regional development bank to accelerate the economic and social progress of the less affluent, financed, in part at least, by revenues provided by the nations richly endowed with oil reserves.

As for human rights and political freedom, recent history and the immediate prospect in the Middle East does not encourage easy optimism; but if political settlements and arms control agreements could be achieved, the little-noted rise of the educational level in the region in the past generation and an enlarged middle class may yield a move towards political moderation, human rights, and democracy along the line of the recent trend in Latin America.

This analysis could be extended to think about regional policies for South Asia and the Pacific Basin. The point is simple. Regionalism offers a way of moving towards the fundamental objectives of the UN Charter, which appear beyond the reach of the central organization itself, and the most important of these regional functions is to maintain a regional balance of power such that no government can judge regional hegemony a realistic objective.

Global Functions and the Regions

Turning to the third point, one could predict that a splendid arena for doctoral theses in the future will be the relation between the global international institutions and the major organizations in the regions. There is a range of useful specialized agencies whose continued operation on a global basis is not likely to be seriously questioned: the World Bank and IMF; the food and agriculture groups and World Health Organization; and the institutions responsible for telecommunications, certain aspects of the environment, and other inherently global tasks. Even in such cases, practical work and key projects often require intimate cooperation among global, regional, and national institutions. In the mid-1960s, for example, the Inter-American Committee on the Alliance for Progress (CIAP) coordinated the flow of World Bank, IMF, Inter-American Bank, and the US Agency for International Development (AID) funds to particular countries on the basis of agreed criteria for external assistance.

As for the United Nations, the release of that institution from the corrosive constraints of the Cold War is beginning to develop a new common law. An ad hoc coalition, for example, ran a regional war in the Gulf on the basis of Security Council Resolutions (but no UN Command), and it returned to the Security Council for peace terms and their implementation. What is worth noting is that the Security Council needed the ad hoc military coalition and vice versa. The case of the Haitian junta poses another kind of problem. The formal commitment of the OAS to political democracy is somewhat more explicit than that of the United Nations, a fact reflecting the greater heterogeneity of the latter's constituency. In both cases, however, there have been in the past sovereignty reservations about external interference in domestic politics, even in political events regarded as unsavory by a majority of member states. The Dominican Republic crisis provides a possible model for UN and OAS involvement in situations such as the Haitian junta; in that instance the OAS provided the leadership of the regional task force (after unilateral US action) but the United Nations participated tangentially.

In short, if chaos is avoided and the objectives of the United Nations Charter approximated, a common law federal structure is likely to emerge in the post-Cold War world. That structure will provide for purely global, purely regional, and an array of mixed enterprises. What, then is the ultimate purpose of the rather complex federal structure envisaged here? It is to tip the balance of forces at work in the world arena away from chaos towards order, and to do so by implementing the UN Charter under these headings:

- To deter aggression by the maintenance of regional balances of power rendering grossly irrational thrusts for regional hegemony

- To underpin such balances with political settlements of major inflammatory issues, with sedulously-monitored arms control agreements including—again as in Europe—agreements on weapons of mass destruction (an issue which will continue to rise on the global as well as regional agenda)

- To buttress the process as a whole with a setting of general economic and social progress which narrows the gap in real income among states, and by enlarging the sway of human rights and political democracy

- Finally, should deterrence fail, to defeat aggression.

The US Role

If this is a roughly correct view of the common task in the world of palpably diffusing power that has succeeded the Cold War, what is the appropriate role of the United States given our abiding interests? Those interests are that no single nation dominate the balance of power in Europe or Asia and thereby gain control of the Atlantic or the Pacific; that no major external power emplace itself in this hemisphere with substantial military force; and that we deter the use of weapons of mass destruction against ourselves or others. Out of our heritage and ideals we are also committed ideologically to advance the cause of economic and social development, of human rights, and political democracy.

The fact is that we have acted, often with vigor, to defend these interests when they were under acute threat, but we have not been notably forehanded. Indeed, we Americans even resisted accepting the fact that, like other nations, we had abiding interests. As a result, we have confused our adversaries from the Kaiser to Stalin. The problem of the 20th century lay not in the mysterious East, but in inscrutable Washington. The practical problem before Americans is, then, to come to consensus on our interest in the world as it is and is evolving, and then to act steadily to advance or protect those interests.

How much influence on the course of events do we command? A few years ago there was a good deal of talk in the United States and around the world about the decline and fall of the United States as a great power. Lately there has been a good deal of talk about the United States as the single remaining superpower. Both images of the United States are misleading. We have had and still have a considerable array of serious domestic problems, but we are a big, resilient, creative society, with many centers of initiative and experiments and a saving, skeptical sense of humor. We are committed by our origins as a nation to ideals beyond our reach—perhaps beyond human reach. But we keep striving. Our most serious social problem has been the building of a multiracial society of equal opportunity. Great progress has occurred in the past several generations, but obviously we have a great deal more to do. The increasingly multiracial character of American society will prove to be a source of US strength in the next century. Furthermore, in time we shall overcome the economic problems— mainly self-inflicted—that have weakened the foundations of American society. In short, the United States will prove a viable nation in the coming generations.

It has been clear, for at least the past three decades, that power has been systematically diffused away from both Washington and Moscow and that the notion of a superpower is an illusion, and it is progressively becoming more of an illusion. The United States represents a significant margin of power and influence when it does the right thing. If the United States seeks to do something that runs against the grain of majority thought and feeling in the world, it can be easily frustrated or, indeed, vetoed. When its view conforms to the common view or majority interest, the United States can still play a critical catalytic role in the enterprise, as in the Gulf crisis.

We are the "critical margin." At the margin, the quiet, purposeful presence of the United States is required to sustain the balance of power in Europe, the Middle East, Latin America, and the Pacific, and the case could be made as well for Africa. The United States cannot impose its will on others as a hegemonic power, but big things can't get done in the world without our active participation. There is no contemporary power that can now perform our role. Europe is not sufficiently unified to do the job on its own as the crises in the Gulf and Yugoslavia underlined; nor the Soviet Union, in extraordinary disarray as it makes the triple transition from single-party dictatorship to democracy, from central command to a market economy, from an empire maintained by force to a federal system governed by consent; nor Japan, by reason of its history in the 20th century and because its rapid transition from insular isolation to a comfortable leader in the world community is still incomplete; nor yet China or India. Perhaps someday, but not for the foreseeable future, can any other nation play this limited but important role of critical margin. If we fail at the task, the alternative is likely to be chaos and quite particular dangers to the American interest, as well as to humankind as a whole. Despite the higher priority certain domestic problems clearly deserve, this is not a world from which we can safely withdraw into isolation.

Continuity and Discontinuity in US Foreign Policy

This chapter began by accepting the legitimacy of the title of this book. Clearly the shift in the locus of danger from Moscow to, say, Baghdad and Pyongyang is a real phenomenon and likely to persist over coming decades. However, this final section argues that we have been talking prose all along; the end of the Cold War is not as clear a benchmark as it may appear. The Cold War challenges have been essentially regional. In meeting those challenges, the United States acted with others to strengthen cooperation in and with the regions, but a good deal of US regional policy was determined by considerations transcending the Cold War, considerations still relevant and likely to become even more compelling.

The Cold War started in Europe and centered on a regional question: Should post-1945 Europe be split on the Elbe between Communist East and democratic West or unified, including a democratically united but disarmed Germany? Although somewhat schizophrenic, US policy sought a unified solution, but accepted the schism when it became apparent that Stalin's policy was to go as far south and west as he could go: in Greece and Turkey, Italy, France, and Germany. US policy went into high gear, in fact, only when the East had been nearly consolidated by Stalin and the West was distinctly on the defensive. In shoring up the West, the governments of Western Europe and the United States confronted a truly great question—part of the fabric of the Cold War but with much longer roots and much longer consequences: How should Germany, the most powerful nation in Europe, relate to its neighbors? More narrowly, how should France relate to its old enemy Germany? The answer was found in the Coal and Steel Community, NATO's combined command (SHAPE), the Common Market, and EURATOM; that is, Germany became a full-fledged member of multilateral political, economic, and military organizations governed by even-handed rules and explicit common purposes. This formula strengthened Europe in the Cold War confrontation—as it was meant to do—but it was addressed to a quite independent problem. The formula must now be elaborated in the post-Cold War setting, with the unification of Germany, the problem of relating Eastern Europe to the West, and dealing as constructively as possible with the melodramatic transition through which the former Soviet Republics are passing.

The point is, then, that much of the future is continuous with policy toward Europe that evolved during the Cold War but was addressed to problems that remain on the agenda now that the Cold War has faded into history. There is a similar mixture of discontinuity and continuity in the Middle East. The discontinuity is, of course, that the Soviet Union has ceased to conduct a Cold War policy in the region. Its policies, however, may well reflect interests somewhat different from those of the United States and Europe, for example, interests flowing from its role in global oil and gas markets and its Moslem border populations. The central fact remains that an array of old festering problems exist: the Arab-Israeli issues, the problem of the Kurds in Iraq and Turkey, and above all, the recurrent tendency of the region to breed seekers of hegemony: Gamal Abdel Nasser, Ayatollah Khomeini, Saddam Hussein. It is almost as if the Cold War was a transient framework for problems with long histories and a momentum of their own. As in Europe, one can hope that the removal of the Cold War framework and the passage of time may make the resolution of these stubbornly assertive problems more possible, but the fact is that in 1992 Secretary of State James Baker, in his peripatetic search for peace in the Middle East, was treading a path familiar to a number of predecessors.

Perhaps the most important illustration of this proposition lies in the Pacific Basin. Here the continuity of the problems reaches back to 1941 at least and stretches almost certainly far into the next century. Indeed, the dynamics of power in the Pacific Basin and its modes of expression may determine in the generations ahead whether we experience another major war. The Pacific Basin is an arena containing China, Russia, Japan, and the United States as well as an increasing array of medium powers, including Indonesia, which may emerge to major power status by the middle of the next century. As it comes to technological maturity, India could become a quasi-Pacific power if it achieves stable, peaceful accommodation with its partners on the subcontinent. India aside, the Pacific Basin now contains something like half the human race, depending on how the region is defined. As nearly as we can estimate, it is likely to remain the most dynamic region of the world for some time as it rapidly moves to the global technological frontier and consequently experiences high real growth rates. This dynamism will inevitably shift the locus of economic influence and potential military power. The art of peace will, therefore, consist of so organizing this vast arena as to accommodate the emerging new powers without tempting them with the possibility of achieving regional hegemony or otherwise enlarging their power by the use of military force. The tragedy of the 20th century can be defined as a failure to fulfill these two conditions—a failure that yielded two world wars and some 40 years of Cold War.

An American policy that seeks stable peace in the Pacific under the circumstances envisaged here, however, will find much on which to build: the United Nations Economic and Social Commission for Asia and the Pacific (ESCAP, created 1947); the Asian Development Bank (ADB, 1926); the Association of Southeast Asian Nations (ASEAN, 1967); and the Association for Asian and Pacific Economic Cooperation (APEC, 1989). To these should be added the Pacific Economic Cooperation Conference (PECC, 1980), an private organization but closely monitored by the region's governments. The quiet success of its efforts helped pave the way for APEC, an intergovernmental institution.

In addition, there is a complex network of security pacts linking the United States with New Zealand, Australia, Taiwan, Thailand, the Philippines, South Korea, and Japan. These pacts are, of course, a product of the Cold War (although the link to the Philippines has older antecedents). As in the case of Europe, the regional organizations that emerged in the 1960s were also, in part, related to the protracted Cold War struggle in Southeast Asia. A remarkable group of the region's leaders, however, looked far ahead and acted purposefully on the perspective: Harold Holt of Australia; Lee Kwan Yew of Singapore; Adam Malik and Tun Abdul Razak, who settled extraordinarily sensitive issues between Indonesia and Malaysia and made ASEAN possible; Thanat Khoman of Thailand; President Park of Seoul; a succession of Japanese leaders who launched and helped carry forward the intense dialogue on the concept of an organization for the Pacific Basin; and, above all, Lyndon Johnson, who, from the late 1950s at least, viewed the emergence of modern Asia and its relation to the United States as perhaps the most important challenge the United States would confront in the generations ahead. In the midst of the struggle in Southeast Asia, when Johnson whistlestopped through East Asia and the Pacific for 3 weeks in October 1966, his theme was not Vietnam but the regional organization of Asia—a fact not understood in the United States at that time and perhaps not understood even today.

In the short run, these leaders—and others of like mind—behaved in the spirit of Lee Kwan Yew's admonition to a group of protesting Singapore students on June 15, 1966. He said the United States was "buying time" for the nations of Asia and " . . . if we (in Asia) just sit down and believe people are going to buy time forever after for us, then we deserve to perish." The vision of an Asia and the Pacific that institutionalized methods of cooperation and mutual conciliation was attractive to the several nations of the region, however, for more specific reasons of national interest. For example:

● For Japan, a Pacific Basin organization was viewed as a route back to acceptance and freedom of action on the Pacific scene, with memories of 1931-1945 dimmed if not erased, much as the European organizations performed that function for post-1945 Germany.

● For South Korea, the attraction was different. Pinned down for virtually all its history among larger powers— recently Japan, China, and Russia—Korea sought the safety of a large multilateral organization as a base for survival in independence, without excessive direct dependence on the United States.

● Similarly, Indonesia, Thailand, Malaysia, Singapore, and the Philippines sought safety in numbers via ASEAN, but looked beyond to an organized Pacific Basin when its own economic and social progress and the gathering of cohesion in ASEAN made participation in the larger venture unthreatening.

● For Australia, destined to be anxious about modernizing Indonesia with a rapidly growing population many times its own, and acutely dependent on freedom of the seas in waterways it cannot directly control, a successful Pacific Basin organization embracing the United States is an optimum base for national security.

These are among the abiding national interests, flowing mainly from geography, that will suffuse the work of a Pacific Basin organization; evidently, they transcend the Cold War.

Postscript

As we move into the post-Cold War world we find ourselves neither at the end of history nor at a clean-cut fresh beginning. But we are at the start of the third conscious attempt to provide for the human race and by common endeavor, a framework of stable peace, human freedom, and civilized levels of human welfare. It is worth recalling that it was just 75 years from the beginning of the First World War to the dismantling of the Berlin Wall. In that time, taking up most of the 20th century, the first effort to create a peaceful world community—the League of Nations—failed, yielding the Second World War. That disaster gave way to a protracted Cold War, somewhat less bloody, but which gravely inhibited the pursuit of the purpose of the United Nations Charter. On this third try, in a world where the capacity to manufacture weapons of mass destruction is rapidly diffusing, we had better succeed.

Strategic Implications of Population Change

Nicholas N. Eberstadt

*F*or better or worse, ours is a time of rapid and pronounced demographic change—at least, by comparison with any earlier period in history. For hundreds, if not thousands of years before the Industrial Revolution, the overall pace of global population change was negligible. Any rapid population change was then characteristic principally of communities visited by catastrophe. Between the years 1000 and 1750 A.D., by some estimates, the human population grew by roughly 14 percent per century.[1] At current estimated rates, the same proportionate growth is achieved in fewer than 8 years.[2] Over the past few generations, demographic change has not only radically altered human numbers in the aggregate but has also profoundly affected their composition and international distribution. Further changes are expected in the generations immediately to come; one may anticipate these to be consequential as well. It is small wonder that students of world affairs should wish to harness demography—the study of population change—in their quest to understand the vicissitudes of state power and the mysteries of national security.[3]

Yet while the role of population in world affairs may seem to be intuitively self-evident, its actual pertinence to the specific assessment of state power and national security is often far from obvious. Power and security are highly complex quantities. Demographic change is but one of many possible consid-

Nicholas N. Eberstadt has been a visiting fellow at Harvard University's Center for Population Studies, as well as a consultant to the World Bank, the State Department, and the Agency for International Development. Mr. Eberstadt received an A.B. from Harvard College, an M.Sc. from the London School of Economics, and an M.P.A. from the Kennedy School of Government at Harvard University.

erations limiting a state's ability to impose its will abroad, or to maintain itself at home. It need not be a major factor—nor should one presume that demographic forces typically pull together to exert a single pressure on a society or state when they do come to bear.

Careful examination and reasonable use of population data may nonetheless shed at least a bit of light on some of the problems facing a few of the participants in the global arena today. Although these indications for the most part are fairly elementary, they may draw attention to neglected weaknesses, or may help correct erroneous impressions that would prove costly if embodied in policy.

Reassessing Population Assessments

Within intellectual and policy circles in Western countries, rapid population growth in the Third World is commonly viewed as a serious problem, sometimes as a pressing one. Population growth, moreover, is envisioned as "eating away" at economic growth in poor countries, reducing or altogether canceling potential improvements in living standards and aggravating such conditions as poor health, malnutrition, illiteracy, and unemployment. The political implications of such trends are also held to be ominous. By some assessments, rapid population growth threatens to destabilize governments in low-income countries—through food shortages, for example, or by overwhelming the state with social service demands, or by creating an unmanageable and volatile crush in urban areas.[4] By creating major new demands for global resource use, it is sometimes said that rapid population growth in low-income countries pushes all of mankind toward an era of scarcity, perhaps even toward an unsustainable overshoot of our environment's "carrying capacity."

The fervor that such visions arouse notwithstanding, there is considerable empirical evidence to suggest that the consequences and implications of the contemporary pattern of rapid population growth are significantly different from those

144

commonly supposed. Take the notion that rapid population growth has prevented economic progress in low-income countries. Angus Maddison, long the Director of the Development Research Center at the Organization for Economic Cooperation and Development (OECD), has recently produced estimates of economic growth rates over the course of the 20th century for a sample of 32 countries, whose populations comprise about three-fourths of the current estimated world total.[5] His sample includes such places as China, India, Indonesia, Brazil, Bangladesh, Pakistan and Mexico, although for want of reliable data it excludes all of sub-Saharan Africa. By Maddison's reckoning, per capita output for his sample rose by a factor of over four between 1900 and 1987. Although the populations of his nine Asian countries more than tripled during this period, and the population of the six Latin American countries he covered rose by a factor of nearly seven, per capita output is estimated to have risen dramatically as well—by a factor of more than three for the Asian group, and by a factor of nearly five for Latin America. Moreover, despite Latin America's highly publicized economic problems in the 1980s, per capita income in the Latin American countries in Maddison's sample—countries accounting for roughly three-quarters of the total population for Central America, South America and the Caribbean—more than doubled between 1950 and 1987. Whatever else it may have done, rapid population growth has evidently not prevented major improvements in productivity in many of the societies most directly transformed by it.

Such a cautiously optimistic conclusion might seem to be challenged by the current example of sub-Saharan Africa, where troubles abound and population growth rates are thought to be the highest on earth. Many observers attribute the social, economic, and political ills of the region directly to its rapid population growth. They seldom stop to consider whether this may be a fallacy of composition. Sub-Saharan Africa does have the highest rate of natural increase of any large region of the world at the moment, and its pace apparently continues to accelerate, but sub-Saharan Africa is also characterized by what might be described as pervasive misrule. Tribal animosities are widespread and sometimes incorporated into government policy by the dominant group. State involvement in the local economy is often far reaching, and mismanagement and misappropriation are often the norm. Some governments have set about systematically uprooting their subjects and overturning their livelihoods, even when such groups are on the barest edge of subsistence.

Under such circumstances, one would expect societies to report economic problems, irrespective of any contribution population growth might make. Under current state policies and practices, in fact, most serious social and economic problems currently attributed to rapid population growth in the sub-Sahara would be expected to beset those same societies even if their population levels were entirely stationary. A "population problem" that proves in practice to be independent of a society's actual demographic conditions is a problem misdefined.

What of the concern that continued population growth will place a devastating burden upon the global environment, endangering the well-being of all? When public opinions are as strong, and popular emotions as inflamed, over any issue as they seem to be over global environmental degradation today, a few words will be unlikely to change many minds. One may note, however, that modern man has been worrying about impending resource exhaustion and environmental catastrophe for more than a century. Today's attention to the "ozone layer," the "greenhouse effect," and the destruction of the Brazilian rain forest has precursors in 19th-century England's alarm that it would soon run out of coal (as the eminent economist Stanley Jevons had prophesied) and President Theodore Roosevelt's warning of a "timber famine"—disasters, we now know, that failed to materialize. While the inaccuracy of such past predictions does not invalidate current environmental concerns, it should raise questions about why such dramatic forecasts in the recent past have been so recurringly amiss.

One possible explanation is that such assessments have paid inadequate attention to the economic process, which generated the demand for resources and put them to use. Between 1900 and 1987, by UN estimates, the world's population more than tripled, and its level of economic output, to generalize from Maddison's sample, may have increased more than a dozen times. Despite such growth of demand, the inflation-adjusted prices of many primary products—ore, farm goods, and the like—are lower today than at the turn of the century.[6] By the information that prices are meant to convey, many resources would appear to be less scarce today than they were at the turn of the century!

How could this be so? Quite simply, because the economic process prompts responses to shortage and scarcity. To oversimplify greatly, the price mechanism identifies scarcity through the agency of higher prices, thereby encouraging substitution and rewarding innovation within the limits of human preference. Previously worthless materials are brought into use (bauxite, petroleum); previously plentiful resources are more likely to be husbanded (German forests).

One may note in passing that environmental degradation is reported to be a serious problem in a number of countries today—China, the former USSR, and the various states of Eastern Europe among them.[7] There is reason to believe that misuse of resources has been so severe in some of these countries as to contribute to an overall worsening of public health. These territories have been governed by Marxist-Leninist regimes that constructed planning mechanisms that deliberately ignored price signals in the national allocation and utilization of resources. One may additionally note that population growth in all of these territories is relatively slow today; some of them even register slightly negative rates of natural increase.

The laws of thermodynamics, it is today believed, ultimately constrain the "closed system" we take the universe to be. As for earthly constraints, however, the only nonrenewable economic "resource" for which there exists no possibility of substitution is the time of human beings. The value of human time has generally and substantially increased over the course of this century, despite the multiplication of human beings. Affluent populations around the world, moreover, have revealed a distinct preference for a cleaner environment. Even if environmental protection were to be regarded purely as a luxury, it is one that prosperous peoples are willing often eager to pay for.

There is one implication of rapid population growth that has not occasioned much commentary, though it may bear directly upon the balance of world power and prospects for national security. The rapid growth of Third World population, and the attendant rise in per capita output in low-income areas, have been affecting the distribution of global economic output—and not in the direction currently presumed. Maddison's sample points to the tendency. By his estimate, the 16 OECD countries in his study—call them "industrial democracies" as a shorthand—accounted for about 68 percent of the total output for his group in 1950. By 1987, these same industrial democracies were estimated to account for only 58 percent of the group's output.[8] The declining relative potential of the countries currently defined as "Western" may indeed have important political and security implications, as will be noted in concluding comments.

Fertility, Mortality, and Migration

The immediate impact of the population factor on national power and international security is best illustrated in specific examples. At the national level, population change is propelled by three demographic forces: fertility, mortality, and migration.

Fertility as a Factor in World Affairs

The mathematics of demography can easily demonstrate fertility's tendency to dominate other demographic forces in the shaping of "closed" populations. Under all but the most catastrophic circumstances, neither wartime losses nor mass movements of people will have as much impact on a population's evolving size and structure as will ordinary shifts and fluctuations in fertility.

While the instances of contemporary China and Japan can be used to demonstrate the possibility of adducing political significance to either "high" or "low" levels of overall fertility, political consequences more typically devolve from fertility differentials among social groups within a country. In some places, differential fertility may have actually contributed directly to the collapse of the state. (Lebanon comes to mind in this context.) Israel is another Middle Eastern country facing fertility-driven security pressures. Though vastly outnumbered by its typically hostile and often militant Arab neighbor states, Israel has succeeded in preserving, even enhancing, its security since its establishment over four decades ago, fighting and winning three major wars in the process. For reasons of state, Israel occupied the territories of Gaza and the West Bank during the "Six Day War" of 1967, and has maintained administrative control of these areas ever since. Maintaining control of these regions beyond the "Green Line" (pre-1967 boundaries) is still viewed as essential to Israel's security prospects by both major blocs in Israel's Knesset, or parliament, yet the arrangement engenders its own security dilemmas.

Although above replacement, and indeed higher than rates for almost all other contemporary "Western" populations, the fertility level of Israel's Jews has been distinctly lower than that of Israel's Arabs. Fertility rates for Palestinians in the occupied or administered territories are higher still. In 1981, by one estimate, Jewish fertility in Israel averaged under three children per woman, about half the rate for Israeli Muslims.[9] In the 1970s, total fertility rates were as high as almost nine children per woman in Gaza and the West Bank.[10] Within "Green Line" Israel, almost five-sixths of the population was Jewish in 1989;[11] within the boundaries of "Greater Israel," however, the ratio was barely over three-fifths.[12] Despite renewed Jewish immigration from abroad, the rapid fertility among Palestinians in the West Bank and Gaza means Jews could become a minority population within "Greater Israel" within a few decades.[13]

Israel has been constituted as both a Zionist state and a Western-style democracy. In the near future, under current administrative boundaries, Israel will be forced to sacrifice one of those two principles. Surrendering either would change the very character of the state and might have far-reaching effects upon its relationship with its Western allies. Resultant changes, in effect, would likely force a redefinition of the country's security situation. The ongoing *intifada* in the administered territories illustrates the tension that exists between Zionist political authority and large elements of the Palestinian population under its jurisdiction. Demographic trends did not create that tension, but they are likely to make it increasingly central to the definition of state power in Israel.

Even more than Lebanon or Israel, the former Soviet Union can be seen as a tangle of demographic problems. Although the terms "Soviet" and "Russian" are sometimes used interchangeably, ethnic Russians accounted for barely half (50.8 percent) of the enumerated population in the USSR's 1989 census. Like South Africa, the USSR assigns each citizen a state-determined race or ethnicity (in Soviet parlance, "nationality"). More than 100 nationalities were recognized in the country's 1989 census. By that same census, less than half of the USSR's non-Russian population reported itself to have a command of the Russian language; the proportion was actually somewhat lower than in the previous census.[14] The Russian population is separated by language from the life of other Soviet nationalities, but not by language alone. Consequential fertility differences are also evident, for example, between the USSR's Russian population and its populations of Muslim heritage.

According to estimates by Anderson and Silver, "Russians" outnumbered "Muslims" in 1959 by a ratio of 4.6:1.[15] Between 1959 and 1989, the USSR's Russian population rose by about 27 percent, but its "Muslim" population grew by an estimated 125 percent, reducing the ratio of Russians to "Muslims" to 2.6:1. By early 1989, the USSR's population of persons of Muslim heritage might have exceeded 55 million. If these people were counted as actual Muslims (not all students of the subject would do so), the USSR would today contain the world's fifth largest Muslim population. The USSR's "Muslim" population, in fact, would presently outnumber the populations of such places as Egypt, Turkey, and Iran.[16]

Despite doctrinally stipulated equality of all nationalities, Russians have been the dominant element to date within the USSR's multi-ethnic configuration. As in the Imperial order that preceded it, Russians have provided the Soviet Union with its official language and have supplied the overwhelming majority of political personalities within the country's ruling circle. Fertility change will directly challenge prevailing assumptions about the administration of Soviet power. Russians no longer constitute a majority of Soviet men of military age (18-25). Within a decade, they will no longer form the majority of the working-age population, and may by then account for less than two-fifths of the country's children. Such changes have implications for Soviet military, labor, and linguistic policies. If the Russian Republic substantially underwrites living standards in Central Asian Republics, as some analysts in the USSR and the West believe,[17] these changes will have consequential budgetary implications as well. Note that none of these incipient difficulties presumes or requires concerted political action on the part of "Muslim" populations. Under the best of circumstances, government in the former Soviet Union is likely to become a more complex task.

In themselves, it should be emphasized, the USSR's fertility differentials do not consign the country to domestic disorder or even to a reduced international stature. As the 19th century example of Prince von Metternich should emphasize, the decline of a fractious multi-ethnic empire can be forestalled or even reversed for a period of decades through skillful leadership by a single individual. The impending shift in Soviet population composition will by definition be gradual and is therefore unlikely to set immediate constraints on the day-to-day options of Soviet leadership. Over time, however, it may just as surely alter the boundaries of the possible. Today, when central authority in the former USSR seems to be relatively weak, centrifugal ethnic passions have come to the fore and seem to be assuming a prominence in events currently unfolding. Such forces are likely only to be enhanced by the current momentum of differential fertility.

Mortality in World Affairs

The 20th century has witnessed a revolution in health. Very possibly, three-quarters of the total improvement in lifespan in the history of our species has occurred since 1900.[18] So powerful have been the forces promoting improved health that even the advent of total war has not to date been capable of counterbalancing them. Despite the terrible loss of life and attendant devastation, life expectancy for both women and men was higher in France in 1920 than before World War II; higher in Spain after than before the Spanish Civil War; and higher in Japan and West Germany in 1950 than before World War II. [19] The same factors that have contributed to the health revolution have also evidently established the possibility of amazingly rapid recuperation from wartime destruction. The recent histories of West Germany, Japan, and South Korea, among others, demonstrate that the loss of significant portions of the working-age population, and the wounding, debilitation, or episodic starvation of some considerable fraction of surviving cohorts does not now preclude rapid restoration of prewar levels of output, or a rapid subsequent pace for material advance. Moreover, despite the severe privations its people suffered during and immediately after World War II, Japan currently has the longest expectation of life (and generally the lowest age-specific mortality rates) of any country—arguably suggesting that the Japanese are today the healthiest people on earth!

In the future, health progress might be halted by some cataclysm or catastrophe. Imaginably, a plague or pestilence against which human populations could not develop immunity might strike. (Some current commentators believe the AIDS epidemic to be just such an affliction.) One need not look to a hypothetical future, however, for instances of interruption and even reversals of health progress in national populations. The Soviet Union and Eastern Europe provide us with real-life examples today.

In the 1950s, the Soviet Union enjoyed a rapid drop in overall mortality and a corresponding increase in life expectancy. So dramatic was this health progress that the United Nations Population Division estimated life expectancy to be slightly higher in the USSR than in the US in the early 1960s;[20] before World War II the American level was estimated to be about a decade and a half higher. In the mid-1960s, however, mortality reductions came to an abrupt halt, and death rates for men in certain age groups began to rise. As the 1960s and 1970s progressed, death rates registered a rise for all adult cohorts, male and female alike. Mortality rates apparently even began to rise for Soviet infants. Though the immediate official reaction was to withhold data on these trends, the *glasnost* campaign has provided recent evidence on their scope. Between 1969/70 and 1984/85, for example, Soviet death rates for persons in their late forties were reported to have risen by over a fifth; for those in their late fifties, by over a fourth. Between the mid-1960s and the mid-1980s, in fact, Soviet life expectancy at birth is now reported to have fallen by almost three years, and to have registered a decline for women as well as men.[21]

Although the USSR was apparently the first industrial society to suffer a general and prolonged deterioration of public health during peacetime, it is no longer unique. Similar, though less extreme, tendencies have been reported in Eastern Europe over the past generation. Between the mid-1960s and the mid-1980s, life expectancy at 1 year of age fell by an average of slightly less than a year for the European members of the Warsaw Pact;[22] for men at 30 years of age, life expectancy dropped by an average of over 2 years during the same period. According to the estimates of the World Health Organization, by the late 1980s, total age-standardized death rates (adjusted to the WHO's "European Model" population) were higher for the USSR and the countries of Warsaw Pact Europe than for such places as Argentina, Chile, Mexico, or Venezuela![23]

Whatever the etiological origins of these trends, the implications for state power are unmistakably adverse. Rising adult mortality rates reduce the potential size of a country's work force. Between 1977 and 1988, the US Census Bureau reduced its projection for turn-of-the-century population aged 25-64 in Eastern Europe by about 2 million persons, or 3 percent. Insofar as the cohort had been born by 1977, and migration was negligible, the revision basically reflected a reassessment of the impact of health trends. With deteriorating health, moreover, the economic potential of surviving groups might be constrained. To the extent (if any) that attitude and outlook factor in the decline, far-reaching and not inconsequential problems of popular morale may be indirectly indicated.

There is nothing immutable about the former USSR's and Eastern Europe's unfavorable mortality trends. To the contrary, at a time of generally improving health potential, it would seem to require special effort to prevent health progress. Evidently, these states were up to the task. At the very least, they have proved to be unwilling or incapable of embracing the sorts of policies that would have forestalled such declines. One may wonder whether acquiescence in such long-term attrition does not in itself speak to a brittleness or decay in presiding polities—and thus directly to political prospects for the states in question.

Migration in World Affairs

Paradoxically, even as our evolving economic process has been increasing the scope for, and role of, human mobility in material advance, the demographic significance of international migration has decidedly diminished in recent generations. The "Age of Exploration" is finished; the territories of the globe are now divided among standing governments, virtually all of which limit the absorption of new citizens from abroad in some fashion, many of which presume to regulate even the right to travel.

Given the reluctance of most foreign governments to welcome immigrants, opportunities for voluntary migration remain limited today for most "Third World" populations. Increasingly, therefore, 20th- century emigration has become a response to catastrophe—the *Aussiedlung* of millions of ethnic German refugees into what was West Germany during and after 1946, or the movement into what has become the State of

Israel. Upheavals and turmoil have also given rise to a distinctly new form of "migration"—the long-term refugee housed for decades or more in a country not his own. Millions of such people may be found today in such places as Lebanon (Palestinians), Pakistan (Afghans), and Thailand ("boat people" from Vietnam). Modern flows of migration thus often serve as an unhappy barometer of instability and tensions in the emigrant's native land.

For a country accepting migrants, national security may be affected greatly by the manner in which the state encourages newcomers to involve themselves in local economic and political life. Saudi Arabia and other Gulf states have inducted a total of several million foreigners to man and operate their oil economies; in some of these places, mercenaries from abroad even flesh out the security forces. Evidencing as they do little interest in (or perhaps capacity of) incorporating guestworkers of Palestinian, Pakistani, or Korean extraction into the local social fabric, the governments of these countries must engage in a complex balancing game to assure that national power is augmented more by the presence of these foreigners than domestic stability is compromised.

By contrast, the United States has had a markedly different approach to immigrants. Qualifications and exceptions noted (the enormous exception of slavery, for example), it may be fair to describe the traditional US attitude toward immigrants as universalistic, predicated on the assumption that one can "become American" by coming to share a particular set of political, social, and economic values. (Note that the universalistic presumption is not invalidated by current official US restrictions on numbers of new immigrants.) Without ignoring the problems manifest in the assimilation of its newcomers, one may still judge the process to have been successful.

Since the founding of the Republic, more than 50 million persons have voluntarily immigrated to the United States. Though initially a product of an English-speaking population and English political theory, the American system proved capable of absorbing large numbers of persons from Ireland, from German cultures, and from successively more remote Southern and Eastern European cultures. More recently, non-European groups have figured prominently in the flow of persons adopting a new "American identity." To no small degree, US international power and national security today can be traced, both in a specific sense and more broadly, to its approach to immigration. For reasons intrinsic to its political order, migration has to date, on balance, dramatically enhanced US security. Immigration, in fact, has made it possible for the United States to transform itself from a small political experiment into a "superpower."

Strategic Implications

The role of the population factor in world affairs is both limited and diverse. Demography is the study of human numbers, but it is the human characteristics of those numbers—their individual and collective capabilities, outlooks, and actions—that define events in the world of politics at any given time. Divorced from an understanding of those human beings themselves, population studies can provide little insight or guidance for statesmen, diplomats, or generals contemplating an uncertain future.

One may nevertheless suggest that today's prospective trends highlight an impending problem, which may just as accurately be described as a moral and intellectual problem that is taking demographic form. Regardless of their exact calibrations, virtually all current global population projections anticipate comparatively slow population growth in today's "more developed regions" and comparatively rapid growth for the "less developed regions." As such, with variations, they envision a general continuation of trends that have been in evidence since the end of World War II. (While projected trends are of course not immutable, their near-term alteration would necessitate major demographic changes, and perhaps not at all pleasant ones.) If these trends do continue another generation or two, the implications for the international political order, and the balance of world power, could be enormous.

Current population trends are redistributing global population, and mostly away from today's industrial democracies. The significance of this tendency may first be considered when one ranks the world's countries by their size. State power is a complex quantity. Even so, today, as in the past, great powers have relatively large populations. (As A.F.K. Organski once noted, "A large population does not guarantee a large armed force, a mighty production machine, or a large market, but it is a prerequisite for these important means to national power."[24]) In 1950, two of the top five and seven of the top 20 countries by population would be currently described as industrial democracies. Their combined populations accounted for nearly a quarter of this big country total. By 1985—35 years later—today's industrial democracies accounted for only one of the top five, and six of the top 20; they made up less than a sixth of the group's total population. In the year 2025—fewer than 35 years from today—not one of today's industrial democracies is projected to rank among the top five, and only two—the United States and Japan—are projected to remain among the top 20. (Even reunited, Germany's projected population would be too small to be included.) In this future world, today's industrial democracies would account for less than one-fourteenth of the total population of the big countries. Today's industrial democracies would figure prominently only within the world's population of geriatrics. By one recent U.S. Census Bureau projection, for example, today's industrial democracies would account for 8 of the top 18 national populations of persons aged 80 and older by the year 2025.[25]

Whatever their ultimate accuracy, current UN projections for the year 2025 depict an American population slightly smaller than Nigeria's, an Iranian population almost as large as Japan's, and an Ethiopian population almost twice the size of France. Today's industrial democracies would almost all be "little countries." Canada, one of the so-called "Big Seven" today, would by these projections have a smaller population than such places as Madagascar, Nepal, and Syria. In aggregate, the population of today's industrial democracies would account for a progressively diminishing share of the world total. Where they made up more than a fifth of the world's population in 1950, they were only a sixth by 1985, and prospectively stand to be only a tenth some 30 years hence. By such projections, the total population of all of today's Western countries would be considerably smaller than those of either India or sub-Saharan Africa in 2025 and would not be much greater than those of the Latin American and Caribbean grouping.

Projected shifts in birth totals are perhaps even more striking. Though these projections posit a slight rise in fertility in "more developed regions," and a steady drop in "less developed regions" to near net-replacement levels, women in today's Western countries are projected to bear fewer children in total than mothers in the Islamic expanse from Casablanca to Tehran by the year 2020. They are projected to be bearing a third fewer children than mothers in Latin America and the Caribbean; less than half as many mothers as in India, and less than a third as many as those from sub-Saharan Africa. By such projections, a very different world would seem today to be in the making. Naturally, there may be much about this world that would be difficult to imagine today. Weapons, political arrangements, or other innovations that would seem fanciful today might be taken for granted a few decades hence. To the extent that one can impute a continuity from our world into the one projected, however, such trends speak to pressures for a systematically diminished role and status for today's industrial democracies. Even with relatively unfavorable assumptions about "Third World" economic growth, the Western countries' share of global economic output could be anticipated to decline. With a generalized and progressive industrialization of current low-income areas, the Western diminution would be all the more rapid. Holding current governments fixed, but projecting demographic and economic growth forward, one can easily envision a world more unreceptive, and indeed more threatening, to the interests of the United States and its allies than the one we know today.

In this exercise of the imagination, it does not require much additional imagining to conjure up conditions in which the international situation would be even more menacing to the security prospects of the countries of today's Western Alliance than was the Cold War of the past generation. Even without the rise of new blocs or alignments, one can under these trends envision the rise of a fractious, contentious, and often inhumane international order in which liberal precepts have steadily less impact on international action, and Western notions about "human rights" prove to be a progressively weaker constraint upon the exercise of force in the world arena.

Imagine a world, indeed, very much like the United Nations today, but with today's rhetoric informing policy on a global scale, directing actions affecting the lives of millions of people on a daily basis. Even without an aggressive or hostile Soviet bloc, or the invention of new weapons, this would be a very dangerous place.

In our day, the proximate guarantor of ultimate Western security has been American force of arms, around which the various Western security alliances have been arranged. Security, however, is a matter not only of power, but of the ends for and means by which power is exercised. American power has been guided by a distinctive set of principles and precepts. Very broadly speaking, these principles and precepts are shared by all the governments, and populations, in today's Western countries. Their particulars include a respect for individual rights, including the right to private property; adherence to a genuine rule of law; an emphasis on the civil rights of the citizen; an affirmation of the propriety of limited government; and a belief in the universal relevance of these principles. These values and precepts are not shared, or only intermittently acknowledged, by the states presiding over the great majority of the world's population today. The distinction, in large part, defines our security problem today—and points to our security problems tomorrow.

How to increase the share of the world's population living under such "Western" values? Some writers have endorsed the notion of pronatalist policies for the United States and other Western countries. Imaginative as such proposals may be, their results are likely to be of little demographic consequence. To date, pronatal efforts in Europe and elsewhere have proven to be expensive (as might be expected when the state gets into the business of "buying" children for their parents), punitive, or both, and have had only a marginal long-term impact on fertility.[26] A government reflecting the will of the people, moreover, is unlikely to implement measures that would actually transform popular behavior in such an intimate and important realm as family formation.

A narrow focus on pronatalism also neglects and perhaps even undercuts the greatest strength of "Western" values—their universal relevance, and potential benefit, for human beings. Rather than devise means to raise birth rates in societies already subscribing to these values, it might be well to think about how they can be imparted to populations where they are still fundamentally alien.

It is today often argued that "Western" values—the notion of the liberal and open order, and all the notions underpinning these—are culturally specific, and therefore cannot or should not be promoted among non-European populations. Such a view, of course, is widely endorsed by governments hostile to these notions in principle, or unwilling to be constrained by them in practice. In point of fact, however, the political values of the Western order are not decisively limited to populations of European culture and heritage. The example of Japan should demonstrate this. Specialists today argue about the degree to which Japan is in fact an open and liberal society.[27] To the extent that Japan may be described as a liberal democracy, however, the views and arrangements predicated by "Western values" have apparently proved transmissible to a major non-European culture.

Speculating about the future, one may wonder if the future security prospects of the "Western" order does not depend upon our success in seeing two, three, many Japans emerge from the present-day "Third World." Under current Western arrangements, Belgium does not suffer by Germany's prosperity, or her power. Nor should the security of the United States and its current allies be diminished by the economic and demographic rise of countries sharing, and defending, common political principles.

To contemplate the Japanese example, however, is to appreciate the enormity of the task. Japan's present order emerged from highly specific and arguably irreproduceable conditions. Modern Japan's political system, after all, was erected under American bayonets in an occupied country after unconditional surrender. Whatever else may be said about the contemporary international scene, no world wars seem to beckon us at present. Even within Europe, the transition to a liberal order remains far from complete today. The diverse soundings from Eastern Europe suggest that the prospects for such a transition are not imminent.

How can such a transition be implemented in current low-income regions of Latin America, Asia, and Africa? Demographers are unlikely to provide penetrating answers to the question. To contemplate the question, however, is to consider the nature of our ultimate security challenge—a challenge that we may expect to be made all the more pressing by existing and prospective demographic trends.

Notes

1. Estimates by Alexander M. Carr-Saunders, cited in Simon Kuznets, *Modern Economic Growth: Rate, Structure and Spread* (New Haven: Yale University Press, 1966), 35.

2. As derived from United Nations, *World Population 1988* (New York: U.N. Department of International Economic and Social Affairs).

3. This is a condensed version of a chapter from the author's forthcoming book, *Tyranny of Numbers*. The author wishes to thank Jonathan Tombes for research and assistance in this project.

4. See, for example, the summary volume of the National Academy of Sciences, *Rapid Population Growth: Implications and Consequences* (Baltimore: Johns Hopkins University Press, 1971).

5. Angus Maddison, *Economic Growth in the Twentieth Century* (Paris: OECD, 1989).

6. The tendency was most intensively examined in Harold Chandler and Barnett Morse, *Scarcity and Growth* (Washington, D.C.: Resources for the Future, 1963). For a more recent treatment, see the

collection of studies in Julian Simon and Herman Kahn, eds., *The Resourceful Earth* (London: Basil Blackwell, 1984).

7. See, for example, Vaclav Smil, *The Bad Earth* (Armonk, N.Y.: M.E. Sharpe, 1983); Boris Komarov, *The Destruction of Nature: The Intensification of the Ecological Crisis in the USSR* (Frankfurt: Posev Verlag, 1978); and John Lampe, ed., *Environmental Crises in Eastern Europe* (forthcoming).

8. Maddison, *Economic Growth.*

9. Michael Roof, "Detailed Statistics on the Population of Israel by Ethnic and Religious Group and Urban and Rural Residence: 1950 to 2010," (US Bureau of the Census, Center for International Research, September 1984), 3.

10. Gary S. Schiff, "The Politics of Population Policy in Israel," *Forum* (Winter 1978): 186.

11. Foreign Broadcast Information Service (FBIS), NES 89-223, 29 September 1989, 22.

12. Ibid. and FBIS MEA 11 April, 1986, I-7/8.

13. Reinhard Wiemer, "Zionism, Demography and Emigration from Israel," *Orient*, no. 3 (1987).

14. Barbara A. Anderson and Brian D. Silver, "Some Factors in the Linguistic and Ethnic Russification of Soviet Nationalities: Is Everyone Becoming Russian?"eds. Lubomyr Hajda and Marc Beissinger, *The Nationality Factor in Soviet Politics and Society* (Boulder, CO: Westview, 1990).

15. Idem, "Demographic Sources of the Changing Ethnic Composition of the Soviet Union," *Population Studies* (December 1989), 623.

16. Derived from United Nations, *Demographic Yearbook 1988* (New York: U.N., 1990).

17. For example, Nancy Lubin, *Labour and Nationality in Soviet Central Asia* (London: Macmillan, 1985).

18. Nick Eberstadt, *The Poverty of Communism* (New Brunswick, N.J.: Transaction Books, 1988), 11.

19. As verified in *Demographic Yearbook*, various issues.

20. United Nations, *World Population Prospects as Assessed in 1984* (New York: UN Department of International Economic and Social Affairs, 1986).

21. For more details, see *The Poverty of Communism.*

22. Nicholas Eberstadt, "Mortality and Health in Eastern Europe 1965-1985," *Communist Economies*, no. 3, 1990.

23. World Health Organization, *World Health Statistics Annual 1989* (Geneva: WHO, 1989), table 12.

24. A.F.K. Organski, *World Politics (New York: Knopf, 1958), 147.*

25. Barbara Boyle Torrey, Devin Kinsella, and Cynthia M. Taeber, *An Aging World*, US Bureau of the Census Report, series P-95 87 (September 1987), 11.

26. Under communism, Romania's Ceaucescu regime implemented forceful and harsh pronatalist policies, but these were inadequate to keep the country's fertility rates from dropping below replacement in the 1980s.

27. For example, Karel van Wolferen, *The Enigma of Japanese Power* (New York: Knopf, 1988).

Environment, Resources, and Security

Peter H. Gleick

*W*e live in a rapidly changing world; every day brings something new and unexpected in the international arena. For nearly 50 years, the Earth has been haunted by the specter of nuclear war and a relentless arms race. Today, as the 21st century nears, the world appears to have awakened. The tensions and alliances that dominated that early period have mostly disappeared, and the risks of war between the so-called superpowers are rapidly receding. Indeed, even the very form of what is now being called the "former Soviet Union" has been fundamentally altered.

But even as the threat of nuclear conflict is disappearing, a new period of international frictions, tensions, and conflict is rapidly opening, and during this new era we will see a realignment of interests, new alliances, and new forms and causes of regional violence. The seeds of this growing discontent will be found, not in traditional territorial disputes, or religious and ethnic hatreds, or ideological competitions, but in growing economic disputes between rich and poor, transnational environmental pollution, and diminishing quality and quantity of resources. For the first time in history, the interactions between the geopolitical and the geophysical realms are reaching global proportions.

This is not to say that international peace and security will no longer be affected by traditional security threats.

Peter H. Gleick is the Director of the Global Environment Program at the Pacific Institute for Studies in Development, Environment, and Security in Berkeley, CA. In 1988, Dr. Gleick was selected as a MacArthur Foundation Fellow; he used this grant to look at the implications of climate changes for international water resources and international security. Dr. Gleick received a B.S. from Yale University in Engineering and Applied Science and his M.S. and Ph.D. degrees from the the Energy and Resources Group of the University of California, Berkeley.

Indeed, while the focus here is on the links between environment, development, and security, traditional threats remain. Conflicts between nations are caused by many factors—religious animosities, ideological disputes, arguments over borders, and economic competition. The disintegration of the Soviet Union raises questions about the control of nuclear weapons in that region. The continued spread of weapons of mass destruction (including nuclear, chemical, and biological weapons), particularly in the developing world, raises wide concerns about the potential for severe regional conflicts. The civil war in Croatia and Bosnia threatens to spread throughout the Balkan zone. And conflicts and confrontations in the Middle East continue to make that region volatile and violent.

In addition to these traditional concerns, however, we are now entering a period in which unrestrained population growth, inequitable and wasteful use of natural resource, and the degradation of critical environmental services will increasingly affect international behavior and relations and threaten the goal of common security.

There are many reasons for this de-emphasis on arms and military security: The bold initiatives of former Soviet President Mikhail Gorbachev, a better understanding of the political limitations of military strength, and the growing economic and social realization that the world can no longer sustain the voracious military-industrial complex.

Past Relationships Between Resources and Security

We have only a poor sense of how to bring these issues into our deliberations over security, and there has been far too little discussion about the nature of environmental threats that might actually lead to confrontation and conflict. In the past, resources have played a definite, but very limited role in international security and politics: resources have been used as strategic goals, they have been targets during conflict, and they have been tools of war.

Resources as Strategic Goals

The drive for access to scarce minerals has been described as a major underlying motive of the foreign policies of states, because many such resources are essential to the economic prosperity of a nation, because there are great variations in the physical distribution of such resources, and because of the threat of intentional constraints and embargoes on their international trade. Thucydides, writing nearly 2,500 years ago, described the conflict between the Thasians and Athenians over access to a mine. Part of the motivation of Japan and Germany during World War II was reliable access to oil and mineral resources. Part of the motivation of Saddam Hussein was access to the oil reserves (and the economic power these resources provide) of Kuwait. The response of the industrialized world to the invasion of Kuwait was due largely to our reliance on that oil. While attention has begun to shift away from the role of direct access to resources, these will remain a concern of military analysts for a long time to come.

Resources as Targets

Certain strategic resources, including power plants, hydroelectric dams, and energy distribution facilities such as oil pipelines, pumping stations, and electrical transmission facilities have always been considered legitimate targets for attack in the event of war. Nuclear plants and research reactors may be particularly attractive targets because of their importance for electricity grids and for the multiplicative effect of the explosive release of the highly radioactive core materials, and because of their links to weapons production. Such was the case in June 1981 when Israel attacked the Osirak nuclear plant outside Baghdad in an attempt to stop a suspected Iraqi nuclear weapons program.

Other examples abound. Irrigation systems in North Vietnam were bombed by the United States in the late 1960s. When Syria tried to stop Israel from building its National

Water Carrier in the early 1950s, fighting broke out across the demilitarized zone, and when Syria tried to divert the headwaters of the Jordan in the mid 1960s, Israel used force, including air strikes against the diversion facilities. These military actions contributed to the tensions that led to the 1967 war. During that war, oil and power facilities in Syria were targeted. Most recently, dams, desalination plants, and water conveyance systems were targeted by both sides during the Persian Gulf War. As water supplies become increasingly valuable in water-scarce regions, their value as a military target also increases.

Resources as Tools

Increasingly, nonmilitary tools are being used to achieve military ends, including economic and trade embargoes and a variety of resource "weapons." In extreme situations, the direct manipulation of resources or environmental services can be used either as political threats or for actual military advantage. President Carter imposed an embargo on grain sales to the Soviet Union in response to their 1980 invasion of Afghanistan. The United Nations (UN) imposed more comprehensive embargoes on Iraq after its invasion of Kuwait.

Water offers many interesting examples. In the Middle East, recent development on the Euphrates River has been the source of considerable international concern. This river flows from the mountains of southern Turkey through Syria to Iraq, before emptying into the Persian Gulf. In 1990, Turkey finished construction on the Ataturk Dam, the largest of the dams proposed for the Grand Anatolia Project, and interrupted the flow of the Euphrates for a month to partly fill the reservoir. Syria and Iraq both protested, despite advance warning from Turkey of the temporary cutoff, that Turkey now had a water weapon that could be used against them. Indeed, in mid-1990, the Turkish President threatened to restrict water flow to Syria to force it to withdraw support for Kurdish rebels operating in southern Turkey. While this threat was later disavowed, Syrian officials argue that Turkey has already used its power over the headwaters of the Euphrates for political goals and could do so again. When the Turkish projects are complete, the flow of the Euphrates River to Syria could be reduced by up to 40 percent, and to Iraq by up to 80 percent. Iraq is dependent for 50 percent of its water from sources that originate outside its border. In the early days of the Persian Gulf War, there were behind-the-scenes discussions at the United Nations about using of dams on the Euphrates River in Turkey to shut off the flow of water to Iraq in response to its invasion of Kuwait. While no such action was ever taken, the threat of the "water weapon" was made clear.

Similarly, the possibility that Ethiopia will build dams along the Blue Nile has long been viewed with suspicion and fear by Egypt, and the Egyptian Foreign Minister said in 1985, "The next war in the region will be over water, not politics". An odd twist on the water resource issue also occurred in 1990 when North Korea threatened to build a dam on the Han River immediately upstream of Seoul. This, in turn, led South Koreans to begin construction on a dam to prevent any intentional flooding the North Koreans could cause. In other areas, oil exports have been used as nonviolent political tools, such as the OPEC oil embargo.

Resource Inequities and Environmental Degradation

Traditional assessments of resource threats have focused on three issues—resources as goals, targets, and tools. Of growing importance, however, are two new concerns: large and increasing inequities in resource use and distribution, and the deterioration of global environmental services and conditions. These new global environmental problems affect not only traditional East-West concerns but also the relationships between the industrialized countries of the so-called North and the developing countries of the South.

What constitutes inequitable use of natural resources, and how might international frictions and tensions result? One major issue is leading to a political split between the "haves" and "have nots": the growing economic discrepancies between the rich and the poor, characterized by the enormous per capita use of resources in the North and the much more modest use of resources in developing countries.

The use of energy is perhaps the best example. Industrialized nations use energy at nearly seven times the rate, per person, of developing countries—the gap between the richest and the poorest countries is even larger. Without addressing this gap, poor countries will be unable to escape from poverty. But the massive use of fossil fuels to drive the economies of the industrialized nations is primarily responsible for a wide range of global environmental problems, particularly the greenhouse effect. If all the world's 5.3 billion people used energy at the rate of those in the industrialized countries, the result would be intolerable environmental costs and possible ecological catastrophe.

We thus have a situation where the amelioration of this rich-poor gap is necessary, but the environmental costs of doing so with traditional energy sources could be prohibitive. This sets the stage for continuing misery, despair, a sense of frustration for billions of people, and inevitably, social and political instability.

The other concern is the rapid deterioration of global environmental services and the gap between who is causing the problems and who will suffer the worst impacts. In the two decades since the 1972 UN Conference on the Human Environment in Stockholm, the principal environmental worries of the public and policy makers have been air and water quality and the overexploitation or degradation of nationally held resources with only local consequences, such as air pollution and soil erosion. These environmental problems have few international ramifications. On occasion, of course, pollution spills over borders; international rivers become polluted, smelters spew sulfur oxides into neighboring nations. The principal victims however, have been the residents of the same nations responsible for the environmental insult. As a result, the international political dimensions of these problems were modest and often easily resolved.

Now, a new set of pervasive environmental problems has begun to emerge that involve fundamental alterations of biological and geophysical processes at the regional and global scale. These problems include the overexploitation or degradation of nationally held resources with regional or global consequences, such as deforestation and desertification and the abuse of resources held in common, again with regional or global consequences, such as shared fresh water resources, acid precipitation, and degradation of the atmosphere, including climatic change and the depletion of the stratospheric ozone layer.

North-South tensions over these issues may be the most problematic. Take the problem of climatic change. Global climate change—or the "greenhouse effect"—has recently become one of the major concerns of environmental scientists around the world. A wide range of human activities is increasing the atmospheric concentration of greenhouse gases. These gases, which trap heat in the atmosphere rather than allowing it to escape to space, keep the earth warmer than it would otherwise be. Indeed, without any of these gases in the atmosphere, the temperature of the Earth would be 70 degrees Fahrenheit colder than it is today, and there would be no free-standing liquid water. Thus, some greenhouse gases are good. The problem is that industrial activities and deforestation are increasing the concentrations of these gases and thus increasing the amount of heat that is trapped in the atmosphere, hence the term "global warming." Ever-increasing amounts of these gases will lead to a wide range of geophysical problems, including higher temperatures, changes in rainfall patterns, altered frequency and intensity of storms, higher sea level, and so on. We are only now beginning to understand the wide range of possible effects of altering our climate system.

The principal greenhouse gases are carbon dioxide, methane, nitrous oxide, chlorofluorocarbons, and stratospheric ozone. Carbon dioxide comes from the combustion of anything with carbon in it, particularly fossil fuels and trees. All fossil fuels, when burned, emit carbon dioxide, though coal emits more (per unit energy released) than does oil or natural gas. Similarly, deforestation and the subsequent burning of forests leads to both an increase in carbon dioxide emissions and the loss of a "sink" for carbon dioxide, because living trees take CO_2 out of the air and convert it to woody material. Nearly 80 percent of all carbon dioxide emissions from human activities result from fossil fuel combustion.

Methane (CH_4) and nitrous oxide (N_2O) are also greenhouse gases, and they are much more powerful at trapping heat than is CO_2 per molecule, although their atmospheric concentrations are much lower. Methane emissions come from fossil fuel combustion, rice production, cattle, and a wide range of other sources. Nitrous oxide emissions come from changes in land use patterns and fossil fuel use.

Chlorofluorocarbons (CFCs) are the gases responsible for the destruction of the ozone layer—another important global atmospheric problem—and it turns out that they are also strong greenhouse gases. One molecule of CFCs can trap as much heat as tens of thousands of molecules of CO_2. These gases are entirely of human origin, having been created by the chemical industry earlier this century to serve a number of valuable industrial purposes, including foam production, fire fighting, electronic chip manufacturing, and so on. Their very attractive characteristics include nontoxicity and stability, but these characteristics also contribute to their ability to damage the ozone layer. A separate international agreement, the 1987 Montreal Protocol to the 1985 Vienna Convention, has been worked out to eliminate the production and use of CFCs by the end of the century in order to try to reduce damage to the ozone layer. This agreement will also help reduce the CFC contribution to the greenhouse effect.

Among all global environmental threats, climatic change appears to be the most likely to increase international tension. First, the industrialized countries are responsible for about 75 percent of greenhouse gas emissions, while having only 25 percent of the world's population. The other three-quarters of the world's population produce only a quarter of the greenhouse gas emissions. Although this ratio is changing as population grows and as developing countries try to raise their standard of living by increase their energy use, the discrepancy in per-capita greenhouse gas emissions between the rich and the poor will continue for a long time.

The sad reality is that some of the worst societal impacts of climatic change will fall on those nations, and generations, least responsible for the problem. Even assuming that climate impacts are felt equally around the world, the discrepancy between "costs" or climate impacts, and the "benefits" of using the energy that release greenhouse gases will be great. In fact, there is some evidence to suggest that the impacts will not fall equally, and that many developing nations will suffer disproportionately bad effects in some areas.

In addition, developing countries have far fewer technical and economic resources at their disposal than do industrialized nations for adapting to or mitigating the impacts of climatic changes. The richer nations of the world will build sea walls to protect against sea level rise and the effects of storms. Poorer nations, such as Bangladesh and Egypt, with large coastal populations exposed to damaging storms will be unable to protect these populations. Similarly, the richer nations of the world depend more heavily on artificial reservoirs and irrigated agriculture to mitigate the effects of periodic floods and droughts, while developing countries tend to be much more dependent on the vagaries of rainfall in order to produce food. Changes in rainfall patterns due to climate change will therefore affect many developing countries more directly.

Prescriptions

These discrepancies have the potential to worsen existing tensions and to raise new disputes among industrialized and developing nations and between poorer nations themselves. When such environmental degradation is imposed on a state by another country or region—as many of these problems are imposed on the South by the North—conflicts may result. So what can we do? Reducing the risk of environmental and resource conflicts will require addressing several problems simultaneously.

First, *global environmental problems cannot be isolated from underlying economic, political, and social causes.* Indeed, what must now be openly acknowledged is that environmental degradation is intimately connected to other economic and social problems. Deforestation in tropical countries is driven in part by the need to provide hard currency to pay back international debt. Soil erosion and subsequent refugee problems are the result of population pressures, inequitable land distribution, and external investment decisions. The greenhouse effect arises from decisions about how to produce and use energy and food. The connections between and among these issues must be addressed, which requires effective multidisciplinary and interdisciplinary approaches.

Moreover, actions on environment must be translated into tangible benefits for the Third World, where per capita gross domestic product (GDP) over the last 10 years has dropped between 1 and 2 percent annually, where per capita GDP of the countries of sub-Saharan Africa has been dropping at 3 percent annually, and where the net flow of money and resources over the last decade has been from the poor to the rich, rather than the other way around. Failing to address the growing rich-poor gap in a sustainable way will ultimately lead to the failure to solve our environmental problems. The good news is that the issue of global environment and development may finally bring the South fully into the discussion over global security.

Second, *population growth must be restrained.* If the combination of poverty, inequality, and environmental degradation is the vehicle of our destruction, population growth is the engine. In the late 1800s, Malthus offered the insight that no combination of technology and management could hope to offset unlimited population growth on a finite planet. This idea is more relevant than ever, in the accumulating evidence of declining quality of resources and environmental services. An uncontrolled rate of population growth can have no positive outcomes and requires the utmost attention and prompt action from all parties, including the world's religions.

Yet there is still no concerted effort to address the problem of population growth. Indeed, over the last decade there has been a disturbing trend away from addressing this problem, particularly by the United States. A distressing proportion of today's population of over 5.3 billion live in extreme poverty in the developing world, and over 90 percent of the future growth in population will be in these countries. Until the people now alive are being decently provided for—a task greatly complicated by the large absolute numbers of people and by the rapid growth of those numbers—it is hard to imagine how conflicts over resources and continued environmental degradation can be avoided.

Third, *there is a need to increase the efficiency of resource use and recycling.* We are living in what may be known in the future as "The Era of Waste"—waste of energy, materials, and human potential. The largest and cheapest untapped reserve of energy and other resources is simply to increase the efficiency of current use. This would go a long way toward reducing demand on raw materials, reducing the discrepancy between rich and poor per capita resource use, and reducing the severity of a wide range of environmental insults. The subsequent easing of international tensions could be enormous. For example, an increase in average U.S. automobile efficiency of only 1.5 miles per gallon, a paltry amount, would reduce the US consumption of petroleum by more than the United States used to import from Iraq and Kuwait combined, while also reducing carbon dioxide emissions, the severity of acid rain, and a host of other local and regional environmental problems.

We must also develop renewable energy resources to the extent technology and economics permit; nuclear to the extent that technology, safety, economics, and weapons proliferation concerns permit; and mechanisms to transfer these technologies widely. Some complain about how much these technologies might cost. Yet compared to the enormous costs of military preparedness and the intervention in the Middle East, an emphasis on renewable energy and increased energy efficiency seems much more reasonable. Why not pay for research and development of energy efficiency and nonfossil fuel energy sources for our own and developing countries to eliminate the need for oil imports. The problem is not a shortage of money. The entire US budget for energy efficiency and renewable energy development in 1991 was about 1 percent of the costs of the Persian Gulf war. To be blind to this fundamental issue is to be blind to the true threats to security and the true costs of oil dependency.

Fourth, *we must transfer money from the military sector to the human sector.* The huge financial, intellectual, and geophysical resources devoted to the military sector must, in part, be transferred to other sectors of society. Unless this occurs, the limited capital available for economic development and environmental protection will be insufficient. The entire budget of the UN Environment Programme is under $50 million a year. Huge resources are available: over a trillion dollars are spent annually on the military, with NATO and the former Warsaw Pact countries responsible for about 80 percent of that. The dramatic changes in military tensions in the last few years permits us to seriously consider the diversion of financial, human, and materiel resources out of the military sector. For it to be effective, however, in solving the urgent problems of North and South, these resources must not disappear down the black hole of increased military intervention in the Third World, or into other financial drains of the industrialized countries such as the savings and loan crisis.

Last, *while some environmental problems are amenable to national and regional solutions, there is a group of global problems that cannot be addressed successfully unilaterally or in ad hoc fashion. For these issues, greater cooperation at the international institutional level is essential.* There is a growing trend toward such international cooperation, as more and more problems appear to transcend traditional borders and policies. In the last two decades, for example, recognition of certain global commons problems encouraged negotiations on the UN Law of the Sea Convention, the signing of treaties covering use of outer space, the sea bed, and Antarctica, and the Montreal Protocol on Substances that Deplete the Ozone Layer, among others.

International law and intergovernmental institutions must play a leading role. There have already been some attempts to develop acceptable international law protecting environmental resources. For example, the Environmental Modification Convention of 1977 (negotiated under the auspices of the United Nations) states:

> "Each State Party to this Convention undertakes not to engage in military or any other hostile use of environmental modification techniques having widespread, long-lasting or severe effects as the means of destruction, damage or injury to any other State Party." (Article I.1)

In 1982 the UN General Assembly promulgated the World Charter for Nature, supported by over 110 nations (but not comparable in force to a treaty), which states:

> "Nature shall be secured against degradation caused by warfare or other hostile activities" (Article V)

and

> "Military activities damaging to nature shall be avoided" (Article XX).

Other relevant international agreements include the 1977 Bern Protocol on the Protection of Victims of International Armed Conflicts (additional to the Geneva Conventions of 1949), which states:

> "It is prohibited to employ methods or means of warfare which are intended, or may be expected, to cause widespread, long-term and severe damage to the natural environment." (Article XXXV.3)

and

> "Care shall be taken in warfare to protect the natural environment against widespread, long-term and severe damage. This protection includes a prohibition of the use of methods or means of warfare which are intended or may be expected

to cause such damage to the natural environment and thereby to prejudice the health or survival of the population." (Article LV.1)

Unfortunately, these agreements carry less weight than might be desired in the international arena when politics, economics, and other factors in international competition are considered more important. Until such high-sounding agreements have some enforcement teeth and are considered true facets of international behavior, they will remain ineffective.

In the area of conflict over water resources, there are also important roles for international water law and intergovernmental institutions. Unfortunately, the history of international water law is incomplete and offers only limited guidance. More effective means are the wide range of water treaties negotiated and signed by a small number of parties in an affected region. There are dozens of major international river treaties covering everything from navigation to water quality and water-rights allocations. These treaties have helped reduce the risks of water conflicts in many areas, but they are imperfect and cannot be applied easily to other regions. In addition, some of them are beginning to fail on their own accord as changing levels of development alter the water needs of regions and nations.

To make both regional treaties and broader international agreements flexible, detailed mechanisms for conflict resolution and negotiations need to be developed, basic environmental data need to be acquired and completely shared with all parties, and strategies for sharing shortages and apportioning responsibilities for damages need to be developed before conflicts begin to emerge.

A new era in international cooperation may be dawning. The United Nations, considered moribund for many years, now shows signs of life. A Framework Convention on Climate Change was signed in 1992 at the UN Conference on Environment and Development (UNCED) in Brazil. To address the issues of environmental security, it might be attractive, for example, to establish regional institutions, or to strengthen the UN Environment and Development Programs, which have been successful recently in coordinating various international environmental protocols and agreements. Other official fora devoted to traditional security issues might be effectively broadened to include issues of environmental security. And nongovernmental organizations with international political influence and the ability to provide high quality, independent analysis and advice must play a role.

The thawing of the Cold War between the East and the West provides an unprecedented opportunity to begin to address global environmental problems and fundamental resource inequities, just at a time when these problems are assuming new, frightening prominence. The world cannot be considered "secure" where billions live in poverty while others waste valuable resources, where the struggle for basic human services is a dominant factor in life, and where global environmental services are being degraded and destroyed. If we are to move toward a secure world in the 21st century, we must truly begin thinking in a new way.

United Nations Forces and Regional Conflicts

William J. Durch

*T*he end of the Cold War has not only given the United Nations (UN) a greater opportunity than at any time in its history to play its intended role as the centerpiece of the international collective security system, it has also opened up new possibilities for UN-organized cooperative security measures for keeping the peace, fostering voluntary democratic change, and promoting respect for human rights. Although it is fashionable, since the end of the Gulf War, to speculation about the United Nation's future role as a fighting organization or accreditor of just wars, this chapter will focus more on cooperative than collective security issues, particularly the United Nation's operational role in conflict containment and conflict resolution. Conflict containment is generally known as "peacekeeping," and this paper looks at what it does for regional conflicts, why it works, and what the United Nations does when it fails to work or otherwise encounters adverse conditions in the field, something worth knowing as its large reconstruction operation in Cambodia gets underway. We then review the coupling of the more complex peacekeeping operations to conflict resolution, which together have produced UN missions of recent years, of which Cambodia is the culmination. The paper closes with a look at the increased emphasis on human rights in UN peacekeeping and suggests some future possibilities.[1]

William J. Durch is Senior Associate at The Henry L. Stimson Center in Washington, D.C. He is former assistant director of the Defense and Arms Control Studies Program at the Massachusetts Institute of Technology, research fellow at the Center for Science and International Affairs at Harvard University, foreign affairs officer in the US Arms Control and Disarmament Agency, and analyst at the Center for Naval Analyses. Dr. Durch holds a doctorate in political science from MIT and a B.S. from the Georgetown University School of Foreign Service.

Basics of Peacekeeping

Peacekeeping was invented at the United Nations when the Cold War put collective security temporarily beyond the organization's reach. The standard image of peacekeeping comes from operations in the Middle East and shows peacekeepers monitoring a no-man's land between two states recently (or not so recently) at war. Although the image is partly valid, it is incomplete and out of date. UN forces have indeed played some role in the aftermath of most conventional, cross-border wars since 1945, including the Arab-Israeli and India-Pakistan wars, the Korean war, and both Persian Gulf wars. But such conflicts have been outnumbered in the past 45 years by civil wars and decolonization struggles, some of which have also drawn peacekeeping operations. In dealing with such conflicts and their termination, peacekeeping has evolved into a more-than-military operation. Always highly political in nature, it has in recent years taken on new functions that can best be described as "nation-building" —demobilization of fighting units, de-mining of agricultural land, securing and monitoring of elections, and human rights oversight, among others. In short, over the years, the UN has evolved from guardian of the status quo (collective security being a fundamentally conservative concept) to midwife of political transitions. The end of the Cold War has accelerated the demand for UN missions, particularly where regional conflicts were sustained by countervailing US and Soviet support.

Traditional peacekeeping adds to the self-help system of international politics a formal element of disinterested outside assistance intended to help conflicting local parties disengage. At base, it is a confidence-building measure. By observing both sides' behavior, reporting on what they see and resolving violations before local military reactions can escalate, peacekeeping forces can assure conflicting parties, for example, that a cease-fire will remain a cease-fire, or that one side's willingness to lay down arms is reciprocated by the other. In the newer, nation-building operations, they help to assure that election processes are free from bias and voter intimidation, and that election outcomes are valid reflections of votes cast.

Integrity, more than military power, has been key to the peacekeepers' success in the field. (Indeed, case histories of peacekeeping demonstrate that, with rare exceptions, fighting strength has been a relatively unimportant factor in determining the success of a mission.) Aside from personal integrity and impartiality, peacekeepers' effectiveness derives from the moral authority of their sponsoring organization; from their ability to dispel misinformation that could otherwise lead to renewed conflict; and, a most important element historically, from the supportive role of the great powers, particularly, in the case of UN operations, the support of the United States.

US Support

US support has been a prerequisite for peacekeeping in the past. In 44 years of UN operations, all that have gone forward have had US support, while some of those that have been stillborn suffered from a lack of it. Nicaraguan requests for observers to monitor the activities of Contra guerrillas, for example, or France's proposal to have UN troops secure the PLO's withdrawal from Beirut in 1982, were both blocked by the United States. As it demonstrated in the runup to the Gulf War, Washington can marshall an awesome array of political, military, and financial resources when its governmental machinery is bent to the task. In the new era, however, that leadership may sometimes be most effective when exercised quietly, behind the scenes, and in concert with other powers. Such efforts can and have spelled the difference between success or failure of a peacekeeping mission at a critical juncture.

For example, when deployment of the military components of the UN force for Namibia were delayed in late March 1989, fighters of the Southwest African People's Organization (SWAPO) poured into Namibia from their bases in Angola in violation of the settlement agreement. UN leaders on the scene felt compelled to let South African military forces leave their

Namibian bases to contain the incursion, resulting in several hundred casualties. Only intercession by the Joint Commission of Angolan, Cuban, and South African officials established by their tripartite agreement of December 1988, on which US and Soviet officials sat as interested observers, brought the fighting to a halt, induced SWAPO to withdraw with promises of safe passage back into Angola, and allowed the peacekeeping mission to proceed. The political leverage of the Joint Commission proved decisive, and a similar Commission is now watching over UN implementation of Angola's more recent settlement of its own internal conflict.

Local Consent

Although such support by the great powers, and especially by the Security Council's five permanent members, is necessary for successful peacekeeping, it is far from sufficient. "Consent of the local parties," although recited often enough to appear a clichffi, is also crucial if an operation is to be both politically effective and financially supportable. Peacekeeping is cheap compared to war because it does not require expensive military accoutrements such as armored brigades, advanced air forces, or a 30-day supply of smart ammunition. It doesn't require these things because it doesn't have to force its way in. Consent makes an operation more effective politically, moreover, because an operation can build trust faster with parties who want it than with parties who don't. The more complex the situation into which the UN deploys, however, the more opportunities to lose the consent, or diminish the trust, of one or more local parties.

Dealing with Difficulties

When faced with a difficult field situation, the UN's options are to soldier ahead regardless, withdraw, or seek a revised mandate that is weaker or stronger than the one that is not working. How it has tended to come down on these options tells us what we can expect of it in future situations.

Soldier Ahead

Iran was deeply ambivalent about accepting a United Nations peacekeeping force (the UN Iran-Iraq Military Observer Group, or UNIIMOG) as part of the Security Council's package to halt the fighting in the bloody Iran-Iraq war. UNIIMOG was an unarmed, 300-strong military observer group sent to monitor the two countries' 1,400-km border.

Having never dealt with a peacekeeping operation, and trusting few foreigners in any event, Iranian authorities regarded UNIIMOG with suspicion. They were especially wary of communication links between UNIIMOG elements in Iran and those in Iraq, concerned perhaps that military secrets derived from UN inspections were being funnelled to Iraqi authorities. As a result, it impounded the operation's main INTELSAT transmission dish, used to talk to New York, and shut down the smaller INMARSAT satellite terminal used to communicate with UNIIMOG-Baghdad. Ground observers assigned to the Iranian side of the international border could not cross into Iraq, nor could observers on the far side cross into Iran. Indeed, ground observers were restricted to a very narrow strip of border zone, and generally not allowed to venture inland. Even when permission came down from Tehran to allow such visits, local commanders often failed to act on it. Observers were usually accompanied by members of a specially raised group of escort-interpreters.

UNIIMOG also didn't manage to hire a substantial fraction of office staff and other support personnel it had hoped to recruit locally, a common UN practice that provides jobs that are usually well paid by most local standards but cheap compared to importing UN personnel on New York salaries. Local recruitment in Iran proved difficult because Iranians consorting with foreigners were subject to harassment and arrest.

Restrictions applied to air patrols as well. The United Nations was forbidden to bring any of its own observation helicopters into Iran, and suitable Iranian helicopters were not always available when needed. Having had only their removable doors painted "UN white," they could be reassigned to military tasks on short notice.

Ironically, in light of subsequent events, Iraq was in most instances a model host for UNIIMOG, allowing inspections where requested and providing aircraft when needed. And despite Iranian reticence, and gross cease-fire violations on both sides (including Iran's flooding of the southern marshlands), UNIIMOG managed to keep the war from flaring anew. It was not, however, until Iraq's invasion of Kuwait that real progress began to be made toward a final disengagement agreement, as Iraq rapidly came to need its eastern forces on other fronts.

The premier example of "soldiering ahead," however, is Cyprus. Communal strife on the island in late 1963, and the country's refusal to accept a NATO peacekeeping force, led its Greek Cypriot-dominated government and guarantor power Great Britain to request establishment of the UN force in Cyprus (UNFICYP). This operation, intended as temporary palliative, has become a political fixture. Inserted to separate conflicting parties, the force has treated the symptoms of strife so well that the local parties have lost incentive to treat the causes. The human cost of political recalcitrance has been reduced without any accompanying changes in basic local attitudes. UNFICYP's presence removes the need for compromise.

However, the United Nations has chosen to stay in Cyprus rather than leave and force the local parties to resolve their dispute or face further bloodshed. Because the United Nations does not wish to risk further bloodshed, for which it might be blamed, the force is stuck, as might be any foreign object thrust between carefully nurtured ethnic grudges.

Withdraw

Withdrawal under pressure is a rarely exercised option, yet UN forces may be known, to those with but a passing familiarity with peacekeeping, as the forces that flee. The organization has withdrawn just one peacekeeping force under pressure, and still smarts from the experience. Charges of dereliction were levelled at the organization when Secretary General U Thant withdrew the UN Emergency Force (UNEF) from the Sinai in 1967, just before the outbreak of the June war. The United Nations had no legal recourse but to leave Egyptian territory when Cairo requested it, under the terms of its status of forces agreement. Further, because Israel refused to permit a UN presence on its soil, UNEF had nowhere to go but home. Since then, UN forces have been overrun by superior forces (in Cyprus by the Turks, and in Lebanon by the Israelis) but they have not withdrawn. Indeed, the desire to live down the 1967 episode may keep UN forces locked in place when a purely rational calculus might send them home.

Trim the Mandate

An alternative to pulling out or bulling ahead is trimming the mandate to fit altered circumstances, an option applied to operations in Central America and Lebanon. Sometimes the local party objecting to an operation is not a government. In 1987, the five Central American presidents signed an accord, Esquipulas II, that called for an end to cross-border arms aid to insurgent movements in the region. The UN operation in Central America (ONUCA) had the job of monitoring regional compliance with the agreement. Once it had demobilized the Nicaraguan Contras (after the Sandinistas' ouster in February 1990 elections), ONUCA's principal remaining mission was, in effect, to abet the shutdown of arms supplies to El Salvador's Farabundo Marti National Liberation Front (FMLN). The FMLN rightly perceived the UN force to be contrary to their interests, and informed ONUCA's leadership they did not want to see any sign of ONUCA on or over their areas of influence—and they haven't. When the Salvadoran conflict reached the stage where a settlement seemed possible, an entirely separate UN operation was established to help implement it.

ONUCA's implementation of its mandate was reinterpreted in another way as well. Its original job, watching for gun runners, is one in which UN forces historically have not excelled. The United Nations sent observer groups to Greece in 1947, Lebanon in 1958, and Yemen in 1963. The latter two groups, in particular, found nothing. ONUCA found nothing. Populations along porous borders are not prone to talk freely to strangers, even (or perhaps especially) polite strangers. And UN contingents are not prone to patrol at night. Since late 1990, ONUCA has realistically adjusted its emphasis from border patrols to monitoring how well the Central American countries' own authorities implement provisions of Esquipulas II.

A second example of sail-trimming is the United Nations Interim Force in Lebanon (UNIFIL). Prevented from carrying out its original, arguably impossible instructions to restore the authority of a then-crumbling government in the southern part of the country, and unable effectively to resist Israeli power, UNIFIL became an essential provider of basic services and political protection to the populace within its area of operations. When the force first deployed in 1978, the population in its area was about 50,000. As fighting in and around Beirut escalated during the 1980s, the UN area's population peaked at 300,000, serving as a sanctuary from Beirut's violence. This is a population that the United Nations is loathe to abandon. The Lebanese government, gradually rebuilding its power since the Saudi-brokered Taif accords of 1989, prefers a weak buffer force in the south to none at all, so UNIFIL is likely to remain in place despite the fact that many consider the lack of respect accorded it by most Lebanese "armed elements" (including the Israeli-supported South Lebanon Army) añ embarrassment to the United Nations. The United Nations can handle embarrassment. What it does not want is blood on its hands.

Strengthen the Mandate

Before UNEF became the dominant trauma of peacekeeping, there was the UN Operation in the Congo (1960-64), as searing an experience for the United Nations as Vietnam became for the United States. Initially deployed with the wispiest of mandates, its marching orders were successively strengthened to include the use of force. It is treated at length both because it is the largest UN operation prior to Cambodia, and because the conditions into which it deployed prevail again, in what is now Zaire.

In July 1960, leaders of the newly independent Congo issued several calls for UN assistance to repel "external aggression" when army mutinies threatened internal order and triggered Belgian military moves to safeguard European lives and property in the former Belgian colony. With a peak strength of 20,000 troops, ONUC was the largest peacekeeping force ever deployed by the United Nations. Its initial mandate of July 1960 authorized Secretary General Hammarsjkold to:

> provide the Government with such military assistance as may be necessary until . . . . the national security forces may be able, in the opinion of the Government, to fully meet their tasks.[2]

ONUC had the strong support of the United States and initially the support of the USSR, until it became clear that UN troops were not going to suppress the foreign-supported secession of the country's richest province, Katanga, as desired by Patrice Lumumba, the country's radical nationalist prime minister. (Among other things, in Hammarskjold's view, ONUC did not then have the authority to use force.) Lumumba sent his own troops toward Katanga in Soviet-provided transport aircraft. When they killed large numbers of civilians en route, Lumumba was sacked by the Congo's pro-Western president and attempted to fly his troops back to the capital to seize control. UN officials closed the capital's airport and seized its radio station. In the ensuing political turmoil, the government dissolved, Soviet General Secretary Nikita Khrushchev's shoe pounded the podium at the General Assembly as he called for Hammarskjold's resignation, and ONUC occupied itself trying to minimize death and destruction in the country while nudging its fragments back together. When ONUC failed to prevent Lumumba's assassination in early 1961, a third of its troop contingents were pulled out by their governments, but within a month, its mandate was expanded to include the deport-tation of foreign mercenaries and the use of force to prevent civil war.

These options were not exercised for 6 months while the Congo's central government was re-formed under UN protection. When ONUC officials in Katanga did act to seize and deport European mercenaries, as their revised mandate directed, they did so haltingly, since whatever they did displeased some faction in New York. Partly as a result, three separate skirmishes over a period of 16 months, and a further mandate amendment (in November 1961) explicitly ordering an end to Katanga's revolt, were needed to enable ONUC to complete the task.

ONUC's experience suggests that, to make effective use of a strengthened mandate, one with quasi-enforcement powers, for example, several political-military conditions must be met. The UN force must operate throughout a country's territory and not just in a border region, must have substantial military power relative to local combatants or be able to invoke such power, have the cooperation of other regional powers (to deny the uncooperative party sanctuary and support), and the cooperation of the relevant great powers, particularly the permanent members of the Security Council.

The military balance in the Congo was no more than adequate from ONUC's perspective. In 1960-62, the country was nearly surrounded by European colonies, including Portuguese Angola and British Northern Rhodesia (now Zambia), through which Katanga's leaders could receive arms and mercenaries. France and the Soviet Union were largely hostile to the operation (refusing to support it financially), and British and Belgian official opinion was divided. US support was consistent, but its attention was not, as it weathered both the Berlin Wall and the Cuban Missile Crises while ONUC wrestled with Katanga. All of these factors contributed to the uneven and hesitant manner in which ONUC went about its tasks.

The Congo was traumatic for the UN not only because of the political turmoil it caused, or the fact that it took the organization to the brink of bankruptcy, but because it cost Secretary General Hammarskjold his life, in a plane crash en route to Katanga to mediate an end to the initial round of fighting between ONUC and the rebels. Thirty years would elapse before the organization would undertake a peacekeeping operation remotely as large or as broad in scope.

Of the newer UN security operations, those in Iraq (the relief operations, the weapon-hunting of the Special Commission, and UNIKOM) meet most of the conditions for mandate expansion. That prospect may serve to deter direct Iraqi challenge of UN operations; even so, Iraq continues deceptive practices to inhibit Special Commission inspectors and conducts raids into the Iraq-Kuwait DMZ to recover cached weapons. The Cambodia operation, where the risk of field resistance to UN plans is also greater than zero, may also meet some of the conditions for mandate expansion.

Conflict Resolution and Nation-Building

The Security Council will continue to take the initiative periodically to quell major cross-border conflict, and peacekeepers are likely to be part of the cease-fire package, but the real future of UN field operations does not lie in simple buffer-zone monitoring (although we may yet see such a mission deploy to Yugoslavia, and it is unlikely to be simple). Rather, the future lies in the sort of complex nation-building operations of the sort first undertaken in Namibia in 1989.

These operations implement political settlement agreements that are usually the products of several years of negotiation coordinated by UN, Western, or most recently, US and Russian mediators. Rather than buy time for a peace process, they implement its results. The new UN nation-building operations have civilian as well as military components, and manage political transitions to democratic governmental institutions. Being more complex and ambitious, they have greater annual costs than traditional missions of a similar size.

The first of these, the UN Transition Assistance Group (UNTAG), arrived in Namibia in the spring of 1989 to oversee the election of delegates to a constitutional convention. Its deployment was more than 10 years in the making, although the struggle over the former Southwest Africa's independence goes back much further than that. Soviet pullback from regional conflict involvement and US-led mediation of Cuban and South African withdrawals from Angola set the stage for Namibia's UN-supervised independence. UNTAG adapted to the still-unsettled politics of the territory, quintupling the number of its international police observers when it was clear that right-wing elements of the old Southwest Africa security police continued to harass potential voters. South African security forces worked covertly to manipulate the election, and bus loads of "Namibians" were brought across the border from South Africa to help dilute the electoral majorities of the Southwest African Peoples Organization. Still, with extensive publicity to "sell" the concept of free and fair elections to the Namibian population, with a program that repatriated some 40,000 refugees, and with close monitoring of election procedures, UNTAG emerged as one of the great success stories of UN peacekeeping, folding its tents and going home.

UN mediation also produced the UN operation in El Salvador (ONUSAL), a multi-part mission launched in July 1991. ONUSAL will first verify compliance of the government and FMLN with the July 1990 San Josffi agreement on human rights, with powers to receive and investigate human rights complaints from any Salvadoran and "visit any place freely and without prior notice." It will make extensive use of mass media to publicize its findings and to improve the climate of human rights in the country. Implementing the human rights agreement in El Salvador was considered sufficiently important by all parties, including the UN, that it went ahead prior to the signing of a cease-fire in the 12-year civil war. Eventually, ONUSAL will oversee the cease-fire, the reintegration of the FMLN into national life, and national elections.[3]

In Cambodia, UN oversight responsibilities will be even greater. UNTAC will essentially take over governmental functions that could influence the political transition, including the preparation, conduct, or outcome of free and fair elections to a constitutional assembly that will draft a constitution, transform itself into the national legislature, and create a government. As part of its mandate, UNTAC will repatriate over 300,000 refugees, most living in Thai border camps, with the cooperation of the UN High Commissioner for Refugees. Before significant numbers of people can be repatriated, the United Nations must engage in a major mine-clearing operation, as roads and agricultural lands alike are infested with mines that have given Cambodia the highest per capita rate of amputees in the world. Because Cambodia's transport and communications infrastructure has been all but destroyed by two decades of warfare and neglect, the United Nations will need to mount a major infrastructure development program as well. The country's Supreme National Council, the interim committee of all national factions chaired by Prince Sihanouk, has pledged to adopt a national constitution that explicitly guarantees basic civil, political, and religious rights in the context of a liberal, multiparty democracy, as stipulated in a draft settlement agreement of 26 November 1990.[4]

In late 1991, the preliminary UN Advance Mission in Cambodia (UNAMIC) began deploying to establish communications links between the headquarters of the rebel factions and UN headquarters in Phnom Penh. UNAMIC's mine-awareness unit will help educate Cambodian refugees on mine avoidance. Finally, the advance team will set about arranging the construction of facilities for the larger UN operation to follow. The Secretary General asked the Permanent Members of the Security Council for an immediate $300-million contribution to defray the operation's startup costs.[5]

There is always the risk, in such an operation, that a party will bolt, or perhaps hope to use the settlement as a Trojan Horse. Where a settlement calls for the United Nations to disarm and demobilize "armed elements" like the Contras (or the Khmer Rouge), it is difficult to verify whether they have actually done so. In Nicaragua, the United Nations understood that significant quantities of arms (perhaps equal to what had been turned in by Contra fighters) would remain in the bush once that it had neither the authority nor the manpower to search or seize. In Cambodia, it is widely assumed that the Khmer Rouge have even larger caches. That assumption was one reason why the Hun Sen government in Phnom Penh was unwilling to agree to the total disarmament proposed by the Permanent Five's draft agreement of late 1990. Thus each faction will have the right to hold back 30 percent of its arms and men, although these are supposed to be held under UN custody.[6]

UNTAC's ability to adapt to problems in the field (for example, growing lawlessness or cheating on the settlement accord) will depend on whether its modest military capability can be reinforced; on the willingness and ability of Thailand, Laos, and Vietnam to seal their borders against weapon infiltration; and on the continued support of the permanent members of the Security Council, China in particular as chief external patron of the Khmer Rouge. All of these factors are, as of this writing, uncertain. Given what we know of UN preferences in past difficult operations, it will want to hang tough if mission conditions deteriorate and, if things go wrong, it may need significant military assistance.

Extrapolation: Safeguarding Human Rights

The operations in El Salvador and Cambodia, and one in Angola that is quietly monitoring the political restructuring of that country along democratic lines, are significant departures for the United Nations both because they involve the organization heavily in traditionally internal affairs, and because of the emphasis on human rights and democratic principles. Emphasizing the right to vote in free and fair elections, the new UN operations by definition advance the cause of civil and political rights. The newest accords make human rights an explicit focus, and they are likely to function as precedents for future agreements. What begun perhaps as lip service in the

General Assembly, on the part of a majority that is neither democratic nor possessed of a shining human rights record, has been implemented as policy by the Secretariat and fed back to the organization in settlement accords mediated by the Western democracies, or its own diplomats. The organization then implements and the Assembly agrees to fund. From the standpoint of a dictatorial regime, it is an insidious process.

As respect for human rights spreads, the United Nations may at some time in the future face a situation of human rights abuses so offensive that they could require corrective action without permission of the perpetrators. Such interventions would have all the earmarks of peace enforcement but without cross-border aggression. To take action in such cases, the Council may need to reinterpret "threats to international peace and security" to include government actions that threaten to create significant numbers of international refugees, thereby restoring a cross-border element to its decision, and cuing the victims of despotic governments to head for the border as their quickest route to international help, with media coverage, if possible.[7] The organization has not yet reached the point where it is prepared to undertake such action, but students of the United Nations note the growth and tolerance of human rights debate within the UN system in recent years.[8] Outside intervention is a sensitive subject with all governments, and such action would initially be constrained to the most egregious cases that truly shock the global conscience.

When the Council is prepared to act in human rights situations, its first decisions may parallel its response to the 1990 Persian Gulf crisis, namely, passage of resolutions authorizing member states to take specified actions on its behalf. Such an approach would avoid both the cost and complication of a UN-directed intervention force. If aimed at only the most egregious of human rights abuses, moreover, such Council actions may find sufficient support in the Assembly to permit the subsequent dispatch of UN peacekeeping operations, not to participate in the enforcement action but to help reconstruct the country when enforcement has run its course.

Governments are not the only source of rights violations. As old authoritarian regimes in the former socialist world and in the developing world continue to fold, the potential for ethnic conflicts within states will grow and along with them the potential for ethnic terrorism, of which Sri Lanka, Yugoslavia, and Liberia are only the most prominent recent examples. Responses to requests for help from beleaguered subnational groups could result in a number of expensive humanitarian operations, whose cost will eventually cause the international community, and the United Nations, to face difficult questions that pit moral against fiscal responsibility. In advance of such requests, the Organization and its members need to devise tools and techniques for defusing ethnic tensions, especially within states—a potentially important task for preventive peacekeeping that has received little attention.

The United Nations has come a long way from the Middle East model of peacekeeping. With the end of the Cold War, it became an active champion of democratic principles and basic human rights in the conflict settlements it mediates and the field operations it mounts. This is a development perhaps unexpected by anyone who last paid notice to the United Nations a decade or so ago, when sharing the wealth of the seabeds, touting the New International Economic Order, and condemning Zionism preoccupied the majority of its member states. The Secretariat remains a poorly organized operation, with limited ability to adapt to its own growing role without wholesale reform, but it is doing valuable work. As work in the field of cooperative security bears fruit, there may be much less need in the future to implement the original, collective kind for which the Organization was intended.

Notes

1. The Stimson Center recently completed a report for the Ford Foundation on United Nations peacekeeping, for which the author was the principal researcher. The study is based on more than 80 interviews conducted by the author with UN and US government officials, members of UN-accredited diplomatic missions in New York, and experienced peacekeepers. It is also based on case studies done by the author and by Karl Th. Birgisson, V. Page Fortna, Mona M. Ghali, and Brian

D. Smith. The Study Director was Stimson Center Chair Barry Blechman.

2 Security Council Resolution S/4387, July 14, 1960. The Republic of China (Taiwan), France, and the United Kingdom abstained.

3. See United Nations, General Assembly, A/44/971, annex, July 1990; Security Council Resolution 693, 20 May 1991; General Assembly, A/45/242 and Add. 1, 30 May 1991; and General Assembly A/45/1055, 16 September 1991. Also, New York Times, 26 September 1991, A1, and 4 October 1991, A9.

4. See 26 November 1990 Draft Agreement, UN Document S/22059, and the Supreme National Council's letter to the Secretary General, contained in UN Document A/46/494, 24 September 1991.

5. *New York Times*, 11 November 1991, A1; National Public Radio, *All Things Considered*, 11 November 1991.

6. UN Document S/23066, 24 September 1991, 2.

7. Live television coverage of the Kurds' plight on the mountains between Iraq and Turkey certainly helped to stimulate reluctant Western governments to intervene forcefully on their behalf, much as it has stimulated volunteer contributions for past victims of disaster or famine. The fact that Turkey was a Western ally also clearly figured prominently in Western calculations, as nearly comparable numbers of refugees fleeing into Iran did not receive the same degree of Western support. Of course, neither did Iran invite CNN to cover the story.

8. For discussion of the UN in a broader context of human rights issues, see David P. Forsythe, *The Internationalization of Human Rights* (Lexington, Massachusetts: Lexington Books, 1991), especially ch. 3.

America's Role
in the New World Order

Patrick M. Cronin

*A*merica assumed an internationalist role only reluctantly, after economic predominance had been established for a half century, after a crushing military assault on a US territory in 1941 catalyzed the Nation out of its isolationist torpor, and after the globalization of the Cold War kept America engaged. For 150 years prior to the Japanese bombing of Pearl Harbor, Uncle Sam was quite a shy and retiring fellow, at least in terms of foreign policy. When it came to alliance politics, he seemed particularly reticent. The Founding Fathers' injunctions against "permanent" and "entangling" alliances had such a far-reaching legacy that America fought World War I as an "associated power," ostensibly unencumbered by the sordid obligations of multilateral coalitions. Given this persistent strain of isolationism in the American ethos, it should surprise no one that today an increasing number of well educated observers are calling for America to come home again.[1] Perhaps the most striking evidence of this growing anti-internationalist consensus among America's policy elite is the recent rhetoric emerging from the respected Council on Foreign Relations—an organization that, ironically, was established in the interwar years to combat US isolationism. For instance, William Hyland, editor of the Council's journal, *Foreign Affairs,* opines as how "We need to start selectively disengaging abroad to save resources and seize the unparalleled opportunity to put our house in order." He stated

---

Patrick M. Cronin is a Senior Fellow at the Institute for National Strategic Studies, National Defense University. Dr. Cronin, who holds M.Phil. and D.Phil. degrees from Oxford University, is also Associate Editor of *Strategic Review* and Professorial Lecturer in International Relations at Johns Hopkins University's School for Advanced International Studies.

that the United States cannot afford not to take a radical turn inward because, "The enemy is not at the gate, but it may already be inside."[2]

America's Reluctant Internationalism

It is important to put current calls for American disengagement from its central alliances with Europe and East Asia in a broader perspective. Despite the fact that geography then provided a safer buffer and strategic technologies posed no significant threat, the early leaders of the American Republic adhered to an alliance policy that did not arbitrarily stop at the water's edge. Indeed, America has never been as steadfastly anti-alliance or as isolationist as often portrayed. The Founding Fathers enthusiastically embraced foreign powers in alliance when it was consonant with the national interest to do so; for example, America aligned with France, Holland and Russia during the War of Independence, with Britain at the time of the Louisiana Purchase, and with Britain again as the *eminence grise* underwriting the Monroe Doctrine.[3]

In his Farewell Address of 1796, President Washington proclaimed that "It is our true policy to steer clear of permanent alliances with any portion of the foreign world . . . . "[4] Popular interpretations aside, he was not so much professing a universal truism as he was expressing a particular fear: that the Franco-American alliance during the War of Independence might be misconstrued to represent unflinching allegiance to France in any future war. The first president calculated that US involvement in an Old World conflict on France's behalf against England would unleash the centrifugal forces of Anglo-Franco factionalism in the fledgling Republic.[5]

Similarly, President Jefferson's inaugural admonition of "honest friendship with all nations, entangling alliances with none"[6] has created the misimpression that Jefferson deplored international security commitments. What is overlooked is that Jefferson discreetly discussed the need for a British strategic naval umbrella to defend the young Republic, an idea that

200

ultimately manifested itself in a de facto "Concert of the Atlantic" with England. Thus, from well before the pronouncement of the Monroe Doctrine in 1823 until the end of the Spanish-American War in 1898, America's interests were safeguarded by a combination of geography, British naval mastery, and a common Anglo-American interest in blocking European intervention in the Western Hemisphere.[7] By aligning with the world's greatest maritime power, America was insured against external security threats, and American foreign policy achieved an ends-means equilibrium. For its part, Britain realized the balance of power in Europe and stability in the Western Hemisphere were indivisible.

In the complex world of international politics, even successful policies often spawn unintended consequences. Ironically, the enduring Anglo-American alliance produced unwarranted American complacency with regard to the foundations of national security. America had been a free rider, enjoying security on the backs of a *Pax Britannica*. When it came to foreign policy, Americans had been unmindful of life's hard edge. At the turn of the century, however, the United States was increasingly unable to ignore its inextricable relationship to other regions of the world. While America added commitments in the Pacific after its war with Spain, its unspoken alliance with Britain was being devalued as a result of the rising German challenge to British maritime supremacy in the Atlantic. In short, as Walter Lippmann wrote, the chasm between America's commitments and its power to fulfill them was growing ever wider.[8] The seismic shifts in the strategic environment of the day meant the old order of US security policy was no longer valid. America required larger armed forces to defend its new Pacific interests and to offset surging German military capabilities in the Atlantic. Yet, for the first four decades of the 20th century, Washington policymakers refused to jettison the obsolete policy of near-isolationism and the delusion that alliances were a malign instrument of foreign policy. This peculiarly American brew of antipathy toward alliances, like the ardent desire to outlaw war, found expression in the Wilsonian concept of collective security and the organization of the League of Nations. But the League's successes could only be a derivative of alliance-like behavior, for only an alliance—based on common interests and equipped with a credible military force to compel aggressor states to comply—could muster the means for fulfilling the League's myriad promissory obligations.[9]

It was with reference to the early decades of the 20th century that Lippmann developed his concern about the need for a balance between objectives and resources:

> Without the controlling principle that the nation must maintain its objectives and its power in equilibrium, its purposes within its means and its means equal to its purposes, its commitments related to its resources and its resources adequate to its commitments, it is impossible to think at all about foreign affairs.[10]

Lippmann was restating a classic maxim, a maxim that retains its validity today. Anyone who fashions a national security policy for the United States in the 21st century must address the need for such harmony between ends and means. During the past half century we have been learning that neither our ends nor our means are inexhaustible, and that "superpowerdom" is a relative concept.

The American Half Century: 1941-1990

America was ill prepared for hegemony, and yet for the past half century much of the world, but particularly Europe and East Asia, has welcomed and depended on American participation and leadership in the international community. American foreign policy architects played a key role in designing the economic and security institutions still in place today. These institutions—from the United Nations, the North Atlantic Treaty, and the US-Japan security relationship, to the General Agreement on Tariffs and Trade (GATT) and the International Monetary Fund—are those through which countries with democratic and free-market orientations cooperate.

Throughout the postwar period, America remained the only great power with strength in economic, political, and military spheres, including that singular superpower attribute of deliverable nuclear weapons.

Many speak of this period of *Pax Americana* with derision. Clearly, American alliance policy is not unblemished. The acquisition of 42 allies in the span of a decade, from 1947 to 1956, was bound to lead to overcommitment (beyond our means to defend), miscommitment (to authoritarian or corrupt regimes), and mismanagement (lacking consensual mechanisms for burden and power sharing).[11] In particular, the Dullesian pactomania of the 1950s violated the rule of striking a balance between what we were committed to doing and what we could do. This alliance-making spiral reached its apogee with the Central Treaty Organization (CENTO) or Baghdad Pact, and the Southeast Asian Treaty Organization (SEATO), both of which represented unsustainable symbolic American commitments.[12] CENTO and SEATO lacked a unified purpose among their members, relied disproportionately on extraregional states, and were never organized to function as true multilateral fora, much less combined military entities.

However, the US-led postwar order has succeeded far beyond what we had a right to expect. More than any other nation in the world, the United States has created the basis for an unprecedented degree of international cooperation, prosperity, and freedom among the modern industrialized nations of the world. In a limited sense, we can be grateful that a Soviet threat propelled the United States to move from the "closet internationalism" of Franklin Roosevelt to overt internationalism, from unilateralism or collective security to collective defense. Given that for 40 years American national security strategy has revolved around the need to contain Soviet and Communist power, it may seem rational to conclude that the eclipse of communism unshackles the United States to return safely within its owns borders. However, having spearheaded the effort to defeat one of the dominant ideas of our century, it is now our responsibility to help establish a new world order for the post-Cold War era.

Confronting an Altered Strategic Environment

At the twilight of the 20th century as at the inception, the international system is on the brink of a fundamental transformation because of technology and political realignment. The old certainties have receded, but no unified set of assumptions has yet filled the void. In US security policy, the only idea that tends to generate widespread agreement is that the strategic rationale for the old order appears increasingly irrelevant to the new. Before Americans can arrive at a broader compact regarding the new course, we must first understand why the world of the next decade will or will not resemble the previous four, to recognize what is changing and what is not. At the risk of oversimplification, the most important changes can be captured in four trends, each of which provides a motive for reassessing America's grand strategy:

- The decline of communism

- The emergence of new centers of economic power

- Lingering instability in the developing world

- Growing interdependence, especially among the industrial democracies.

First, the terminal illness of communism and the disintegration of its chief patron must have a profound effect on the prescription administered to deal with them—the grand strategy of containment. Whatever else happens, it is currently difficult to imagine a return to the virulently ideological Cold War, if only because the Leninist model has all the appeal of AIDS. At the same time, however, prudence suggests that the United States be on its guard against both a bankrupt ideology and its still militarily powerful ex-benefactor. If power corrupts, the loss of power may corrupt absolutely. US interests in global stability are too great to ignore either substantial military capabilities or authoritarian regimes that might resort to the arbitrary use of force: Russia retains the former and has not yet finally succeeded in throwing off the yoke of the latter. The breakup of empires can be dangerous.

Hence, while the central front war scenario is a relic of a bygone era, no one can predict with a high degree of assurance that the former Soviet Union's path to economic and political reform will be linear and peaceful. No one knows who will follow democratically elected Boris Yeltsin, although many suspect he will not be a democrat. At the same time, further outbreaks of civil unrest in Russia and the other former Soviet republics would further hinder their likely eventual integration among the world's industrial democracies. Thus, the prudent path is to support Yeltsin and other democratically elected republic leaders. In early 1991, the notion of a "grand bargain" with Russia still seemed premature. In early 1992, however, it seems that the bigger danger would be for the industrialized democracies of the world to move too cautiously in helping to transform Russia into a free market, liberal democracy.

A second salient trend that seems to be bulldozing the international landscape beyond recognition lies in the emergence of competing financial power centers in the economically integrated European Community and in Japan. Two goals underlying US postwar containment policy were to help unify a vibrant Western Europe and to anchor the defeated Axis powers to the international community (and hence to avoid a repeat of Versailles). That these objectives are now reaching fruition is a masterpiece of accomplishment. But it is one that now dictates a reassessment of the distribution of costs and benefits being borne by the United States and its allies.

The new tripolar balance of economic power will need to be matched by a reapportionment of burdensharing and decisionmaking responsibilities among the leading industrial democracies. Notwithstanding Operation *Desert Storm,* economic power is likely to count more in the future calculus of international strength, if only because increased economic interdependence among industrial nations requires closer allied coordination of foreign policies and the collapse of communism means that leaders in Eastern Europe and elsewhere are turning to the West for economic assistance. It is worth asking whether or not the United States would have intervened on Kuwait's behalf absent serious financial and political support from America's allies. In any event, the rise of Germany and Japan to global stature requires a new means of ensuring that both their voices and their bank accounts be constructively incorporated into the international system.

Volatile trends in the developing world can be seen as a third factor forcing American security policy and the global order to undergo sober review. To be sure, there are some hopeful signs in the developing world. For instance, new information technology is increasingly reaching the farthest corners of the globe, making it virtually impossible to isolate people in or near developed democracies. While the rising flood of information may have something of a numbing effect on people (compassion fatigue), the information surfeit still makes more readily known the plight of oppressed peoples and the potential for alternative economic and political systems. Another positive sign in the developing world is the increasing rejection of political extremes. Not only is Leninism being abjured wholesale, but from Latin America to Asia and perhaps to the Middle East and Africa, right-wing dictatorship also seems to meet growing opposition. Finally, the label "Third World," never very precise, appears even less applicable than before to some "lesser developed countries" (LDCs)— such as Brazil, Argentina, and Taiwan; other states soon may follow their path.

Unfortunately, for all the positive trends in the developing world, there are at least as many negative countervailing trends. These trends suggest that the basic causes of instability in the developing world are unlikely to disappear in the foreseeable future. Compared to most of the industrial democracies, which have had centuries to evolve into legitimate political entities, states in the developing world generally are postwar creations, lacking cohesion or a single national consciousness. One legacy of colonialism is that many borders, especially in Africa and the Middle East, were arbitrarily drawn, without regard for ethnic and tribal identities. In addition, authoritarian politics continue to dominate LDCs, with power vested in the hands of dictators or oligarchies. Furthermore, the dearth of external threats to most LDCs has denied them a catalyst for overcoming divisive subnational loyalties; consequently, many weak LDCs persist (in fact, not a single one has succumbed to external aggression since the end of World War II).[13] These weak regimes, however, are unlikely to close the widening gap between the have and have-not nations. Moreover, while the rich get richer, the poor get more people. The continuation of high birth rates predicted for the developing world over the next few decades militates against a happy outcome for most LDCs. In fact, some such as historian Paul Kennedy have suggested that the bleak forecast by Malthus—that geometric population growth will surpass the arithmetic growth in the means of subsistence—is at last on the verge of being realized. The vicious cycle of indebtedness and poverty, coupled with the proliferation of weapons of mass destruction, could provide a breeding ground for what Charles Krauthammer dubs the "weapon state," of which Iraq is but the most recent.[14]

These conflicting trends in the developing world pose a paradox for the United States. On the one hand, more and more of what happens in the developing world transcends national borders; at a minimum, neglecting large-scale suffering and chaos anywhere in the world will exact an increasing price on our collective conscience. The newly independent countries in Eastern and Central Europe and some of the incipient democracies deserve greater support from the wealthier developed states. As the Cold War ebbs, the United States must shift some resources to meeting the problems of the South, in order to assist the current losers in the developing world out of their current predicaments and to prevent local instability from becoming regional or systemic.[15]

A fourth aspect of the altered strategic environment is implied by and applicable to all of the aforementioned factors: growing interdependence. Our prosperity and freedom are increasingly intertwined with those of the rest of the world, but especially among the democratic states of the North. The global dimension of longstanding issues is expanding, from ecology to economy, from demographics to drugs. Natural sovereignty clings to a shrinking if still dominant position in our interdependent societies. For example, consider the price of membership in the informal Concert of Europe against the perceptible degree of sovereignty sacrificed in the Conference on Security and Cooperation in Europe (CSCE) and the major derogations in the European Community (EC). The security component of contemporary alliances is often inseparable from the domestic policies of their signatories. This diffusion of power from the states suggests the need for a more enlightened concept of self-interest, beyond our borders, and a more sophisticated policy of global management than was permitted by the rigid bipolar era. These broad developments, perhaps with the exception of the entombment of Leninism, did not just occur in the past 3 years. What is important is not whether they have been evolving over time, but that they together imply a fresh opportunity for American leadership, to redefine what it means to be a superpower, to play a leading role in establishing a new global order in the post-Cold War era. The Bush Administration asserts that in foiling the brutal elimination of a member of the comity of nations, Kuwait, American leadership may provide the crucible for establishing a new world order that protects and promotes political and economic freedom in a world of law.[16] While that remains a laudable aspiration, it is clear that changes in the strategic landscape are at least compelling us to rethink and revise, and possibly even discard, old assumptions. In recasting the framework, we should not be beguiled by "declinists" who argue that America is in the throes of inevitable decline and incapable of a leading role, or by those who believe that we are at "the end of history," that radical ideology is extinct, and that therefore the United States can be apathetic about and insulated from foreign affairs.[17]

The Emerging Paradigms

The loss of communist containment as a *raison d'être* in American foreign policy has planners groping for an alternative strategic framework. The folllowing discusses four emerging paradigms in which America's role is: isolationist and inward-looking (Fortress America); internationalist and unilateral (Unipolar Moment); internationalist and totally multilateral

(Comprehensive Globalism); and internationalist in concert with other key industrial democracies (*Pax Consortis*). Their fundamental differences lie in one of two realms: the extent to which the United States pursues nationalist rather than internationalist goals; and the degree to which the United States executes its external policies unilaterally or multilaterally. Looking ahead from 1991, it is disturbing how much the end of the bipolar contest is obscuring our perception of America's global role. Most alarming are two plausible consequences stemming from this blurred vision:

● That the isolationist strain of the American ethos reflexively will force the United States to disengage from its leading international role without fully considering the consequences (something the United States has already done to differing degrees twice this century).

● That, whether by design or neglect, we will allow our core alliances to atrophy without understanding the consequences.

Fortress America: The Isolationist Seduction

The first paradigm calls for a "Fortress America," an isolationist nationalism of which Patrick Buchanan is the most notable proponent. Having undertaken an "agonizing reappraisal" of US policy, Buchanan calls for American troops to come home from Europe and Asia alike. For instance, regarding America's commitment to help defend South Korea, Buchanan sends an unequivocal message to our Korean allies: "If Kim Il Sung attacks, why should Americans be the first to die?"[18] The short answer, of course, is that our presence deters such an attack from occurring in the first place. But Buchanan's advocacy of American retrenchment is just one facet of his larger conclusion, namely that "What we need is a new nationalism, a new patriotism, a new foreign policy that puts America First, and not only first, but second and third as well."[19] Such rhetorical flourishes only conceal that what Buchanan truly espouses represents the antithesis of a US global role. Unhappily, there seem to be a growing number of Buchanan-like, born-again isolationists who, in the wake America's reputed shellacking of its Cold War adversary, are underwhelmed by the current stable of demons.

There are three major problems with Fortress America as a guiding principle for US national security policy. One, it fails to comprehend fully the achievements of US postwar engagement. An appreciation of America's postwar role and achievements cannot help but highlight the fact that the world of 1992 would look much different if American leaders in the 1940s had not exhibited so much foresight.

What would the international system look like today if Americans had not made the sacrifice and provided the leadership to steer it out of the ashes of World War II? In a self-help international system, who would have helped make sure that some despots—from Stalin to Saddam, and Qaddafi to Castro—did not help themselves too much? The system is not self-regulating, governed by simple laws of physics; active US participation is essential if that system is to reflect, to some extent at least, our values and aspirations and not just those of others. If Buchanan and others really believe in our past accomplishments, then they should give greater weight to the need to remain actively engaged for the sake of what we can accomplish in the future, in concert with our allies.

The second problem with Fortress America is that it underestimates how much disorder there is in the post-Cold War order. "The new world order," as one commentator notes, "is not very new and certainly not very orderly."[20] Certainly the Gulf War should have alerted us to the dangers of a multipolar era—an era in which the superpowers let regions be regions. This thought was spoken by the Chairman of the Joint Chiefs of Staff, General Colin Powell: "I've been chairman for 18 months . . . and I've had . . . six opportunities to use the armed forces of the United States and no one had predicted [any] of them 18 months and one day ago."[21] Threats are now both more diffuse and more difficult to anticipate than in the recent past. While we no longer require a massive peacetime ground force scaled for a sudden global conventional war, the United States must retain a range of flexible, mobile military forces for a wide spectrum of contingencies, some at least as intense as the recent combat in the Persian Gulf area.

Thus, it is not only a question of past achievements, of what would have been if we had not been actively engaged, but also a matter of realizing what will be if we disengage now. Do we want others to calculate, as perhaps did Saddam Hussein, that the end of the Cold War invites regional hegemons to fill the vacuum of power? Hussein's aggression aimed at Kuwait exposed how regional conflicts could impinge on the U.S. national interest. Iraq's potential control of Middle East hydrocarbons threatened to put too much power in the hands of an outlaw regime, enabling Hussein to wage "petrowarfare" against the industrial democracies of the world, and, at a minimum, irrevocably shifting the region's balance of power.[22]

The third problem with Fortress America is that it requires an excessively truncated interpretation of American purpose. For example, having derided America's alliances with Europe and East Asia, Buchanan advocates a strong defense and posits that "As we ascend the staircase to the 21st century, America is uniquely situated to lead the world."[23] He adds: "But America can only lead the world into the twenty-first century if she is not saddled down by all the baggage piled up in the twentieth."[24] But what's the point? What are we leading and, hence, what are we defending? Much of which he pejoratively calls "baggage"—including foreign aid and forward deployments of military forces—in fact is what makes us well suited to leadership. While it may be impossible to explain the range and weight of the various factors that went into President Bush's decision to intervene in the Gulf in support of Kuwait, one significant determinant that went beyond simple national self-interest was this: Americans do not let bully regimes batter little states so long as something practical can be done to prevent or correct it. At the very least, blatant aggression by a relatively strong state against a relatively defenseless state makes US intervention easier to justify to the American public.

Isolationists tend to be virulently allergic to the notion of championing democratic values abroad, almost regardless of the circumstances. After all, writes Buchanan, that substitutes "a love of process for a love of country." Apparently concerned that not all democratic leaders are conservatives, Buchanan distorts Schumpeterian logic to support his argument: "When we call a country 'democratic,' we say nothing about whether its rulers are wise or good, or friendly or hostile; we only describe how they were chosen." Besides, Buchanan asserts, "How other people rule themselves is their own business."[25] But does Buchanan's dictum apply only to Serbian communists, rather than Slovenian or Croatian democrats? Buchanan veers in the direction of myopic nihilism by contending that there is no higher goal in international relations than a narrow definition of national interest. *Realpolitik* must be tempered by higher moral goals, goals which Buchanan glibly dismisses as "messianic globaloney."[26] As demonstrated by the plight of the Kurds fleeing Iraq, the international community does not have to sit idly by and tolerate mass suffering. Life's hard edge can be blunted. I am not arguing that we, even in concert with allies, can do everything or that internal repression everywhere is a "vital interest." There are a wide range of options between a wholly moralistic foreign policy and a self-interested one; the prudent policy combines moral concerns and interests.[27]

The isolationists' ends are too restrictive for our increasingly interdependent world, too selfish for idealistic Americans. For it is no longer sufficient for a superpower to have merely the super power of ICBMs; it must be able to galvanize political, economic and military forces outside its borders to address the challenges that confront us now and will only multiply in the years ahead. The time has passed when America could retreat to enclavism. Rather than solving our problems, disengagement would only exacerbate them. A policy that thinks only of "America First" is one that, in tomorrow's altered strategic environment, will guarantee that America is not first, second, or even third.

The Unipolar Moment

A second paradigm wishes not only to continue American leadership but to pursue an alleged "unipolar moment," to take advantage of a *Pax Americana* in which the United States is the sole superpower. "There is but one first-rate power and no prospect in the immediate future of any power to rival it," columnist Charles Krauthammer declares.[28] While this statement may seem irrefutable, Krauthammer and others who adopt this line of reasoning often wind up advocating a unilateralist global hegemony that is unsustainable even over the generation or two Krauthammer suggests. It, too, fails the litmus test of ends and means.

The critical problem with trying to carry *Pax Americana* into the 21st century is that it overstates our means. Even if it were not prohibitively expensive in monetary terms, it would be politically counterproductive in terms of America's alliance policy and legitimacy in the international arena. If we do not move further in the direction of genuinely reciprocal alliances, of equal partnerships, as opposed to unilateral security guarantees based on inferiority-superiority relationships, we risk becoming a country without friends. One might reasonably deduce this from considerable grousing from allies (e.g., France and Japan) and nonallies (e.g., China and Iran) about an American superpower monopoly in the aftermath of the Gulf War. Krauthammer brands the US-led coalition that liberated Kuwait a form of "pseudo-multilateralism" designed principally to give legitimacy to US intervention.[29] While not minimizing the importance of a validatory instrument for US military intervention, Krauthammer's cynicism towards the coalition understates the value of both allied contributions and the shared concept of legitimacy, especially among the industrial democracies. Multilateralism is not a virtue in and of itself; but surely there is merit in a relationship in which costs are widely distributed. Moreover, international legitimacy not only bolsters America's current external policy, it also provides greater latitude for that policy in the future.

Ironically, Krauthammer had earlier appeared to recognize the need for some devolution of US power toward its chief allies in Europe and East Asia. For instance, in an allusion to the ongoing revolution in the means of communication, he proposed "the politics of the fiber optic cable." I agree with this earlier Krauthammer:

> As the industrialized democracies become increasingly economically, culturally, and technologically linked, they should begin to think about laying the foundations for increasingly binding political connections. This would require the depreciation not only of American sovereignty, but of the notion of sovereignty in general.[30]

He sagely appreciated the need to build on our strengths in an era of uncertainty, building on "embryonic mechanisms . . . such as the G-7 and the G-5, which are beginning to act as a finance committee for the West."[31] But Krauthammer's more recent "unipolar moment" hypothesis seems to imply more unbounded unilateralism than a super-sovereign entity of North America, the European Community and democratic Asia. Germany and Japan would not be likely to subscribe to more burden sharing without a concomitant sharing of power and decision-making.

Comprehensive Globalism or Regionalism

A third paradigm focuses on the hope embodied in the phrase "new world order," especially the potential for the United Nations or regional organizations to cope with the multiplicity of security issues that arise in the future. An extreme version of these world-order idealists intimates that human behavior has progressed beyond war.[32] A more earth-bound variant of a liberal institutionalist world is offered by Ambassador Richard Gardner of Columbia Law School. Among other things, Ambassador Gardner advocates a system of collective international security centered on the United Nations; assisting the former Soviet Union's transition to democracy and a market economy; and a Helsinki-type Conference on Security and Cooperation in Europe (CSCE) for Asia (CSCA).[33] While there is something to be said for these goals, Gardner and other liberal institutionalists place undue emphasis on the importance of strict adherence to international institutions at the expense of a US leadership role.

All three of these major pillars for a brave new world are founded on quicksand. First, collective security is a laudable goal in the long run, but, for the foreseeable future at least, it remains too romantic. It would be more realistic to let the United States finish its lap in the race for world order and leadership before it hands off the baton to a United Nations currently incapable of dealing with the gravest challenges to international order. The Permanent Five members of the Security Council invariably would not agree on any course of action that would jeopardize their national interests. Indeed, their general harmony over the Gulf crisis was often unrelated to the crisis itself (e.g., the Soviet Union's desire for Western aid and China's wish to restore its pre-Tiananmen relationship with the United States). The nub of the problem, as an only mildly hyperbolic Krauthammer writes, is that "The United Nations is guarantor of nothing."[34] Nor are those five members representative of the world's only power centers. Moreover, there is yet one more basic problem with entrusting the United Nations with so much authority. As Jeane Kirkpatrick asserts: " . . . it is probably not yet safe for democracies to vest the definition of the most fundamental rights of citizens in the votes of an international body, most of whose members still do not enjoy such rights."[35]

The prospects for comprehensive regionalism, outside Europe, are not much better than globalism. The notion of an effective pan-Asian collective security organization remains problematic at best. In the foreseeable future, such a Helsinki-like CSCA organization could do little more than provide a forum for airing grievances.

Pax Consortis

The fourth paradigm is also outward looking, choosing active engagement rather than isolationism. But unlike the previous framework, a *Pax Consortis* places less faith in comprehensive regionalism or globalism and instead focuses on expanding core alliances with European Community states (especially Germany) and democratic Asia (especially Japan). As the name implies, peace (at least at the systemic level) will be maintained by equitable subsidies by the United States, EC, and Japan. This is meaningful in an era when no single industrial power seems capable of fulfilling the role connoted by the term "hegemon." Together, these three entities (which in 1988 accounted for some $600 billion in foreign exchange every day) could sustain a trilateral concert of power that preserves their mutual interests at a realistic cost. Calling for the United States to acknowledge the need for a new set of special relationships, one analyst writes, "Washington should move quickly to fully engage Tokyo and Bonn . . . in all major discussions about the shape of the post-Cold War world."[36]

Although much of the rationale for this paradigm is suggested throughout this essay, there are a pair of reasons for positing this as a general model for US engagement in international affairs. First, it appreciates our stake in the global order and provides a means of achieving our objectives given the potential threats to global security. Second, a *Pax Consortis* provides realistic means, because we cannot afford to go it alone (unilateralism), and the world is not yet ready to go it together (collective security). Here is a practical community—which combines power and wealth and a range of shared goals—that can become the basis for a new world order. The more that these three communities can serve their common interests, then the more each will benefit.

Precisely how might a *Pax Consortis* operate? In one sense, *Pax Consortis* is an affirmation of present trends: it means more of the same. For instance, much of the collaboration (for example, on foreign aid, trade and finance, and development initiatives) will continue to be effected through international organizations such as the IMF and the World Bank. Furthermore, on foreign policy and security issues, unity may have to be forged by one of the three power centers (United States, Germany, and Japan). The United States, as the only country with sturdy links to both others, retains an exceptional position in this loose trilateral alliance. As Peter Tarnoff observes:

> The potential for American leadership in dealing with Germany and Japan is premised in part on closer American ties to both than either has with the other. Of all their foreign partners, only the United States today enjoys sufficient standing in both Japan and Germany to be in a position to discuss fully with either the essential elements of a common course for the West . . . . [37]

Hence, although the United States has lost primacy, it has no equal; America remains *primus inter pares* among the advanced industrial countries. Even so, trilateralism is not a nostrum for all international ills. Hindrances to coordinated trilateral policy similar to those that have arisen in the past will continue to apply. But the assumption here is that these states will generally overcome their differences—such as those in the Uruguay Round of the GATT talks—based on a sober analysis of costs and benefits. The common agenda of these states, from global economic growth, to concerns over energy means and protection of the ecology, are substantial. Thus, appellations such as "trilateralism" or "*Pax Consortis*" are only broadly accurate, just as the United States never really enjoyed an absolute *Pax Americana*. Collective efforts among Europe, Japan, and the United States provide a judicious path for protecting their common security goals with reasonable means, while also creating a means for responding to the increasingly urgent needs of the developing countries. Ultimately, the goal would be to enlarge the circle of industrial nations to include Russia and, in some areas, China.

The Case for Active Engagement

The assumption that the United States ought to be engaged in the international arena despite the attenuation of the Cold War centers first and foremost on what this author perceives to be the national interest. But given that the "national interest" is a heavily value-laden concept, what is meant here? On the one hand, this represents a broader definition of national interest than that implied in the Cold War epoch. On the other hand, it encompasses a less stressful threat in terms of warning time and scope of potential armed conflict. Second, the case for active engagement can be made based on the larger goal of international order, especially regarding the role of great powers and the importance of international norms.

US Interests At Stake

US interests argue for active engagement. Our foremost priority must remain the survival of the United States, with its institutions and people free and its values intact. In the past, we have relied on military deterrence of the greatest external threat, the Soviet Union, through forward-deployed forces and a global alliance network. In the foreseeable future, this will increasingly become a task of general deterrence of multiple threats, including a large element of reassurance to our allies, rather than immediate deterrence against a single potential adversary. While "multiple-threat deterrence"[38] requires fewer forward-deployed forces than immediate deterrence of the Soviet Union, because an even larger part of its mission is psychological rather than strictly military, forward forces must be (a) sufficiently present so as to demonstrate American commitment to stability in a given region or subregion; (b) capable of a swift response to a variety of crises; and (c) represent the trigger of a credible rear-echelon force that could be rapidly mobilized in order to deter, compel, or defeat an enemy. Immediate deterrence of a specific threat remains in order in a number of areas, including strategic nuclear deterrence of Russia and on the Korean peninsula and, in the short run at least, deterrence of Iraqi aggression in the Gulf. Otherwise, general deterrence is sufficient to retain relative stability in Central and Eastern Europe, Latin America, and the Asia-Pacific region.

Today, a connection is frequently made between US well-being and international stability. While no value inheres in stability—which can be either good or bad depending on the merits of the system we are trying to keep stable—there are a number of instabilities the United States should be trying to thwart. They might include: unbridled arms races; the rise of regional hegemons or other large imbalances of regional or subregional balance of power; wholesale human rights violations; flagrant breaches of international law; subversion of democratic and free-market institutions; and threats to the sea-air-land-space lines of communication. Obviously US policy makers will have to be selective in where and how to respond, measuring US interests on a case-by-case basis.[39] For instance, instability on the US-Mexican border should rank far above an insurrection in Burma. Furthermore, the interest here is principally with international instability, not domestic instability (such as riots and insurgencies). There is no foolproof set of criteria for pre-selecting which crises to respond to, but the United States has more leeway for selecting where and when it wants to make a stand than it did during the Cold War, when a zero-sum mentality dictated a response to every Soviet incursion anywhere. As we broaden the concept of security, less traditional elements of American power must be placed beside the military component. Foreign policy hinges on a solvent domestic policy. Economic vitality is part and parcel of a strong and free nation. As the US economy becomes more interdependent with the global economy, we have a larger stake in an open, inclusive and stable international economic system. As we labor to salvage GATT, we also must remain competitive with our main allies, at the same time keeping in mind that even a limited industrial policy would need to be conducted in such a manner that it did not threaten to bring down the entire edifice of trilateral cooperation upon which the industrial nations of the world increasingly depend.[40] The undisturbed flow of oil from the Persian Gulf is only the most obvious common interest shared by almost all of the industrial democracies. Moreover, forward military presence provides a ready means of protecting economic interests. Without trying to revitalize a mercantilist rationale for military intervention, it is important to recognize the security-economic linkages between our military presence and large markets. For example, the fact that Taiwan is the fifth-largest American trading partner suggests concrete interests that might need to be protected. The United States also may bear some responsibility for protecting countries converting to free-market principles. In short, our economic and foreign policies are inextricably linked. Economic strength and military power can be mutually reinforcing.

Some believe these two goals of domestic strength and international engagement are mutually exclusive. America's domestic agenda is beyond the scope of this essay, but it is necessary to be explicit about these assumptions. It is the contention here that America's current economic situation is not incompatible with a global leadership role. If the American economy is in worse shape than many contend, then we may have no alternative but to curtail our international activities. The worst case would be to forsake our global position not out of necessity, but because of economic mismanagement at home. Above all, we must understand that the new basis of economic power lies more in our people than in the number of durable goods produced. As Robert Reich contends:

> The success of American capitalism no longer depends on the private investments of highly motivated American capitalists. Our nation's future economic success depends instead on our unique attributes — the skills and insights of our work force, and how we link those skills and insights to the world economy. . . . The government's role is not just to spread the wealth. It is to build our human capital and infrastructure, and to bargain with global capital on our behalf.[41]

Reich's bipartisan approach toward increasing revenues in education, infrastructure, and research and development, without wiping out the US defense budget, seems a good start for dealing with the Republic's long-term economic needs.[42] In brief, domestic weal is not only an end in itself but also a means toward a security posture that can protect that state.

A sound security policy also must be mindful of America's resources. America's economic resilience will depend in large measure on a wise energy policy. In the short term, there seems little hope of reducing US dependence on Persian Gulf oil, ascribing an even greater importance to maintaining Gulf stability in the future. In the longer term, however, we must follow a two-track policy of conservation and alternative-energy development. At the same time, threats to our environment endanger more than the US economy. From deforestation to ozone depletion, a world in which resources are increasingly sparse is a recipe for volatility. The consequences might range from massive population movements across national boundaries to recurrent international crises as states compete with renewed urgency for scarce resources. There is no single answer to these challenges. The best insurance policy—and a policy with reasonable premiums—is one that combines economic and technical assistance to help mitigate the consequences of these environmental and energy problems, while maintaining sufficient military force to defend US interests from others and to ensure access to the global resources America needs.

The Case for US Leadership

Having made the case for US global engagement, why must America play such a commanding leadership role? There are several answers to that question. First, allowing the international system to drift amorphously without leadership is fraught with danger. Second, there is no better alternative to US leadership available in the impending future. Third, leadership in the security realm plays to America's strengths, given US military and political clout. Finally, a broad swath of public and elite opinion, not only in the United States but also in Europe and Asia, supports a robust US role.

221

The Dangers of a Leaderless World

If Americans want the world to be a relatively congenial place, a world in which their values find full expression and can flourish, the United States must assume a position of leadership. The absence of US leadership would likely engender even greater disorder than already exists in the world. The world's ills are such that they can be exacerbated by an American retreat, but they are unlikely to be mitigated without active American engagement.

Power confers responsibility, and much of America's unique role is rooted in her multifaceted and far-reaching power. History teaches us that the code of conduct that prevails at any given point within the international system is heavily influenced by the rules supported by the system's most powerful members. Inis Claude states it simply: "Singly or jointly, the great powers are responsible for managing the international system."[43]

Their postures toward international obligations and alliance commitments reinforce the norms others follow and that threaten to become applicable to all.[44] For example, treaty-compliance issues dominated diplomatic discourse in the United States in the 1980s because adherence to agreements was perceived to be so ambivalent. This was spurred in part by America's proclivity for rugged individualism, a tendency expressed in Charles Krauthammer's repudiation of American attempts to marshall multilateral action as a "a long and dismaying list of failures."[45] Even if allies have failed to act in concert with US initiatives at times, the answer seldom lies in autonomous action. The United States cannot afford to forget that when the world's most powerful country challenges the fabric of international legal institutions, the whole panoply of treaty and international law norms risks being upset. Once again, Inis Claude sums it up best:

> In the final analysis, it is not clear that the United States really has the option of renouncing its status as a great power, or that it would in fact exercise that option if it were available. The fantasy of retreating to the sidelines from

which Americans could resume their old habit of judging the iniquities of states engaged in the political arena has its attractions, but in truth most Americans recognize it as an exercise in nostalgia. It is not the destiny of the United States to be a Belgium or a Paraguay. Having attained the stature of a great power, the United States has unavoidably acquired the responsibilities that accompany that status. The common defense and welfare of the United States and the world depend in large measure upon the way in which it understands its external obligations and seeks to honor them.[46]

In short, America's distinctive role is rooted not only in power, but also in trust. America cannot be responsible for solving all the world's security problems. But it does remain the country to whom others turn when in distress. This faith in the United States creates the burdens of guardianship, certainly. In the Gulf, the United States has shown American leadership must include mobilizing the world community to share all the costs of order, including the risks, but the failure of others to bear their burden still does not excuse us. In the end, we are answerable to our own interests and our own national conscience—to our ideals and to our history—for what we do or fail to do with the power we have.

There are two other ways to illustrate why a leaderless world is perilous. First, while historical analogizing is fraught with pitfalls, a valid comparison has been made between the 1990s and the 1920s, when America was turning inward on the heels of the war to end all wars. Few observers would question the effects of American withdrawal in international affairs during the interwar years. The consequences were disastrous, even though the world was far less interdependent than it is today. On a more theoretical level, it comes down to a question of public goods theory. The public good in this case is regional and systemic stability. As in the building of lighthouses, however, there is no efficient market for international security. States must pool their limited resources together lest the individual parts—their independent defenses—equal no more than their sum. This pooling of resources, however, will not happen without leadership to fashion a consensus, catalyze nations into common action, and coordinate discordant policies. Leadership counts. The question remains, though, who will provide that leadership?

The Lack of Suitable Alternatives

Having established the requirement for *a* leader, the next logical question concerns who would or could fill the vacuum left by American retrenchment? An examination of the potential alternatives to US leadership is a second reason for continuing an energetic American role in global security. The notion that leadership can be provided through an international organization such as the UN has been dismissed above as embryonic. There remain three plausible alternatives: the new economic powers in Bonn and Tokyo, a united Europe, or a US-Russian condominium. None of these options, however, is preferable to US leadership. Will Japan and Germany, the new economic powers, supplant the United States as a catalyzer of international action in the event of a major crisis? The rise of Japan and Germany as important industrial democracies is a triumph of American, Japanese, and German policies. Their affluence, however, was achieved only at the price of a tightly integrated security link to the United States. It is somewhat whimsical to suggest, even in the post-Cold War era, that either country soon could build the kind of power projection forces currently in the US arsenal. While there is little doubt that both countries have access to or possess the sinews of high-technology military might, the only way either could pursue an arms buildup that would be acceptable to domestic public opinion would be if the United States disengaged from its preeminent security role. Tokyo and Berlin are both aware that neighboring states would be very uncomfortable if they became too militarily assertive and independent. Given their historical legacy and their lack of significant power projection forces, then, Germany and especially Japan are likely to remain primarily economic powers for some years to come. The problem is that some of the critical threats to global security cannot be resolved by the power of the purse. In other words, the Gulf War revealed some of the limits of unidimensional power. Like it or not, despite the emergence of new economic power centers, the United States remains the only state with global strength and influence in every dimension: political, military, and economic.

Can Europe lead? Well, if we are to await for a truly whole and free Europe pivoting around a strong pan-European entity, then this seems a dim prospect for the foreseeable future. CSCE has an important role to play in removing barriers that can divide the Europeans, including the muffling of ethnic turbulence. However, any hope for a united Europe would have to follow the achievement of a politically unified European Community (EC). The fact that the EC faces great challenges ahead, even while it moves toward a single market by the end of this year, suggests that a more comprehensive regional institution would be hamstrung by indecision and lowest-common-denominator policy making. It certainly would not likely approve concerted action in a crisis. So what about the EC? The EC, far more than CSCE, will have a vital role to play when it comes to maintaining stability in Europe, including maintaining the vitality of the new democracies sprouting in Eastern Europe. In addition, the trend toward unity, as hinted at by Europe's recent policies vis-a-vis Iraq, may well spur Europeans to take greater responsibility when it comes to Europe's defenses. Regardless of whether a rejuvenated Western European Union comes under the direct jurisdiction of the EC or remains detached, however, it is difficult to see a European military organization that would be willing to take risks, especially outside the immediate borders of their members, without involving the United States.[47] We should encourage the further strengthening of the European "pillar," but we should not expect it to do too much too quickly.

Playing to America's Strengths

A third reason for American leadership focuses on past performance and capabilities in hand, particularly our military preeminence. America's ability to project military, political, or even economic power around the globe is without parallel in any other country. The point has been made repeatedly that no other country could have coordinated, engineered, and executed the operation against Iraq that the US Government did. Of course, the United States was in the ironic position of both mounting the largest conflict in the postwar period and cutting back its power projection forces. Even with forces scaled back some 25 percent, however, from their peak at the end of the Reagan era would leave the United States with a tremendous military force.

Part of America's strength also stems from leadership in various international fora inspired by postwar US architects. It makes sense to utilize existing institutions that are still serving important functions rather than starting over with an unproven design. This is not to preclude innovation, but it does seem more efficient to begin working on the new agenda of international ills with the mechanisms in place. Some critics charge that those American institutions have done at least as much harm as they have done good. For instance, the debate over whether America's purpose ought to be to export democracy rekindled claims that America impoverishes more than it empowers other nations. The United States has the power to do the former; the only certain way to do the latter is by not trying.

Broad International Public Support

Whether one looks at public opinion or elite opinion, whether one asks Asians or Europeans, whether one examines domestic opinion or international opinion, there remains considerable support for the retention of active American engagement and leadership in security issues. First, most countries in the Asia-Pacific region fear the consequences of a mid-Pacific

American strategy in which the US 7th Fleet and other for-ward-deployed military forces fall back to Hawaii, Alaska, and California. For a variety of reasons, the lion's share of diplomatic reporting back from the Asia-Pacific region argues for a continuation of US engagement.

Likewise, most Europeans want to retain a strong US role. Perhaps the most vociferous support for a US-led NATO has emanated from prospective members such as Czechoslovakia, Poland, and Hungary, but even among NATO's principal European powers, there is good reason to support the transatlantic alliance. It is based on common values and not simply a negative reaction to a common threat. To the extent that Fukuyama was correct, that the Cold War was more about an ideological war than an arms race, then NATO's ace in the hole is its shared values. America's engagement in European security, however, will most likely shift to largely multinational naval cooperation in the Mediterranean, rather than any significant presence of ground troops in Europe.[48]

Finally, although Americans are first and foremost about domestic economics, the American public still supports an internationalist role. According to a comprehensive Gallup poll conducted for the Chicago Council on Foreign Relations, despite the virtual disappearance of concern over a worldwide communist threat, Americans remain committed to the active role in world affairs they supported in the 1980s. The nature of the commitment has changed. Fighting ideological battles with Communist states has decreased in priority; protecting American economic interests and maintaining a global military, economic and political position continues as a high priority. When asked, "Do you think it will be best for the future of the country if we take an active part in world affairs or if we stay out of world affairs?" 62 percent of the public said "active" and only 28 percent said "stay out;" of the leaders, 97 percent said "active." When asked whether the United States plays a more important and powerful role as a world leader today compared to 10 years ago, a less important role, or about as important a role as a world leader as it did 10 years ago, 61 percent of the public and 56 percent of the leaders said "more/as important a role." On a list of foreign policy goals, 61 percent of the public and 56 percent of the leaders called defending our allies' security "very important."[49] While public opinion is hardly immutable, significant polling data indicate broad domestic and international public support for US leadership. If this does not constitute a rationale for internationalism, it certainly reduces a potential inhibition.

Leadership with Limited Means

This paper has just put forth the case for carrying US leadership into the 21st century. Having shown that this end is desirable, there remains the question of whether America's means are adequate to the task. Given twin trade and budget deficits, the lingering recession, and warnings of declining productivity and competitiveness; and given the relative increase in economic power of Germany and Japan, coupled with what is often perceived as rising nationalism and reluctance to be subservient to any other global power, how can America maintain a leadership role among the industrial democracies of the world? Four points need to be made on the question of US means.

First, the declinists and their followers have overplayed their hand. The case has been made elsewhere that US economic performance, far from showing signs of incurable decay, is experiencing an historical average; the early postwar period should be seen as the exception, given that European countries were prostrate after the war and Asian newly industrialized countries were not yet developed.[50] For another thing, the historical analogies of Spain's Philip II, France's Louis XIV or Russia's Peter the Great have only limited relevance to the American situation—e.g., with regard to the share of gross national product (GNP) spent on defense.[51] However, the elements of international power are not easily fungible. In particular, willingly abdicating our military preponderance would not likely translate into enhanced economic, social, and political strength at home. This is even more true of the future, given that the defense budget is projected to decline to about 3.5

percent of the gross domestic product by 1995, about half of the postwar average and significantly below the roughly 10-percent benchmark of the Eisenhower and Kennedy administrations.[52] Thus, concludes Henry Nau, America's alleged decline is a myth. It ignores the convergence of purposes in the world today against which American power is applied. It also ignores the choices that America still has to reaffirm its own purposes and rejuvenate its own power.[53]

Second, the United States can maintain its position internationally with fewer resources and less effort than in the past. The key is to create a new division of labor with our European and East Asian allies. New burden sharing means the United States does not have to be ashamed of "going about with a tin cup" to pay for endeavors such as restoring the inviolability of borders in the Gulf. It also means being more constructive when it comes to German and Japanese frustrations about the need for power sharing. Hence, we need a new kind of more pragmatic leadership on the part of all three members of the triad. When taking major actions, the United States must look first to multilateral avenues before unilateral ones. US policy thus should take into account more and more German and Japanese concerns, but those two states also must converge with the United States by developing a more developed sense of global responsibility. The last point is important. The United States will not risk becoming the infantry or the Hessians of the new world order, provided its key allies have a common stake in the risks and costs of major security issues. That means finding ways in which Japan and Germany can contribute people, and not just money, to future situations such as war to liberate Kuwait.[54]

Third, we need a sustainable defense budget. The current Bush Administration recently announced defense program calls for an approximate reduction of one-fourth of the US Armed Forces from their apogee in the 1980s. Whereas defense spending peaked at 6.3 percent of GNP during the mid-1980s, and reached more than 9 percent during the Vietnam war, it will dip to less than 3.5 percent by 1997. Within this constrained defense budget, we should be giving relatively more emphasis to high-technology research and development and reconstitution of our industrial base in order to hedge against long-term threats. Moreover, save for the most Panglossian scenario in which the international environment becomes conflict free, a minimalist force structure designed to maintain a minimal but not hollow US force structure in Europe, the Gulf, and East Asia would differ largely on the margins from the current Bush proposal. For instance, one might be able to shave a couple more active ground divisions from the Army, one of three Marine Corps divisions, several more tactical fighter squadrons from the Air Force, and a couple more aircraft carrier battlegroups from the Navy.

Finally, as stated above, we must also resist the short-sighted attempts to blame our domestic ills on the defense budget. The proposed defense budget leaves room for dealing with our Nation's pressing domestic issues. Harvard University's Robert Reich, for one, put forward a good starting point for national debate over how to locate enough money to invest in our long-term economic future. Through a combination of domestic priorities (such as education, infrastructure, and research and development), some defense cuts, and some tax increases, Reich posits a realistic model for revitalizing American competitiveness in the new economy of tomorrow.[55]

Conclusions

As old certainties crumble, only two things seem certain: The United States needs to modify its national security policy to ensure its interests are protected; and the international order of the future will depart in significant ways from the past four decades. There may be a lesson, however, in our euphoric rush to usher in a new international order. For every opportunity there is a challenge, and the linear trends of today may not hold for long. Consequently, America must not abandon her hard-fought and hard-earned achievements of the post-war era so eagerly. As William Hyland writes, the United States might do well to prepare for more surprises that will defy any carefully crafted vision, a centrist policy between "indiscrimi-

nate isolationism and an equally indiscriminate internationalism or globalism."[56]

A second conclusion is the need to be clear about
America's purpose and to understand that we deserve a special
seat at the head table of international affairs—and not mis-
placed as a result of the war in Iraq.[57] If the premise was that
America had exchanged a Vietnam syndrome for an Iraqi
syndrome, then the tone of this essay would be dramatically
different. Instead, one must guard against the opposite, a return
to indiscriminate isolationism. The significant domestic
agenda facing us will invariably continue downward pressure
on our defense forces and budget and an inward-looking posture because of mounting problems at home and because of the
perceived difficulties of maintaining allies who seem to wax
while we wane will make such a conclusion increasingly tempting in the future. It is because these appear to be the emerging
trends in America that this paper emphasizes both an internationalist perspective and a strong alliance posture; if we neglect
either one of these, then we jeopardize our long-term security.
At the same time, we must not overlook the notable role we
have played and should play. More than any other nation in the
world, the United States has created the basis for an unprecedented degree of international cooperation, prosperity, and
freedom among the modern industrial nations of the world.

Finally, we must return to a central focus on ends and
means. If there is a single measure of effectiveness for a satis-
factory grand strategy for the future, it comes down to the
following: 50 years from now I would like my children and my
children's children to say that their mothers and fathers—
today's architects of American power and purpose—had
brought them another half century of prosperity and freedom.
Without trying to minimize the role that other states and
peoples must play, I believe a policy of active engagement along
the lines sketched above is the best course for reaching that end.
Whether it is the European Bank for Reconstruction and Development for Eastern Europe's emerging democracies, or a
streamlined NATO reconfigured to defuse "out-of-area" crises;
a mechanism for advancing Arab-Israeli reconciliation, or
measures to curb the proliferation of weapons of mass

destruction in the Middle East; the Association of Pacific Economic Cooperation (APEC) or another innovative panregional forum to increase cooperation in the Asia-Pacific or reduce tensions on the Korean peninsula; a security framework for the Persian Gulf; a North American Free Trade Agreement, or a new partnership to promote democracy in the Western Hemisphere; helping South Africa to stay on its course toward a post-apartheid era or bolstering fragile political and economic institutions of post-independence Africa; or deterring, denying, or defeating armed aggression in concert with our allies and/or the United Nations Security Council: whether it is one or all of these, the United States has a major role to play in erecting the post-Cold War world order.

Americans need to remember that you lose your innocence—and perhaps your preeminence—only once. You can't go home again. The contemporary world does not resemble the 1950s, but neither does it look like the 19th century. Geography no longer provides the *glacis* it once did. The revolution in, and proliferation of, military technology can harm more of our interests faster than ever before. We have too much at risk in the existing global order to pack up and go home or to cede leadership to others not inclined to follow our path. Like the young man who grew up and could never return to that earlier period, we must not delude ourselves into thinking we can return to a period of splendid isolation. In fact, we never could. The next unforeseen crisis would leave us with too little too late. We cannot easily regain our leverage and credibility if we now shatter the patina of American power by disengaging militarily and politically. And yet we can no longer do so much on our own. Thus, I have argued that the best course is to pursue US interests internationally through a concert of power with our key allies, by focusing on what we have done well, by playing to our strengths in a period of extended uncertainty, and by trying to shape the world more to our liking. An era of transnationalism, multipolarity, and interdependence does not permit isolationism on the cheap, but instead prescribes a realistic transnational approach to confront the challenges of the post-Cold War era that lie ahead.

Notes

1. See Earl Ravenal, "The Case for Adjustment," *Foreign Policy* (Winter 1990-1991): 3-19; Patrick J. Buchanan, "A New Nationalism," *Buchanan from the Right* (Spring 1990); Walter Russell Mead, "The 'New Order': Will We Be Its Arsenal--Or its Infantry?" *The Washington Post,* 17 February 1991; and Christopher Layne, "Superpower Disengagement," *Foreign Policy* (Winter 1989-90): 17-40.

2. "William G. Hyland, "Downgrade Foreign Policy," *The New York Times,* 20 May 1991, A15.

3. See Walter Lippmann, *U.S. Foreign Policy: Shield of the Republic* (Boston: Little, Brown & Co., 1943), pp. 48-49, *passim.*

4. Ibid., 61.

5. Ibid., 81-82, *passim.*

6. Ibid., 63.

7. Ibid., 64-67, *passim.*

8. Ibid., 67-80.

9. Ibid., 71-76.

10. Ibid., 7.

11. A point elaborated on by Alan Ned Sabrosky, "Alliances in U.S. Foreign Policy," *Alliances in U.S. Foreign Policy* (Westview, 1988), 1-17.

12. A few recognized this at the time. See Hans J. Morgenthau, "Alliances in Theory and Practice," ed. Arnold Wolfers, *Alliance Policy in the Cold War* (Baltimore: The Johns Hopkins University Press, 1959), 184-212. Note that although the United States retained only observer status with regard to CENTO, it was a driving force behind its creation and existence.

13. I am indebted to Steven R. David for this point.

14. Charles Krauthammer, "The Unipolar Moment," *Foreign Affairs: America and the World 1990/91,* 23-33.

15. Indeed, many future crises in the developing world may be hard for American policymakers to ignore, given the potential influence of international media coverage on US domestic opinion.

16. For example, see President Bush's 1991 State of the Union address in *The Washington Post,* 30 January 1991, A14.

17. I refer here to the tendency toward either ideological or economic determinism, a tendency spawned by over-simplifications of the influential works of Francis Fukuyama, "The End of History?", *The National Interest* (Summer 1989), 3-18, and Paul Kennedy, *The Rise and Fall of the Great Powers: Economic Change and Military Conflict, 1500 to 2000* (New York: Random House, 1987). For some works that generally contend that imperial overstretch has launched America on a course of inevitable and deep decline, see David P. Calleo, *Beyond American Hegemony: The Future of the Western Alliance* (New York: Basic Books, 1987); Thomas J. McCormick, *America's Half-Century: United States Foreign Policy in the Cold War* (Baltimore: Johns Hopkins, 1990); Walter Russell Mead, *Mortal Splendor: The American Empire in Transition;* and Christopher Layne and Alan Tonelson, "Realism Redux: Strategic Interdependence in a Multipolar World" and "America in a Multipolar World--Whatever That Is" in *SAIS Review* (Summer/Fall 1989).

18. Patrick J. Buchanan, "America First--And Second, and Third," *The National Interest* (Spring 1990): 80.

19. Ibid., 82.

20. Meg Greenfield, "A Messy New World Order," *The Washington Post,* 26 March 1991.

21. Quoted in Jim Wolfe, "Iraqi Army's Ruin Makes Drawdown Safer: Powell," *Navy Times,* 15 April 1991, 24.

22. Those who dismiss the "petrowarfare" argument should consider how many more ballistic missiles and nuclear-weapon facilities Saddam Hussein could have bought with the additional revenue of Kuwait's oil fields. That added military prowess, in turn, could then have

a significant influence on the oil production and pricing policies of the fragile Gulf emirates.

23. Buchanan, "America First," 80.

24. Ibid., 81.

25. Ibid.

26. Ibid.

27. Jim Hoagland, "Neither Moral Nor Smart," *The Washington Post,* 9 April 1991.

28. Charles Krauthammer, "The Unipolar Moment,"*Foreign Affairs: America and the World, 1990/91,* 24. Rather than a rare moment in which one superpower reigns supreme, it might be more accurate to say that there are no superpowers left, as William Pfaff argues in his article, "Redefining World Power," in the same issue of *Foreign Affairs,* 34-48.

29. Krauthammer, "Unipolar Moment," 25.

30. Charles Krauthammer, "Universal Dominion: Toward a Unipolar World," *The National Interest* (Winter 1989/90): 48-49.

31. Ibid., 49.

32. See Harry B. Hollins, Averill L. Powers, and Mark Somner, *The Conquest of War: Alternative Strategies for Global Security* (Boulder, Co.: Westview, 1989); and John Mueller, *Retreat from Doomsday: The Obsolescence of Major War* (New York: Basic Books, 1989).

33. *United States Institute of Peace Journal* 10, no. 1 (February 1991): 3.

34. Krauthammer, "The Unipolar Moment," 25.

35. Jeane Kirkpatrick, "Human Rights, 'Territorial Integrity'," *The Washington Post,* 15 April 1991.

36. Peter Tarnoff, "America's New Special Relationships," *Foreign Affairs* (Summer 1990): 67.

37. Ibid., 76-77.

38. I am indebted to my former colleague Daniel Chiu of the Center for Naval Analyses for helping to develop the concept of "multiple-threat deterrence."

39. Ironically, those who argue that "the Third World doesn't matter" fail to differentiate among various countries in the developing world. See Steven David, "Why the Third World Matters,"*International Security* 14, no. 1 (Summer 1989): 50-85.

40. Here I am impressed by the arguments of Chalmers Johnson and James Fallows. See James Fallows, "Containing Japan," *The Atlantic* 263, no. 5 (May 1989): 40-48, 51-54.

41. Robert B. Reich, "The REAL Economy," *The Atlantic* (February 1991): 36.

42. Ibid.

43. Inis L. Claude, Jr., "The Common Defense and Great-Power Responsibilities," *Political Science Quarterly* 101, no. 5 (1986): 727.

44. See Charles W. Kegley, Jr. and Gregory A. Raymond, *When Trust Breaks Down: Alliance Norms and World Politics* (University of South Carolina Press, 1990).

45. Charles Krauthammer, "The Multilateral Fallacy," *The New Republic* (December 9, 1985), 18. This article provides further evidence that Krauthammer's "unipolar moment" implies unilateralism.

46. Claude, "Common Defense," 732.

47. I have argued recently that the WEU is indeed the proper bridge between NATO and the EC. See Patrick M. Cronin, "Transatlantic Security Cooperation After Maastricht," *Strategic Review* (Winter 1992).

48. See Patrick M. Cronin, "Transatlantic Security Cooperation After Maastricht," *Strategic Review* (Winter 1992).

49. John E. Reilly, ed., *American Public Opinion and U.S. Foreign Policy 1991* (Chicago, Chicago Council on Foreign Relations, 1991), 6, 12-15, 32-33.

50. The studies of Charles Wolf and Herbert Block show that the effect of World War II lasted for about a quarter century and then stabilized. Hence, the US share of global GNP was about the same in 1938 as it was in the mid-1960s--22-24 percent. Cited in Joseph S. Nye, Jr., *Bound to Lead: The Changing Nature of American Power* (New York: Basic Books, 1990), 5-6.

51. Nye, *Bound to Lead.*

52. Ibid.

53. Henry R. Nau, *The Myth of America's Decline: Leading the World Economy into the 1990s* (Oxford: Oxford University Press, 1990), 370.

54. There are some positive signs that this might be happening in the wake of the war with Iraq. See Marc Fisher, "Germany to Send Troops to Iran to Aid Refugees," *The Washington Post,* 24 April 1991, 23; and "Minesweeping Task Group's Sailing Date Advanced to Friday," *The Daily Japan Digest* II, no. 73 (23 April 1991): 1.

55. Reich, "The REAL Economy."

56. The phrase is Hans Morgenthau's. Quoted in William G. Hyland, "Charting a New Course," *Foreign Affairs* (Spring 1990): 12.

57. Some have expressed concern about an Iraqi syndrome, that the United States will be intoxicated with victory and eager to join battle again. The problem, they continue, was that the Gulf victory was too easy and we may soon find ourselves in a different kind of war, say, in Latin America, that bogs down into a drawn-out guerrilla war of attrition. The next Battle of Khafji, a key battle in which Saddam attempted to bloody our nose in order to drag us into a protracted war of attrition on the ground, may not go our way. But I see those occasional excesses tempered by a greater concern for domestic issues. For supporting polling data, see Richard A. Brody and Richard Morin, "From Vietnam to Iraq: The Great American Syndrome Myth," *The Washington Post,* 31 March 1991, B1-B2.

*T*he Burden of Power in a Fragmented World

William Woodruff

*T*he end of the Cold War (wrongly termed a struggle between East and West) concluded an ideological duel between two Western ideas, championed by two great powers—the Soviet Union and the United States. It also terminated a remarkable period of history in which Western power was unquestionably supreme. During the past 500 years, propelled by colossal energy and nerve, by a divine as well as a worldly mission, and with an extraordinary sense of superiority, Western man has triumphed throughout the world. In 1914 the only important states outside Western tutelage were Japan and Ethiopia. In Europe's colonization of the world, existing ethnic, tribal, national, racial and religious traditions were largely disregarded, if not treated with contempt. It is this period of history which some people are currently trying to unlive.

We are now poised between the geopolitics of the Western Age and the geopolitics of a new world order in which regional ethnic, religious, and national aims are reasserting themselves. Relative to the stability of the Cold War, we seem to be entering a topsy-turvy world of unpredictable, regional strife. Yesterday we worried whether the Soviet Union, in an effort to reach the Persian Gulf, would extend its rule to parts of Iran. Today we worry whether Islamic Iran might extend its influence into former Soviet territory.

William Woodruff is the Graduate Research Professor in Economic History at the University of Florida in Gainesville. He holds degrees from Oxford, the University of London, the University of Nottingham, and the University of Melbourne, Australia (honorary). Dr. Woodruff is the author of many books in economics and history, including *Concise History of the Modern World: 1500 to the Present* and *The Struggle for World Power, 1500-1980.*

We are in the process of unliving an extraordinary, unique chapter of world history—one with which we Americans, as the most Western of Westerners, have become identified. We find ourselves carrying the burden of world power we have inherited from the European Age. Within our own country, we have recognized the rights of different ethnic groups; internationally, we remain Western oriented. We think of the Western world as the norm, of Western power as omnipotent, of Western values as universal values. For the time being, the real power of many international organizations still rests in Western hands. Four out of five of the permanent members of the United Nations Security Council are Western. The unusual degree of consensus obtained under the banner of the United Nations during the Gulf War was predominantly Western organized and Western led.

Although there are many aspects of Western civilization that have been embraced by the world, we find it hard to understand the eagerness of some Asians and Africans to unlive or resist Westernization and modernization. For those who have a one-world mentality, the shift of power from the world to the region is equally puzzling. If the world is becoming less stable than it was during the period of *Pax Europa,* it is because the unparalleled and unprecedented consolidation of the world by Western man provided a degree of political and economic centralization that had never been seen before and might not be seen again. It is wishful thinking on our part to assume that this will now be followed by the worldwide triumph of *Pax Americana.*

America's Ascent to Power

We Americans are part and parcel of Western expansion. Our occupation of North America was just as much the outcome of Western European expansion as Russian occupation of Siberia was the outcome of Eastern European expansion. If there is any difference between American and Russian expansion, it was the relative ease and the speed by which our own territory and aggrandizement were obtained. There are few other examples in history of any group of people coming into possession of such a vast, rich area so swiftly and at so little human and material cost to themselves. With overwhelming superiority in weapons and numbers, we needed only a minimal defense to protect what we had won. Peaceful neighbors, distance, and the British fleet were our guards. The threat from the Pacific had still to appear. The only military forces we had abroad at the end of the 19th century were in the Philippines and the Caribbean. There was no ambiguity in those days about our foreign policy: it was supremacy in the Western hemisphere. We left it to the other Western powers to police the rest of the world.

The good fortune we enjoyed in our colonizing age helps to account for our optimism, our sense of uniqueness, and our sense of mission to the world. All Christian nations have shared this sense of mission. We differ in that we were not only messianic but idealistic as well. If we Americans have been historically naive, we have had good reasons for being so. Never has the law of increasing returns operated as well for the Western world as it did in the century before 1914. Small wonder if Western Europe and North America prospered; small wonder if famine was banished from the West; small wonder that the 19th century became a Western age of utopias.

Until the late 1930s, America's business was to look after America. There was a moment with the collapse of European civilization after the First World War when it looked as if we might change our policy from looking after America to looking after the world, especially the Pacific world, where in 1919 Japan had become a great power. The Senate repudiated Woodrow Wilson's support of the League of Nations at Versailles, however, and our policy of isolationism (except on the high seas) remained unchanged. The leading Western powers, particularly Britain, France, and the Netherlands, continued to meet the burden of world defense. In 1919 our troops were brought home from France in record time. In the postwar boom the war was soon forgotten, and our small military and financial losses were quickly absorbed. Relative to our resources, the burden of defense for the First World War, and for most of the interwar years, was inconsequential. After Japan agreed under the London Naval Treaty of 1930 to maintain the status quo in the Pacific, we felt sufficiently reassured not to increase our naval base at Pearl Harbor—a decision we would later regret.

Japan's attack at Pearl Harbor in December 1941 changed our attitude to the world. With the Soviet Union, we willingly led the Allied powers to victory, first in Europe and then in the Pacific. Unscathed by war at home, we poured out blood and treasure in the Allied cause. With the end of the war (with European imperialism in a process of retreat and abdication) and the Soviets and Americans drawn into the vacuum of power created by Europe's collapse, the United States assumed the world responsibilities it had avoided almost 30 years earlier. Convinced that Roosevelt's trust in Stalin had been betrayed, Truman introduced his containment policy. By the 1950s, the Cold War had bifurcated the world.[1] Henceforth, the two "Western" superpowers—the United States and the Soviet Union—ran the world as they thought it ought it to be run, as if the other 90 percent of the world's people did not exist.

The threatened political fragmentation stemming from Europe's collapse after 1945, and the unravelling of its empires, was temporarily delayed by the extension of American and Soviet rule across the world. By the 1950s, US defense policy entailed policing all the continents. There followed the wars in Korea and Vietnam, wars stemming directly or indirectly from the breakdown of European rule in Asia. In some ways, these two wars were a test of strength between a seemingly all-powerful America and a recently liberated Asia. Had Europe remained strong, had its outward thrust not faltered, had it not fought two world wars, had Japan not undermined Europe's Asian empires, had Western ideas not resulted in the bifurcation of first Europe and then the rest of the world, Americans would never have fought in Korea and certainly not in Vietnam. Nor would there have been a Cold War.

Even with the constraining influence of the Cold War, which resulted in the greatest and most perilous arms race human ingenuity and folly have ever devised, most of the world continued its local and regional struggles for independence and influence. As European power in the world declined, a patchwork quilt of separate nations began to appear across the globe. At the Bandung Conference of African and Asian nations in 1954 (in which the Russians were refused participation on the grounds that they were Europeans) a Third World of nonaligned nations was established. Its aim was to break the economic and political ties that hitherto had bound it to the West, as well as to distance itself from American-Soviet rivalry. This world, which was most of the world, was intensely anti-Western. It held an enduring memory of the worst aspects of Western colonialism—an opprobrium we Americans have inherited.

While the gradual substitution of American and Soviet power for European power in the post-World War II period threw an immense defense burden on our shoulders, it was not beyond our ability to bear it. If we showed a remarkably generous and enlightened face to the world from the 1940s to the 1960s, it was partly because we could afford it. We occupied the richest area of the world, and we were the most productive people on earth. (In 1948 we accounted for half the world's gross national product.) Unlike all the other major belligerents of the Second World War, we emerged from the war richer than we had entered it. In the 1950s, President Truman never doubted that we possessed sufficient wealth to contain communism and "to run the world the way the world ought to be run." President Kennedy vowed that America would "pay any price, bear any burden" in the interests of liberty.

We not only felt ourselves able to meet any threat, pay any price, we also intended, under *Pax Americana* to save the world from poverty and hunger. The first law of economics—scarcity—was banished; affluence became the order of the day. With "tricks of growth" we believed that the whole world was headed for linear progress along American lines. Not until the Vietnam War did President Johnson discover that the burden of defense had exceeded what he thought was politically acceptable to the American taxpayer. As President Reagan would do later, he masked his fiscal problems by resorting to large deficit spending. Here lie the origins of the crushing burden of foreign debt our nation bears today.

Challenging Old Assumptions

The collapse of Soviet power in 1991 has suddenly presented us with world problems we had not expected to meet. Our anti-Communist defense stance has become obsolete. The Soviet system (flawed in human and economic terms) is disintegrating. Russian power would probably have disintegrated earlier had not the Cold War forced it to respond to the American challenge. Today, antagonism between the United States and the former USSR has given way to a remarkable degree of cooperation; euphoria reigns.

The positive side of all this is that we have been spared annihilation. The negative side is that the disintegration of Soviet empire will result in further instability. A collapse of Russia's politically consolidating role in the world must bring in its train a growing threat of further political fragmentation and dispute. (A major Islamic threat to Russian rule crushed in Central Asia in 1916 is recurring today). A new Russian storm (not least the threat of an unmanageable flood of refugees in search of food and political freedom) might well become a reality. There has never been a disintegrating empire that did not leave great bloodshed in its wake.

Regardless of the outcome of Soviet disintegration, the world is breaking out of both Soviet and American molds. We are entering a new era in which the West will no longer dominate the world—not even from Washington or Moscow. It is the non-Westerners—many of whom were ignored by the Western powers before 1914—who will increasingly decide whether or not the world will live in peace. For the time being, the collapse of Soviet power has made the world more United States-centric, more unipolar than it was, but this is purely temporary. The change in the geopolitical and geoeconomic equations toward multipolarity has, in fact, been going on since the 1960s. Regional centers of power have reappeared in Europe, the Americas, and Asia. The temporary eclipse of Asia by the West during the past half millennium is over. In some respects Asians are beginning to eclipse us, which is not to say that the impact of Western man will now be followed by a similar impact of Eastern man. We can no longer take it for granted that the "American way" is a universal gospel. Our task is to adjust to a world in which the non-Western peoples (who outnumber the West four to one) are going to influence regional and world affairs more than they did in the Western Age, not only in terms of power but in terms of values. Reality today is multi-power maneuvering and multi-cultural influence.

Our Greco-Roman mental and intellectual traditions are under growing challenge from non-Western ideas. Mahatma Gandhi undid British power in India by expressing the spiritual traditions (the "soul force") of the Hindu. Our tradition of concrete truth, of black or white, of good versus evil, is unacceptable to cultures accustomed to a much greater degree of ambiguity. The Indian god Shiva, for example, expresses a unity of opposites; he is the god of both life and destruction. Death is not something to fear; death is. While some parts of the non-Western world will continue to follow the Western way in ideas, economics and technology, others will tread a very different path. Some will stress the primacy of individual rights; others will place a greater stress on consensus, balancing individual interests with a sense of obligation and public duty. The human family is too diverse to accept one truth in spiritual or material matters. Whatever the basis of future rivalry and accord between humankind, ultimately we shall have to accept the fact the no nation, no continent, no race, no civilization, no religion has a monopoly of truth; that all societies, all human institutions, have their strengths and weaknesses.

Resurgent Tribalism

One thing is certain: We have reached a most paradoxical stage of world history. While science, technology, economics, ecology, health care, and a host of other forces that demand a global order are drawing the worth together, intangible forces such as religion, race, and nationalism are beginning to break the world apart. Resurgent tribalism is blinding us to world needs. Reason points one way, emotion points another. When emotion clashes with reason, emotion usually emerges triumphant. History suggests that the world is not fully capable of rational behavior, and that the West errs in assuming that its own exceptional "Age of Reason" is normal and universal. On balance, an exaggerated belief in reason (e.g., in the French Revolution of 1789, the Russian Revolution of 1917 and the Chinese Revolution of 1949) has proved just as deadly to intellectuals as exaggerated emotion.

Compared with the fractious, regional worlds that are emerging, we might come to look back on the Cold War as one of the more stable periods in modern history. It at least provided a balance, one superpower offsetting the other, one stressing the collective, the other individualism. There was a common basis of understanding; a degree of reason prevailed; regional wars were not allowed to get out of hand. Time and again during the Cold War, the balance of terror saved us from destruction. Unless we can redesign the United Nations so that it reflects the changing power structure of the post-Western Age, and is able to uphold an authentic international law, the world is in danger of becoming anarchistic. In the absence of bipolar tension, the center of gravity of power must shift from globalism to regionalism. The one-time global threat is now replaced by regional threats; new life has been given to age-old national, ethnic and religious disputes.

National aspirations fire the struggle between the Palestinians and the Israelis. In 1990 Saddam Hussein appealed to the ideal, and perhaps illusion, of Arab nationalism. National aspirations lie at the heart of the discord in Northern Ireland, in Belgium, in Spain, in the Baltic States, in Canada, in former Soviet-controlled Central Asia, in Southwest and Southeast Asia, in Eastern Europe and throughout the countries of the Middle East. The present civil war in Yugoslavia is an example of what is to come.

The resurgence of Islamic power throughout the 1980s also threatens conflict. With Moscow's authority disintegrating, and the Central Asian Islamic republics declaring their independence, there is growing fear of civil war. Pakistan promotes the idea of an Islamic economic and military zone (similar to the European Community) stretching from Morocco to

Indonesia. In the countries of North Africa and the Middle East, as well as in the Sudan, resurgent, militant religious fundamentalists, with American modernity as their chief enemy, seek political power. Iran has already been transformed. The overthrow of the Shah is an example of the potential destructiveness of alien cultural elements—in this case Western modernity—when introduced into a traditional cultural environment. Many other countries, including the conservative regimes of Egypt, Kuwait, Bahrain, and Saudi Arabia (whose leaders are pro-American) are threatened by the ongoing Islamic revolution of the masses.

Islam is an austere faith, naturally opposed to many aspects of modernization and the extravagance of some Middle Eastern Arab leaders. In such a volatile region, we need to keep an ear cocked not only to the palace, but also to the bazaar. While a military response by Islam on a worldwide scale is unlikely, Islamic fundamentalists could provide the United States with a lot of trouble, especially within the Middle East. Learning to live with the uncomfortable facts of the Islamic revival calls for greater tolerance and understanding on our part. The more we try to beat down Islam with a military response, the stronger Islam will become. Spiritual issues cannot be settled by the force of arms.

Meanwhile, far from having reached the end of history, ethnic differences, national aspirations, and religious fundamentalism are causing the world to arm to the teeth. The sale of sophisticated weaponry is growing. In addition to the West, China, India, Pakistan, South Africa, Israel, North Korea, Argentina and Brazil either have nuclear weapons or the capacity to produce them. A growing number of nations in Asia, Africa, and the Americas either have or are working to produce stockpiles of chemical and biological weapons. Regardless of American protests and our fixation with Saddam Hussein, ballistic missiles—with ranges far exceeding the Iraqi Scud missiles—are proliferating throughout the world, as are Exocets, Silkworms, and portable anti-aircraft systems like the Stinger, now produced not only by the United States but also by a number of countries including China, South Africa and Egypt. Equally important changes are going on at sea. The new danger is not that the world will be set on fire as a result of great-power rivalry, which for the time being is behind us, but rather as a result of some minor nuclear-armed power losing its head. High-tech conventional weapons can be no match for a madman in possession of a nuclear bomb.

America's Future Global Role

The extraordinary diffusion of advanced weaponry, and the shift of power from a bipolar to a multipolar world, demands from Americans a world outlook different from the one we have held for the past 40 years. As the leading power, we cannot abruptly abandon the responsibilities we accepted during the Cold War (as the Russians are now doing). Nor is there any other great power that can replace us; none has the same global military reach. Yet to try to be the policeman of the whole world is to ensure that the non-Western world will eventually side against us. During the Cold War, with bases throughout the world, we were the solution to the problem of containing communism; now we are looked upon by some as part of the problem as obstructing self-determination. If you read the map of history from the angle of a non-Westerner, things look very different. To dogmatically impose our Western beliefs universally, to be too quick to wave the stick of military might, to go on insisting upon the status quo—these actions run contrary to the historical currents of the last half century. The time has come when, instead of trying to impose our will upon the world, we shall have to critically reexamine our commitments. Certainly we shall have to withdraw from countries where we are no longer wanted, such as the Philippines.

There is a more compelling reason why we have to reduce our burden of world defense. We can only continue it by running the risk of becoming bankrupt. The burden we willingly carried in the late 1940s is not feasible today. As the world's leading military power we cannot avoid the responsibility of leadership, but our power to lead, especially our financial power, is much more circumscribed that it was. A transformation has taken place in our overall economic situation these past 20 years, whereby we have gone from dominating the world economy to being increasingly concerned about the effect of the world economy upon us. There has not only been the economic challenge presented by the resurgence of Germany and Japan (whose economic competition we helped to create); our own mismanagement and fiscal profligacy have brought our nation to the edge of insolvency. Our willingness to excel at the art of war has allowed others to excel at the art of peace.

The indebtedness of the US Government, especially to foreign leaders, has reached a level where it is affecting our political and economic independence. The crippling economic cost of running such a deficit is not as worrying as the loss of world leadership that such a deficit must eventually entail. Debtors never have led the world, certainly not a world where geoeconomics is taking precedence over geopolitics. The United States is still by far the dominant power, but its capacity to govern the world economy has been considerably eroded. One does not need an occult reason why the United States had to pass the hat around to finance the Gulf War. We may cast ourselves as the world's arbiter (as the top cop) but the truth is we no longer have the overwhelming economic, financial, and industrial power to sustain such a role.

There are those who will reject this reasoning on the grounds that the United States is stronger than ever. With only 5 percent of the world's population, it still accounts for 20 percent of the world's goods and services; its share of world GNP today is almost as large as it was in 1970; its portion of gross world product has remained roughly what it was in the late 1960s. All this misses the point. The United States did not rise to greatness by being satisfied with a position it held 20 years ago. At what point in our history were we satisfied with the status quo? The American Dream, the American mystique is one that looks for ever-greater prosperity. Historically, we are not a "marking-time-people." For the first time in our history we have met with the law of diminishing returns. We are suddenly discovering that progress is not linear, that much of life is a bell curve. This is perhaps the first generation of Americans that is not going to enjoy a higher standard of living than its parents. Is it possible that we have been pursuing a mirage of plenty all these years?[2]

None of these things imperils us as a nation as much as the human problems that face our society. Our domestic scene is plagued by growing poverty, a falling standard of living, a crisis in health, education and welfare, a growing army of unemployed and unemployable, drug addiction and lawlessness. It makes no sense to talk about carrying the burden of world defense, of going to the help of others, of setting an example to the world, if our home front is in disarray. The most valuable things we possess are our homeland and our people. For some time now we have focused on high technology while forgetting human values. If we have lost sight of quality in industrial production it is primarily because we have lost sight of quality in our everyday life. The limits of the possible have always been set more by human beings, by human imagination rather than by material wealth. America possesses the necessary human and material resources needed to meet its growing economic and political challenges. Nothing vital has been lost, but what is missing is discernment and political will.

Reordering the Priorities

In deciding what to hang on to and what to let go, our first priority should be the development and consolidation of our own hemisphere. More than anywhere else in the world, it is here that our destiny as a nation will ultimately be determined. Canada, with whom we share the longest peaceful frontier, has become our most important trading partner. There is genuine reciprocity between our two states. In contrast, our attention to Latin America, except for wartime alignments, or actions prompted by the threat of communism, or odd military excursions, has largely been one of benign neglect. Instead of fostering friendly and cooperative relations with the countries south of our permeable border, instead of treating them as partners in a common cause, we have largely ignored them while concentrating attention on Europe, the Middle East and East Asia. Recently, disregarding the Organization of American States (OAS) Charter we helped to create, our policy in Latin America has been one of unabashed unilateral, military intervention. We only have ourselves to blame if some of our Latin neighbors still regard us as an imperialist power ready to use them for our own ends.

Our relations with the countries south of the border are unlikely to improve until we recognize that the southern and northern halves of the American continent are inextricably intertwined and interdependent, that geographical and historical ties bind us inseparably together. We cannot go on neglecting part of the world that has given us the fourth-largest Spanish-speaking population. Latin American debt, illegal immigrants (who, if population trends continue, could well become a torrent) and narcotics threaten the very stability of our country. No nation in the world affects our vital interests as much as Mexico. The seemingly insurmountable social, economic and political problems that wrack that country are our problems as well as theirs. They are not problems that military might can solve. They are problems that call for diplomacy, understanding, and human skills. While we cannot hope to stabilize the whole of Latin America, we can at least ensure that changes in that region do not destabilize us. For too long we Americans have felt too secure in the possession of our homeland; for too long we have taken our southern neighbors for granted. Latin America might well become our Achilles' heel.

Our neglect of Latin America can partly be explained by the attention we have focused on Western Europe. Now that the Cold War is over, the basic military reason for our being in Europe no longer holds. We have to reorient ourselves to a different Europe and a different world. The Europeans themselves are concentrating on the consolidation of their own region—a lesson we should take to heart. What our future military role in Europe will be depends on what happens in Eastern Europe; it also depends on the continued willingness and ability of the American taxpayer to go on underwriting Europe's defense. While the Europeans are hardly likely to refuse help that reduces their defense budget, they cannot expect us to defend them in perpetuity. It is just as absurd for us to have expected French troops, who helped to defeat Britain at Yorktown in 1781, to be garrisoned on American soil in perpetuity. Obviously, the ties that bind us to Europe are too strong and too important to be cut overnight. There is a role for us to play in a redesigned NATO, but not a leading role; that belongs to another period of history. If Gorbachev's idea is realized and Russia and its new commonwealth finds economic and military security within the European house, a new region of 'Euroslavia' might well emerge, stretching from Britain to the Urals. Such a region, with a population of about 750 million and a relatively high standard of living, should surely be able to defend itself.

Our defense stature in East Asia is much more problematical. The resurgence of Asia, after being eclipsed for half a millennium by European colonialism, is the outstanding fact of contemporary history. Few dispute the ongoing shift in the center of gravity of power from the Atlantic to the Indian Ocean and the Pacific. Asia is a region where I doubt that we shall ever be able to control events again—not even in the Middle East. Although we have provided stability to the Northwest Pacific Rim for many years, the chief Asian nations in the area—China, Korea and Japan—are unlikely to continue to accept our leadership. It is an area from which we could be excluded. This region could develop a "Monroe Doctrine" of its own. Certainly, we can expect to meet with growing resistance. While we cannot withdraw our support from Korea and Japan overnight, it is inconceivable that we would be pressed by these nations to keep a military presence there much longer.

The major threat to American interests in this region—despite North Korea's bomb rattling—must come from China or Russia. It is the struggle for power between these states—not talk of democracy and human rights—that will decide the outcome of events. India will try to take advantage of the maneuvering of the other powers but is unlikely to challenge American or Chinese interests. India is much too preoccupied with internal dissension and the ever-present threat of war with

Pakistan over Kashmir. Only the balance of nuclear terror saves the Indian subcontinent from a general conflagration.

China's chief aim is to recover the Maritime Provinces northeast of the Amur River, which Russia took in the 19th century. China still regards itself as the Middle Kingdom and the oldest civilization, therefore we should be sparing in giving advice to the Chinese, or preaching to them on the moralization of politics. Regardless of our protests and Chinese promises, the Chinese are likely to go their own way and sell arms to whom they please. Whoever comes to power when the present old guard dies, the authoritarian tradition (that has been thousands of years in the making) is likely to remain in Beijing. If, however, order collapses and the Chinese empire proceeds to unravel as the Soviet empire has done, there is no telling what might happen to Asia and the world. China, however its history unfolds, must one day become the key player in the politics of eastern Asia. It will eventually challenge the present leading powers in Asia: Russia, Japan, and the United States. Napoleon was right when he said that China would one day move the world. Because of its bitter experience in the 19th century, it will always remain suspicious of Western intrusion.

The unravelling of the Soviet empire might create a vacuum into which, in time, China will move. It would be ironic if the specter of Soviet communism, which has receded, were to be replaced by the specter of Chinese Communism; doubly ironic if China were to contest Russia's access to the Pacific. China cannot rise, Russia cannot decline, without either affecting American interests. Northeast Asia is a region where we might be drawn into a Sino-Russian war, although one wonders on whose side we would fight.

Japan, the country that undid Western colonialism in the East, is today the sheet anchor of United States foreign policy in East Asia. While sensitive to the continued presence of United States troops on its soil, it is not trying to push us out of the region in a hurry. Of all the Northwest Pacific Rim countries, it is the most friendly toward us. It is also the most Westernized and the most reliable. Hitherto a bystander in geopolitics, Japan has now reached a point where it has no choice (as the second most powerful economic nation in the world) but to make its influence felt. The Gulf War—dependent to an great degree on Japanese money and technology—has awakened Japan to the realities of economic power and world responsibility. It is perhaps the last war in which Japan will acquiesce to American decisions. Since 1945 the Japanese have been satisfied merely to respond to world affairs; henceforth they will help to shape them.

Harmonious relations with Japan at this point in history are crucial to American interests, as they are to Korea and other Asian nations. Japan and the United States are very strange cultural partners, with very different world outlooks, yet the pact between them is vital. Japan benefits in trade, investment, and defense; the United States in trade, capital, and world strategy. What endangers the alliance are two views of reality. One is dominated by tradition, the other by the market. Whereas the United States professes to adhere to the laissez-faire philosophy of free trade, Japan regards the market as no more than a guide, one of many factors to be considered. The present controversy over rice is a case in point. We cannot understand why the Japanese would want to pay such a high price for rice when they could obtain much cheaper supplies from California. They do so because rice is not just another commodity, it is their traditional staple; to some it is a cultural heirloom. To say that Japanese business methods are unfair is to disregard the cultural roots of their economic system. The worst error we can make is to assume that the Japanese economic system is like ours, or will become so in due course, provided we apply enough pressure.

Until these cultural differences are taken into account, the Americans and the Japanese will continue to talk past each other. The more we blame Japan for what are essentially our own shortcomings, the more likely it is that Japan will strengthen its ties with Asia. If the world continues to opt for protectionist mercantilist policies (euphemistically called "managed trade") on the lines of the EC and the proposed North American bloc, there is very little that East Asians can do but accept Japanese economic leadership. In the long run, China might well become more important to Japan than the United States is.

Of all the regions, the Middle East occupies our attention most. It is likely to go on doing so as long as the Arab-Israeli dispute remains unresolved, and our country continues to be shackled to that area for oil. Possessing the two essential ingredients of war, motivation and fear, few other territories have taken so much of our time, energy and wealth. Countless empires and nations have fought there, buried their dead and (usually with their military and political objectives unrealized) gone home. The last two great powers to evacuate the area—and whose former defense responsibilities we now carry—were Britain and France. As a result of British colonial history, we ourselves have been drawn to the center of the Arab-Israeli conflict and the area's defense.

Although the United States (under President Woodrow Wilson) had earlier supported Arab rather than Jewish claims to Palestine,[3] it was instrumental in the creation of Israel in 1948. Since then, in war and peace, we have unstintingly supported Israel's cause. In public aid alone, the United States has given more assistance to Israel that it did under the Marshall Plan to the whole of Western and Central Europe. Israel continues to be the largest recipient of United States aid.

Israel presents Americans with a most difficult dilemma. While morals and politics make it impossible for us to abandon it, the task of supporting it financially is becoming increasingly difficult. In the present recession, foreign aid is coming under greater scrutiny and criticism. Our support of Israel not only adds to Arab hostility, it entails the ever-present danger of becoming involved in still another Arab-Israeli war. The British struggled with this problem long before we did; they finally despaired of finding a solution and handed the matter to the United Nations. Growing financial difficulties eventually forced Britain to evacuate the entire region.

Desperate as it is, the Palestinian-Israeli dispute must not be allowed to blind us to the wider problems of the area. The dispute most be seen in the context of the area's resurgent religious fundamentalism and revolutionary nationalism, as well as in the context of the power politics of oil. Despite the Gulf War, the Gulf remains a power vacuum a strengthened Iran may one day try to fill. Explosive tensions exist not only between Arabs and Jews but among the Arabs themselves. The problem of boundaries (which are regarded as an illegitimate legacy of European colonialism) extends far beyond Iraq and Kuwait. There is a danger that a defeated Iraq may now fall prey to its hungry neighbors. If the Palestinians and the Israelis settled their dispute tomorrow, the likelihood of war in the area would remain. We shall be fortunate indeed if we succeed in bringing a comprehensive peace to a region where everybody else has failed.

Toward an Inter-Regional Balance of Power

Sometimes for better sometimes for worse, Americans have become the inheritors of an unprecedented era some of the non-Western world is now trying to unlive. While much of the science, technology, economics, and cultural imprint of Western man will remain, the resurgence of the much larger non-Western world is inevitable. The political hegemony of the world by the West (much of which has fallen to us) is diminishing. The end of the Cold War calls for a change in our whole strategic outlook, especially at sea. Even if the United States had the economic strength it possessed in the 1950s, it is fairly evident that a new world order will have to reflect the whole world, not just Western interests.

We are moving into a multipolar world in which the best we can hope for is a more coherent order based upon consensus rather than Western domination. What will follow is a balance of power between regions. Many of the world's growing ethnic, national and religious problems will have to be settled at the regional level. There would have been no Gulf War if the Arab nations had acted with common resolve. Their failure to halt Saddam Hussein's aggression left the United States with little choice but to persuade the United Nations to intervene. The Gulf War at least confirmed that while the United States is not in an irretrievable decline, it is no longer able to carry a defense burden for the rest of the world. The immediate challenge is to redistribute that burden more evenly. It has become unreal in political, military, and especially economic terms for any nation to guarantee world security.

The United States does not have the financial means to be the sole policeman of the world, nor can the cultural problems that face the world be solved by the sword. Lasting solutions can only be obtained through diplomacy, understanding and political will. Rather than presuming to know what is good for the whole world, we shall have to be much more considerate of other people's aims and values. We cannot possibly teach if we do not learn. As long as we are the leading military power, we cannot avoid worldwide responsibilities, but they are responsibilities we will have to share. The Gulf War was probably the last war where other countries paid the piper while the United States called the tune. We cannot prevent a shift in emphasis from dominance to partnership. Whatever we do, we should keep before us the basic objective of our foreign policy: To maintain the security of the United States and to uphold its fundamental values. In this task we are not faced by a new crisis, but by a new opportunity.

Notes

Author's note: My thanks to Helga Woodruff for her criticism and help in the preparation of this manuscript.

1. One wonders if the real world knew that it had been bifurcated, any more than the world of 1494 knew of the Treaty of Tordesillas under which the Pope divided the world between Portugal and Spain.

2. See William and Helga Woodruff, "Economic Growth: Myth or Reality: The Interrelatedness of Continents and the Diffusion of Technology, 1860-1960," *Technology and Culture 7,* no. 2 (Detroit: Wayne State University Press, Fall 1966): 453-474).

3. The King-Crane Commission (1919).

*A*bout the Editor

*P*atrick M. Cronin is a Senior Fellow at the National Defense University's Institute for National Strategic Studies, where he directs the Asia-Pacific affairs research team. Dr. Cronin also serves as Professorial Lecturer in International Relations at the Paul H. Nitze School of Advanced International Studies, The Johns Hopkins University, as well as Associate Editor of the journal *Strategic Review*. Prior to joining the National Defense University, he conducted analysis for the Center for Naval Analyses, where he was Scientific Analyst to the Director, Strategy, Plans and Policy Division within the Office of the Chief of Naval Operations, and Director, Politico-Military Affairs Symposia Project. In addition, he has held analytical research positions at SRI International and the Congressional Research Service and has taught at the University of Virginia. Dr. Cronin earned his master's and doctoral degrees at Oxford University.